Analysis for Strategic Market Decisions

Analysis for Strategic Market Decisions

George S. Day
University of Toronto

West Publishing Company

St. Paul   New York   Los Angeles   San Francisco

Library of Congress Cataloging in Publication Data

Day, George S.
    Analysis for strategic market decisions.

    (West series on strategic market management)
    Bibliography: p.
    Includes index.
    1. Marketing—Decision making.   2. Marketing—
Management.   I. Title.   II. Series.
HF5415.135.D39   1986   658.8'02   85-13917
ISBN 0-314-85227-1

To Marilyn

Contents

Strategic Issues in Life-Cycle Management

4

5 *The Analysis of Pooled Business Experience: The PIMS Program*

The Growth-Share Matrix and Market Share Strategies

6

Preface

This book offers a comprehensive managerial treatment of the methods and concepts used to support the strategic market planning process. The foundation for the book is built from strategy concepts that are basic to any assessment of the strategic position of a business—including the effect of scale and experience on costs, the relationship of market share and profitability, and the product life cycle. These concepts, when linked to the data banks and models of a decision support system, support the higher-level methods of strategy analysis. At this level we consider a variety of portfolio models and the PIMS (Profit Impact of Market Strategies) approach to the analysis of pooled business experience.

The scope and depth of coverage of these methods and concepts were shaped by three beliefs that come from fifteen years of experience with their application. First, the benefits of the methods are best appreciated when they are seen in use. Abstract discussions are stimulating, but until a manager has seen the insights they deliver in a specific situation, they are not very persuasive. For this reason we have provided several step-by-step applications, so it is apparent how the methods can be applied to resolve pressing strategic issues. The second belief is that informed usage requires sensitivity to the limitations and pitfalls of the methods. There are many conditions in which the methods should not be used. In the right setting these methods can be illuminating, but when mishandled their signals can be seriously misleading. After reading each chapter, readers should have a good appreciation of the underlying premises and the critical measurement and interpretation problems. They then can arrive at their own opinion of their potential contribution to the problems in their strategic environment. Finally, we know that surrounding all the concepts, methods, and tools of strategy analysis are people. People are an integral part of successful applications, for unless the assumptions and insights are fully understood by all those whose actions, organizational roles, and performance are affected, their implications will be resisted and their potential contributions will then be seriously compromised. But when the conditions in the organization are right, these methods and concepts have a powerful capacity to extend the collective strategic reach of management teams.

The organization of the book follows the distinction between the foundation concepts, which are dealt with first, and the higher-level methods of analysis. The first chapter extends this distinction and clarifies the various roles that the methods and concepts can play. This chapter will also help readers better understand why there is so much controversy about strategic planning methods, and why they play a strong support role but can never substitute for strategic thinking grounded in the realities of the business. The second chapter uses the experience curve framework to clarify the dynamic nature of costs and prices. The next two chapters focus on the dynamics of markets with aid of the product life-cycle concept. Chapter 4 is devoted to recent evidence on the need to adjust a strategy as the life cycle evolves. The next four chapters are devoted to integrative planning models. Each model has some capacity to synthesize judgments on the interaction of the capabilities of a business with the threats and opportunities in the environment. The fifth chapter is about the PIMS approach, which seeks guidance from the pooled experience of a large and diverse sample of successful and unsuccessful businesses. Chapters 6 and 7 cover the two basic types of portfolio models. Both models are able to classify and visually display the positions of businesses or products according to the attractiveness of the market and the ability of the business to compete in that market. The growth-share matrix discussed in Chapter 6 is the simplest of these portfolio models and surely the most controversial. It is also a useful framework for analyzing market share strategies. Chapter 6 reviews recent evidence on the complex relationship of market share and profitability. More complex multifactor portfolio models, with greater capacity to support the planning process, are described in Chapter 7. In the concluding chapter the notion of decision support systems is introduced. These systems are combinations of data banks, analytical capability, and models that are tailored to a specific environment or decision. This area promises to hold the greatest potential for development.

Audiences. This book is designed for two audiences. The first is managers seeking to assess the contribution these strategy analysis methods can make to clarifying managers' strategic issues and options in the markets they have chosen to serve. Once they have decided to use these approaches, there is sufficient depth to the chapters to permit implementation and interpretation of the methods.

The second audience is *students* of management with a good knowledge of the basics of marketing and strategic planning, but only a passing familiarity with the concepts and methods of strategy analysis. This book is designed to function on its own or to enhance texts that introduce the basic framework of the strategic planning process. It can be used in executive development programs in strategic marketing or management, and in graduate or advanced undergraduate courses in strategic market management, business policy, or strategic planning.

The West Series on Strategic Market Management

The West Series is a planned series of five books. The first, entitled *Strategic Market Planning: The Pursuit of Competitive Advantage,* also by George Day, appeared in 1984 and serves as the integrating framework for the series. As such, it provides the most appropriate framework to which this book on strategy analysis can be linked. To facilitate integrated usage, a course design manual is available that shows how chapters of the two books can be appropriately sequenced for different types and durations of courses. Also included in this manual are suggestions for cases and computer simulations that support the course objectives.

The forthcoming three books in the series will cover such topics as organization and control of marketing systems and the management of new ventures, and will provide further insights into competitors, customers, and channel members. While each of these books can be treated as a distinct module in a course, they are all designed to be used within the basic planning process framework established by the first book.

Acknowledgments

Many people will recognize their contributions in the chapters to follow, for progress in this field reflects the cumulative experience of researchers and users. Here I want to single out those who made a direct contribution to my thinking or to the content of specific chapters. My first debt is to my clients—both the skeptics and the converts—for they have contributed much more than they suspect. By giving me hands-on opportunities to help them apply the material in this book to their problems, and then by continually challenging the implications, they have helped me better understand both the benefits and the pitfalls of the tools of strategy analysis. Several clients have contributed directly by providing the disguised examples used in several chapters. Their generosity is appreciated.

My thinking has also been expanded by productive relationships with numerous friends and colleagues in the field. They have never failed to share their experience and insights. I have drawn particularly heavily from Dave Aaker of Berkeley, Robert Allio of Robert J. Allio and Associates, Bill Brandt of the Impact Planning Group, Robert Buzzell of the Harvard Business School, Joseph D'Cruz of the University of Toronto, Adrian Ryans of the University of Western Ontario, and Robin Wensley of the London Business School. Bradley Gale and Joe Patten of the Strategic Planning Institute made important contributions to the coverage of PIMS in Chapter 5. Dave Montgomery of the Stanford Business School collaborated with me on Chapter 2 and provided much of the material on strategic decision support systems. My debt to these people is considerable.

Many people have reviewed the material in this book, and made major contributions by challenging the exposition and offering new insights. I am especially grateful to Steve Burnett of Northwestern, John Gwin of the University of Virginia, and Ken Roering of the University of Minnesota. Bart Weitz of the Wharton School deserves special recognition, for he has made major contributions to the structure of both books in this series. Three doctoral students also provided useful criticisms: Ida Berger, Mary Coyle, and Bruce Smyth each helped in numerous ways. Lastly, I would like to give special recognition to Anita Desembrana and Cindy Dixon for their help in the transformation of handwritten notes into readable manuscript.

Of all the contributions that have been made, none are more pleasant to reflect on and acknowledge than the unfailing support and encouragement of my family. I am fortunate to have an exceptional wife and caring parents. Without them this book would not have happened.

George Day
February 1985

Analysis for Strategic Market Decisions

Introduction to the Methods of Strategy Analysis

The past decade has seen widespread adoption of such strategy analysis methods as portfolio classification models and PIMS analyses of profitability determinants. Users were attracted by the logic and relevance of these methods to perplexing questions of strategic direction and resource allocation. A spate of success stories from Mead, General Electric, Borg-Warner, Norton, and other companies helped fuel the initial acceptance.[1] A new breed of strategic planning consultants including the Boston Consulting Group, Strategic Planning Associates, Braxton Associates, and Bain and Company made these methods an integral part of their practice and aggressively promoted them as solutions to management problems.

The new strategy analysis methods were well suited to the emerging planning concerns of the time. During the mid-seventies the orientation of strategic planning shifted from managing predictable growth to conserving scarce resources in a period of sharp discontinuities. Sorting out winning businesses from losers that were draining cash and consolidating strong competitive positions became the primary concerns. The dominant features of the planning systems that were developed in response to these changes are as follows:

- Related businesses and products are grouped into strategic business units (SBUs) or organizational entities large enough and homogeneous enough to exercise control over most strategic factors affecting their performance.

---

1. Cushman (1978), or *Business Week,* "The New Planning." (19 December 1978), or Loomis (1980–81).

■ Strategic direction is provided by strategic market plans that specify the product-market scope and focus of the SBU, the strategic thrust, and the performance objectives for the SBU within the context of the overall corporate mission and strategy.

■ Explicit consideration is given to distinct strategy alternatives, varying in terms of risk-reward profile or the importance of different objectives, such as market share gains versus short profitability.

■ Objectives for different SBUs are tailored to reflect differences in their strategic position and competitive environment that will influence long-run growth and profit potential.

■ A portfolio logic is used to allocate resources in recognition of differences in the contributions of different SBUs to the achievement of corporate objectives for growth and profitability. A key is whether the SBU is designated a net cash generator or a cash user.

A New Environment for Planning Methods

The challenges of the eighties are different from those that originally spawned the strategy analysis methods. Competitive pressures have become even more acute as companies recognize that the maturity of most industries requires them to actively seek new opportunities in order to grow or even hold their position. At the same time, technological advances, deregulation, global markets, changing demographics, a reduced government role, and innumerable other factors are presenting new challenges. As a result, patterns of competition are become more complex, market boundaries are becoming fuzzy, and competitive advantages are increasingly short-lived.

There is also a growing recognition that strategic planning systems emphasizing centralized decisions are unbalanced and ineffective. A pressing need exists for greater attention to the integration of strategic plans and operational planning. Too many conceptually elegant strategic plans have failed from lack of commitment by operating management. As further encouragement to decentralization, adequate funding is usually available for attractive projects. While corporate-level resource allocation problems remain important, they are no longer paramount.

Just as these new requirements for analysis of fast-moving and highly competitive markets emerged, there was growing skepticism of strategy analysis methods in the face of unrealized expectations.

Critics faulted these methods for abdicating management imagination to quantitative factors and thereby suppressing creative alternatives, depersonalizing the resource allocation process, and prescribing strategies that were simplistic, doctrinaire, and possibly misleading.[2]

These criticisms cannot be ignored, but in the main they reflect a misunderstanding of the proper role of these analytical methods. Certainly there is an unavoidable adjustment period in the life of any management concept or method, during which experience is gained and the limitations are appreciated. This is a necessary condition to informed usage and also a useful antidote to earlier overselling. What must be realized is that these methods can facilitate the strategic planning process and serve as a rich source of ideas about possible strategic options. But on their own, these methods cannot prescribe the appropriate strategy or predict the consequences of a specific change in strategy.

For the remainder of this chapter, we develop this theme further by putting the concepts and methods of strategy into perspective in a supporting role in the strategic market planning process. Then we look at some of the important distinctions and relations among the various methods, as a prelude to more detailed discussions in the following chapters.

Perspectives on Strategic Planning

Planning methods and concepts cannot be understood in isolation from the planning process and organizational imperatives that surround them. This section is a brief return visit to the four facets of contemporary planning practice that are more fully articulated in a companion volume in this series on strategic market management.[3] We revisit them here as an antidote to the tendency to get so submerged in the details of the concepts and methods that they become an end in themselves.

The essence of strategic planning is the consideration of current decision alternatives in light of their probable consequences over time. This means identifying foreseeable threats to avoid and opportunities to pursue. Two implications of this perspective are especially important. First, strategic planning is not a way to avoid or minimize risks. If anything, strategic planning should increase risk taking by

---

2. Hall (1980), Palesy (1980), and Kiechel (1981)

3. Day (1984).

ensuring that possible risks are considered and better contained. Second, strategic planning does not require a superior crystal ball in an attempt to outwit the future. The future is unpredictable, but it is not a random walk. In each market are strong likelihoods, built-in dynamics, and even a few near-certainties. Thus, strategic planning is the effective application of the best available information to decisions that have to be made now if there is to be a secure future.

No single definition has been able to capture all facets of contemporary strategic planning practice. Four distinguishing features, however, together shape the accepted meaning. They are linked together in Figure 1.1.

External Orientation: The Strategic Role of Marketing

The primary responsibility of strategic market planning is to continuously look outward and keep the business in step with the anticipated environment. The lead role in meeting this responsibility is played by marketing, for this is the boundary function between the firm and its customers, distributors, and competitors. As a general management responsibility, marketing embraces the interpretations of the environment and the crucial choices of customers to serve, competitors to challenge, and the product characteristics with which the business will compete. But strategic market planning is broader than marketing, for strategies that start with the analysis of market responses will not be effective unless they are fully integrated with other functional decisions.

Figure 1.1 The four facets of strategic market planning

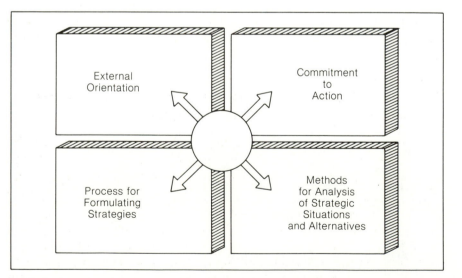

An effective market orientation is not simply a customer orientation that implies a battle for ultimate customers—won by direct appeal to these customers. Instead, the perspective must be broadened to view customers as an ultimate prize gained at the expense of competitors in many ways other than by simply offering a better match of products to customer needs. Additional sources of advantage over competitors can be found in strong distribution arrangements, lower costs, proprietary technology, and so forth.

Strategy Formulation Process

Strategies are the product of a special kind of problem-solving activity. As a result, most strategic planning processes share the same basic steps. Finding a planning process that did not have at least the following steps would be unusual: (1) situation assessment (including specifying the current strategy), (2) setting objectives, (3) generating and evaluating strategy alternatives, (4) selecting the best strategy, (5) developing detailed plans to make sure the strategies will achieve the established objectives, (6) implementation, and (7) performance monitoring.

The strategic planning process seldom resembles a tidy, linear sequence with a clear-cut beginning and endpoint. To be sure, the process eventually yields a set of plans. Because these plans are partially implemented through a regular budgeting cycle, they are usually completed with that schedule in mind. Just as the environment is continually changing, however, so is strategic planning a continuously evolving process. What must be sought is a strategic orientation to environmental change so that when action is taken, it will reinforce rather than compromise the basic thrust of the strategy.

Commitment to Action: The Need for Top-Down and Bottom-Up Dialogue

The output of strategic planning is decisions, implemented by operating managers acting roughly in concert to carry out a strategy they helped devise. Documented plans, analyses, forecasts, and objectives are only a means to that end, for of themselves they have little impact on the ongoing activities of the business.

The decisions themselves will lose impact and support to the extent they reflect a predominance of top-down or bottom-up perspectives on the issues confronting the business. The challenge is to foster a dialogue that blends the top-down corporate concerns with resource allocations and long-run industry position, with the bottom-up understanding of specific product-market opportunities. The decisions taken need not have full consensus; there seldom is. But it is critical that all operating managers understand why the strategic direction was chosen and have a substantial commitment to changing their functional activities in line with the strategy.

Strategy Analysis Concepts and Methods

The fourth facet of strategic market planning is shaped by the methods that are ordered hierarchically in Figure 1.2. The symbolism is reasonably straightforward. The higher one goes in the hierarchy, the more directly the methods speak to the specific decisions to be made by the business unit until the pinnacle is reached, at which point we have the most general and widely applicable method, which is the basic planning process. The foundation of the hierarchy provides the inputs to higher-level analyses, but generally these inputs

Figure 1.2 The hierarchy of strategy analysis methods

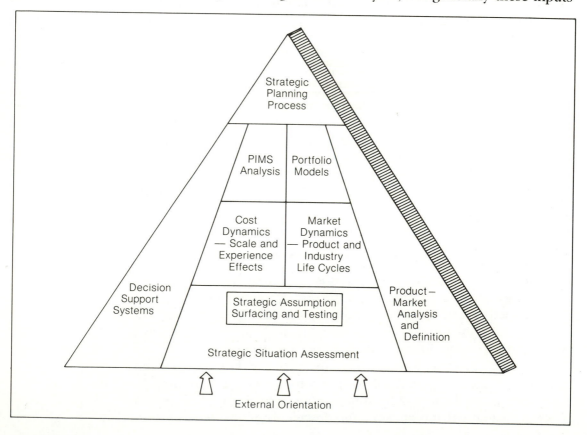

have limited decision relevance. The role of the methods found in the center of the pyramid is to help translate the external orientation into strategies and programs for achieving a competitive advantage. These methods are arranged roughly in ascending order of complexity and degree of integration of external and internal information.

Two methods are shown in a flanking position because they are by nature more flexible. In both cases they are a fundamental part of the foundation analysis, but also provide significant inputs to higher-level analyses. For example, the starting point for a market analysis is a preliminary identification of the product class boundaries and market segments. But part of the market analysis task is to identify and forecast exploitable discontinuities in the market. Also, each of the models in this hierarchy—life cycle, experience curve, portfolio, or PIMS—relies on the proper definition of the market. Decision support systems play an analogous role in turning lower-level inputs into higher-level outputs. These ideas are expanded in the remainder of this section as we briefly overview the basic features.

Foundations of Strategy Analysis

The two related components in the foundation are discussed next.

Situation Assessment. Situation assessment entails the systematic analysis—of past, present, and future data—to identify trends, forces, and conditions with the potential to influence the performance of the business and the choice of appropriate strategies. The relevant data encompass the entire macro-environment, including the industry and market environment, technological trends, and competitive forces, intentions, and internal capabilities. The outcome is a series of explicit and hopefully testable assumptions about internal strengths and weaknesses and external threats and opportunities. These assumptions provide a basis for a critical assessment of the adequacy of the present strategy.

Strategic Assumptions Surfacing and Testing. Assumptions are those data points, facts, or beliefs that are taken as given or true by managers exploring an issue or deciding a course of action. As issues and strategic options are inherently ambiguous and decisions have to be made with incomplete information, assumptions serve to absorb this uncertainty. Otherwise, all those with a stake in the decisions would be immobilized.

A major purpose of all strategy analysis methods is to surface underlying assumptions, critically examine them, and assess their consequences. However, the strategic assumptions surfacing and testing methodology contributes directly to the foundation of strategy analysis, for the outcome is an explicit assessment of relative importance and degree of certainty of each assumption. These judgments serve as useful inputs to the other strategy analysis methods. This method is employed only after distinctive competing strategic options have been identified. The underlying procedure is adversarial in that groups of advocates for each option are formed and asked to identify the pivotal assumptions that are necessary in order for that option to be successful. A subsequent debate among competing groups is designed to identify both shared assumptions and critical issues on which there is no consensus. Further dialogue is necessary to achieve consensus or resolve differences. Details on this method can be found in the Appendix to Chapter 7 of the companion volume.

Planning Concepts and Techniques

The second level of the hierarchy of strategy analysis methods is occupied by experience curves, product and industry life cycles and decision support systems. Each of these concepts and techniques enhances strategic thinking by providing frameworks for organizing the mass of strategic information unearthed in the first level of analysis. They play their role by separating important issues and relationships from those that are unimportant. The methods at this level do double duty by contributing to the conceptual framework for the models found at the next level.

Analysis of Cost Dynamics: Scale and Experience Effects. The organizing framework for dynamic analyses of costs and price is the experience curve. Few strategy concepts have gained wider acceptance than the basic premise of the experience curve: Value-added costs—that have been adjusted for inflation—decline systematically with increases in cumulative volume. These declines in real costs are usually attributable to some combination of learning by doing, advances in technology, or increased efficiency from economies of scale.

Three types of experience curves have been used to support strategy analyses:

- The company cost compression curve relates changes in the company, total value-added costs, as well as individual cost elements, to the accumulated experience of the company with a particular product.

- Competitive cost comparison curves are cross-sectional relationships of the relative cost positions of the competitors in an industry. With this curve it is possible to estimate the relative profitability of each of the competitors at the prevailing price.

■ Industry price experience curves relate the industry average price to industry cumulative experience.

Analysis of Market Dynamics.   Analysis of market dynamics is virtually synonymous with the product life-cycle concept. The notion of distinct stages in the sales history of a product category—from birth to growth to maturity to decline—has enduring appeal because of the biological analogy. What makes the life-cycle concept useful as an organizing framework for strategy analysis is the capacity to reflect the outcome of market, technology, and competitive forces. Its capacity for prediction is much more restricted, and attempts to use it to prescribe appropriate strategies are dubious. This is because the product life cycle can act simultaneously as a determinant of strategy, an enabling condition (in the sense that rapid growth creates opportunities for new competitors), and a consequence of strategic actions.

Analytical Planning Models

The most distinctive feature of analytical planning models is their capacity to synthesize a variety of judgments on the interaction of the capabilities of the business with the threats and opportunities in the environment. They are the most integrative and complex of all strategy analysis methods, and are certainly the most controversial.

The Analysis of Pooled Business Experience: the PIMS Program.
The pooled business experience approach to strategy analysis seeks guidance from the collective experience of a diverse sample of successful and unsuccessful businesses. By 1985 there were over 2,700 businesses in the sample.

The basic premise of the PIMS program is that an individual business can learn as much from the experiences of strategy peers, conducting a large series of strategy experiments from a similar position, as it can learn from industry peers who participate in the same industry but face different strategic situations.

The search for strategically relevant insights is directed toward identifying the controllable and uncontrollable variables that do the best job of explaining the observed variance in profitability and cash flow in the sample of businesses. Three sets of influential variables have been identified: (1) the competitive position of the business, as measured by market share and relative product quality, (2) the production structure, including investment intensity and productivity of operations, and (3) the relative attractiveness of the served market, comprising the growth and customer characteristics. Overall, these variables account for 65 to 70 percent of the variability in profitability. These empirical insights from the data base are used to address a series of strategic questions for each business:

- What rate of profit and cash flow is normal for this type of business?
- If the business continues on its present track, what operating performance could be expected in the future?
- How will this performance be affected by a change in strategy?

Portfolio Classification Models.   The essence of portfolio classification models is the classification and visual display of the present and prospective positions of businesses and products according to the attractiveness of the market and the ability to compete within that market. In the original portfolio model, developed by the Boston Consulting Group, the corresponding dimensions were limited to market growth and relative market share. This simple formulation yields powerful insights, so long as the restrictive premises on which it is based are reasonably well satisfied. A number of alternative portfolio models have been developed to overcome the restrictions by substituting a composite of weighted factors to represent the two dimensions.

Portfolio models are widely used as diagnostic aids for communicating strategic judgments about the position of a business, or for understanding the behavior of competitors. They are being increasingly used to guide the generation of strategic options and facilitate negotiations between corporate and business management on critical questions of feasible objectives and investment strategies. Seldom are portfolio models used as prescriptive guides to the choice of the appropriate strategic option. While all portfolio models can be used to derive natural or generic strategies for a business according to its position in the portfolio matrix, in reality these possibilities are invariably dominated by the specifics of the strategic situation.

Flanking Methods

Flanking methods are utilized during the most basic of preliminary analyses, but are so broad in their potential utility that they also contribute to resolving higher-level strategic issues.

Product-Market Analysis and Definition.   A strategy reflects a pattern of decisions as to how a business unit can best compete in the markets it elects to serve. The chosen market may be defined broadly or comparatively narrowly depending on the choice of customer segments and the treatment of such issues as substitute technologies, geographic boundaries, and the number of stages in the value-added chain. These judgments are pivotal when making assessments of the current performance and the establishment of a defensible competitive position.

A common feature of all strategy analysis methods is their reliance on the choice of product-market boundaries. This is the unit of analysis that is the basic context for the other measures. The choice is complicated by the need to adapt the definition of the product-market to the decision to be made and the reality that there is an element of arbitrariness in all such definitions. Although this topic is the subject of a full chapter in the companion volume, we will revisit it frequently, for each strategy analysis method places different demands on the product-market definition.

Decision Support Systems.   Decision support systems is a generic term for a combination of strategic intelligence and analytical models that are tailored to the requirements of the business. The positioning of decision support systems as a flanking method reflects their versatility and potential contributions to the data base from which all the strategy analysis methods in this book draw for their inputs. Their greatest contributions to date have come from the enhancements to the quality of strategic information gained from the strategic intelligence system. This part of a decision support system directs intelligence gathering, collects the data, and then transforms data into information. Less progress has been made with the development of the models component, but trends in communications and computer technologies are rapidly enhancing their feasibility.

Integrating the Methods into the Planning Process

The four facets of strategic planning can be fitted together in many different ways to suit the needs of the company and the conditions within their industry. The experience of 3M illustrates how an already effective organization adapts its planning system to take best advantage of the developments in strategic planning. In 1981, when management of 3M began to revamp their planning system, 3M had achieved sales of $6.5 billion from over 45,000 products. Most of these products are rooted in the original coated abrasives or pressure-sensitive tape technologies. Subsequent developments have taken the company into markets as diverse as recording equipment, medical products, and pharmaceuticals.

The initial challenge for 3M management was to cope with almost two hundred organizational units worldwide: divisions, departments, projects, and subsidiaries. Most of these units were accustomed to directing their business autonomously, on the basis of their own perceived requirements and opportunities. However, there was a pressing need to coordinate these diverse capabilities to enhance competitive advantage in their markets. The planning systems that emerged in 1982 in response to this need were consistent with the history and culture of 3M in keeping responsibility for strategic decision making with the key operating unit managers. Some of the aspects of this planning system are described in the following boxed insert.

The Principles of the 3M Planning System

Characterizing the Industry:

The first step of the planning process in any SBC or operating unit is to characterize the industry. Managers need to identify factors that will influence the strategies they select—for instance, the size and growth rate of the industry. And what about outside influences—new technology, regulatory changes, and competitive conditions? Who are the key competitors? What share of the market do they hold? What strategies have they adopted?

Determining Key Success Factors:

In order to formulate effective strategy 3M stresses accurate evaluation of the basis of competition. This means understanding the key success factors of a particular industry—the factors that determine ultimate success or failure. For each 3M business, managers need to ask, "Where do I get the competitive edge for long-term success in my industry?" One way of getting these answers is to rank a 3M business against its major competitors in an industry to develop a measure of its relative competitive position. Reflecting the corporate strategy, 3M occupies a strong position in many of its industries, while in others a secure product or market niche provides a favorable position, defensible against competitors with broader product lines.

Selecting Business Strategy:

The strategic condition of an SBC strongly influences appropriate strategies. For example, in embryonic industries 3M businesses emphasize market- or product-oriented strategies to improve their competitive position. As their industries mature, these businesses will very likely emphasize integration, efficiency, and rejuvenation through innovation. In the late stages of maturity, they'll move forward to consolidation and disinvestment. The overall strategic position of each 3M SBC is typically displayed in the form of a maturity/ competitive position exhibit. For a particular SBC or operating unit the product portfolio (Figure 1.3) or market portfolio (Figure 1.4) indicate different strategic positions.

At this point in the planning process, implementation receives priority. 3M believes that the most eloquent strategy statement isn't much use if it's not part of the day-to-day operations of the business. This means that each SBC strategy must be backed up by appropriate action programs that identify the necessary costs, specify expected results, and establish schedules and responsibilities.

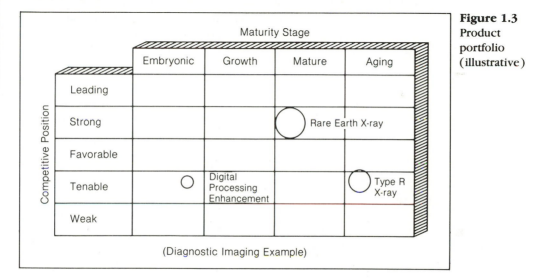

Figure 1.3
Product
portfolio
(illustrative)

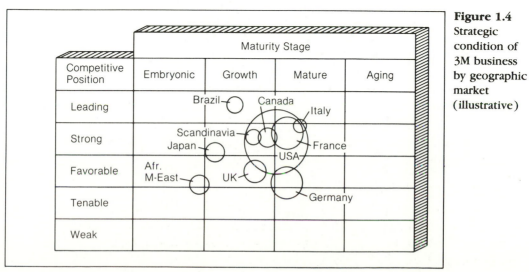

Figure 1.4
Strategic
condition of
3M business
by geographic
market
(illustrative)

The Principles of the 3M Planning System—cont'd

Every SBC is made up of individual operating units. These are usually divisions or departments responsible for specific products or market segments. Some SBCs cover two or more divisions—for example, Tape comprises several divisions, departments, and projects; and Memory Media contains Data Recording Products and Magnetic A/V Products. Other SBCs, such as Pharmaceutical (Riker Laboratories), are a single operating unit. Some of the larger SBCs contain operating units whose main function is to manufacture or market products for other divisions within that SBC or other 3M units.

The planning task for each operating unit is to develop strategic plans that support the overall strategic approach of the SBC. They detail how the SBC strategies will be carried out over the next several years. The responsibility for developing each operating unit's plan rests with the division general manager or department manager and subsidiary management.

Because some organizations, such as the Specialty Chemical and Film Division, provide a critical support function to other SBCs, their plans are necessarily finalized after the other SBC plans. Corporate staff plans (such as R&D and Human Resources) are also completed after SBC plans, although a considerable amount of discussion and integration takes place throughout the planning cycle.

Measuring Strategic Performance:

In determining the expected financial performance of an SBC, 3M managers assess the maturity of an industry, competitive position, and strategy. Although regular operating reviews scrutinize a number of financial health indicators, the key financial parameters for an SBC include return on capital, operating

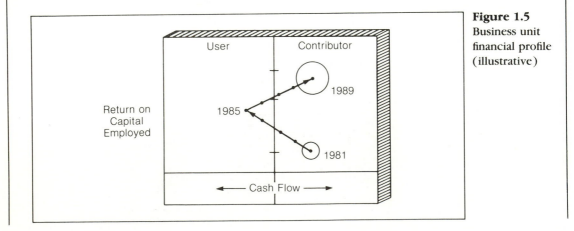

Figure 1.5
Business unit financial profile (illustrative)

income, and cash flow. Figure 1.5 shows how management can estimate the financial consequences of various strategies.

Effective monitoring of performance is based on financial and nonfinancial strategy measurements. For example, market share is a strong indicator of success for a business attempting to penetrate new markets, as are product quality, distribution expansion, and new products. As part of its planning process, each 3M SBC (and its component operating units) identifies a set of strategic measurements appropriate to its strategy. For many 3M businesses, this means that innovation and new product introduction are given high visibility.

Until recently, the corporation's rules demanded that every SBC grow at the same rate each year, that every SBC have 25 percent new products, and that every SBC target the same profit. Although the results were easy to monitor, needless to say, not every business could meet these demands. Now, the old mandate is being replaced by a measurement and reward system consistent with the strategy of each SBC, although overall corporate targets have not changed.

The final step in preparing the strategic plan is assessing risk—what's the probability of the plan's being successfully implemented? A number of factors come into play here, including the characterization of the industry and the competitive position of the business within that industry.

*Source: Tita and Allio (1984). Reproduced with permission of the authors and the *Planning Review* journal.

The Role of Strategy Analysis Methods in the Planning Process

Few generalizations about strategy methods are meaningful in the face of the variety of roles they can potentially play during the planning process. Still, it is safe to say that these methods are limited to supporting and enhancing the effectiveness of the basic process, and should never serve as a substitute for strategic thinking. Our purpose in this section is to describe the feasible roles of the strategy analysis methods to provide a context for more detailed examination in subsequent chapters.

Possible Roles

The contributions of strategy analysis methods are primarily realized during the early stages of the planning process. They play a modest role during the later stages of implementation and monitoring. Among the specific applications where they have been found to be particularly useful are the following:

(A) *Situation assessment*
   1. Provide a *structure for analysis* that enables management teams to separate important issues from the unimportant and identify critical subproblems.
   2. Isolate *information gaps* in order to assign priorities to marketing research and information system activities. One of the most valuable functions of the strategy analysis methods is to provide a logical and comprehensive checklist to ensure key variables are not overlooked.
   3. Provide a common language and mutually acceptable structure that management teams can use to *communicate judgments and assumptions* about strategic issues.
   4. *Evaluate the current strategy and competitive position* in terms of key performance measures such as cash flow and return on investment.

(B) *Strategy development, evaluation, and implementation*
   5. Facilitate the *identification of strategy options* to be given detailed consideration.
   6. *Identify performance trade-offs* involved in choosing among the feasible strategic options.
   7. Provide a logical basis for *allocating resources* across businesses or business segments.
   8. *Test the validity* of forecasts of performance of a recommended strategy.
   9. Facilitate the *monitoring* of actual performance of the chosen strategy and the isolation of reasons for variance from the objectives.

   Although each method may be used for almost all purposes, in practice most methods are much better suited to some applications than others. Table 1.1 shows schematically the preferred patterns of usage. Several generalizations are possible from this table, even though the broad categories of analysis methods obscure some important distinctions (notably among types of decision support systems and varieties of portfolio models). First, we see that the more complex, higher-level methods can assume a greater variety of roles. Complexity here is a function of the number of variables and relationships that are incorporated into the method. This is why PIMS appears to be the most widely applicable. We will find, however, that the usefulness of a method also depends on how readily it can be adapted to a specific setting. Some concepts, such as the experience curve, offer powerful insights within certain industries but are downright misleading in other settings. PIMS and some portfolio models

Table 1.1 Potential Applications of Strategy Analysis Methods

	PRODUCT LIFE-CYCLE ANALYSIS	EXPERI-ENCE CURVE ANALYSIS	DECISION SUPPORT SYSTEMS	PORT-FOLIO MODELS	PIMS
(A) Situation Assessment					
1. Structure for analysis	**	**	**	**	**
2. Isolate information gaps	*	*	**	*	**
3. Communicate judgments and assumptions	*	*	*	**	**
4. Evaluate current strategy		*	*	*	*
(B) Strategy Development, Evaluation, and Implementation					
5. Facilitate identification of options	*	*	*	**	*
6. Identify performance trade-offs			**	*	*
7. Guide resource allocations across businesses			*	*	*
8. Test validity of performance forecasts			*		*
9. Monitor performance against objectives			*		

also suffer in this regard because they are constrained by rigidity in the specification of their variables and relationships.

Creative Combinations of Methods.   From Table 1.1 it seems that several methods serve the same purpose. This does not mean they are substitutes. In most cases, treating them as complements is more appropriate. Each strategy analysis method has a distinctive profile of strengths and weaknesses stemming from differences in orientation, premises, and measures. This is an advantage to the strategy analyst, for the differences in methods permit the examination of the same problem or issue from several perspectives. The hope is that they will give the same signals. If the signals are contradictory, then further analysis must be undertaken to resolve the conflict. In this role, the methods are provocative devices for raising important questions, although the resolution usually lies outside the methods because it is embedded in the details of the particular competitive situation.

The experience of a strategic business unit within a medium-technology manufacturer of alarm and fire security systems illustrates the payoff from vigorous pursuit of contradictions highlighted by the analysis methods. Early in the planning process, each of the six business segments within this business unit was classified in a market attractiveness and business strength portfolio matrix. By all the usual signals, this was a mature "manage for current earnings while holding market position" type of business. But the forecast of the financial and market share consequences of the current strategy was wildly at variance with this portfolio interpretation. The problem was traced to a serious cash flow problem created by an ill-advised decision to carry extensive inventories to buy coverage of a previously unused distributional channel. This situation had been obscured by an unusual one-time improvement in cash generated by the business during the year the new distribution strategy was implemented. Only when management had to reconcile the conflicting signals from two different ways of analyzing their strategic situation did they reconsider their new distribution strategy. The process of reconciliation began with a review of the assumptions made in the performance forecasts, followed by a search for explanations. By the end of the planning process, the management team was committed to a major redirection of their strategy.

Appropriate Level of Analysis.   Methods of analysis may also be distinguished by the level within the organization where they are most appropriate. This will often be related to the relevant role of the method in the planning process, and helps us appreciate why some methods are constrained in their application. The judgments of which methods can be used in which circumstances reflect their inherent limitations and capacity to provide useful insights.

Although the initial impression from Table 1.2 is that strategy analysis methods are widely applicable, a closer look shows that they have little to say about such critical issues as the following:

- Charting new business directions. While the diagnosis may reveal the need for an expanded business definition or diversification into a new business, none of the models say much about where to look for such opportunities or how to assess them.

- Managing shared resource units (such as pooled sales forces and R and D facilities) or taking advantage of synergies that arise when two business units serve related markets or utilize a common technology.

- Directing the specific functional actions and programs necessary to implement a strategy.

Table 1.2 Finding the Appropriate Level in the Organization to Apply Strategy Analysis Methods

LEVEL	PRODUCT LIFE-CYCLE ANALYSIS	EXPERI-ENCE CURVE ANALYSIS	DECISION SUPPORT SYSTEMS	PORT-FOLIO MODELS	PIMS
Corporate			*	**	*
Strategic Business Unit	*	*	**	*	**
Shared Resource Unit		*	*		
Business Segment (Product-Market Unit)	*	*	*	*	*
Product Category	**	**	*		
Value-adding component		**	*		

Implications and Themes for this Book

Strategy analysis methods are no substitute for insightful strategic thinking. Indeed, their greatest weakness is that the superficial appeal of the generic prescriptions may override the careful analysis of fundamentals that are the basis for competitive advantage. The details of the situation will always dominate the facile generalizations of the methods. Yet, without the structure provided by the analysis methods, it is often difficult to know which details require attention and then ensure that managers have a common language for discussing and questioning assumptions.

Many assessments of the value of strategy analysis methods seem to miss this point by focusing solely on the prescriptions. A typical commentary concluded that "clearly, the quantitative formula-matrix approaches to strategic planning developed by BCG in the 1960's are out of favor ... These overly quantitative techniques caused companies to place a great deal of emphasis on market-share growth. As a result, companies were devoting too much time to corporate portfolio planning and too little to hammering out strategies to turn sick operations into healthy ones or ensure that strong businesses remained strong. In too many instances, strategy planning degenerated into acquiring growth businesses that the buyers did not know how to manage and selling or milking to death mature businesses." In the same article, a well-known planner characterized "formula" planning as "a search for shortcuts ... It took the thinking out of what you have to do to be competitively successful in the future."[4]

Blanket criticisms can be just as misleading as the simplistic formulas that they decry, when they confuse the potential contributions of the analysis methods with the undeniable problems of interpreting and applying their signals. What is needed is a change in emphasis rather than a complete break with the past. These changes will be evolutionary—reflecting what has been learned through trial and error to get the most value from the methods. Five directions for change are especially important, and each serves as a major theme tying together the chapters of the book:

1. *Integrate the methods into the planning process.* Strategic decisions are shaped during an ongoing dialogue between functions and levels. Strategy analysis methods are no replacement

---

4. *Business Week,* "The New Breed of Strategic Planner," (17 September 1984).

for this dialogue, but can facilitate it by providing frameworks for sharing and challenging strategic insights and assumptions. From shared understanding comes the commitment to action, which is an essential ingredient of effective implementation.

2. *Watch for misleading signals.* All methods and concepts impose discipline on strategic thinking through some amount of quantification. This is both a source of strength and a potentially crippling weakness. The problem is their dependence on input measures and assumptions that may themselves be inaccurate, invalid, or inappropriate. Bad measures will invariably lead to poor results. The measurement of market boundaries and structure, competitive positions, and costs are notorious problems. The problems may be more fundamental, as when the basic premises of the analytical models are violated or inappropriate. Informed usage requires a good understanding of these pitfalls, and may sensibly lead to the conclusion that the concept or model should not be used. Much of this book is devoted to examining these limitations and suggesting ways of overcoming them.

3. *Avoid the "planning priesthood" barrier.* Resistance—if not outright sabotage—by line managers is assured when planners are viewed as an elite group with their own dogma and arcane language of matrices, PIMS models, and SBUs. Whether planners construct this barrier inadvertently in an effort to show their analytical prowess, or deliberately use independent data and mysterious models to second-guess line managers, their effectiveness can be markedly reduced. To avoid this situation, planners and their methods need to be mainstreamed into the early stages of plan formulation. The models and concepts should be used only when they are understood and accepted by the line managers. This requires a commitment to education in strategic thinking and the capabilities of the methods by the planners. Planners should then act as internal consultants, offering guidance and answering questions.

4. *Focus on exploitable advantages.* The source of a competitive advantage for a business is often found in the unique complexities of a market and the skills and resources that have been assembled to exploit that evironment. Yet by design, strategy analysis methods are myopic about these specific possibilities. The narrowing of vision comes about from the need to put order into complex situations. This means using mea-

sures that can be generalized across many different businesses. When these simplifications are not recognized, the temptation is strong to derive equally generalized strategy statements that are not relevant to the business. Such statements as the following provide little useful guidance.

■ Dominate the market for zippers through aggressive capacity expansion.

■ Gain market share through development of a position as the golf ball industry's low-cost producer.

■ Manage the business for cash as it proceeds from maturity to decline over the planning horizon.

Such generic strategy prescriptions have a limited role to play in the planning process and should be avoided by all users of planning concepts and methods. The argument against formula-based planning that yields these prescriptions has been made forcefully by Carroll in a critique of planning manuals that force all strategies into a common mold.[5]

The author of the manual has attempted to reduce all the possible courses of action for any company (in any business, in any competitive situation) into a very limited number of options. Each is given a name. A simple decision rule then guides the company into the appropriate category. [But] suppose customers rate service important . . . and installed base has a pronounced effect on the ability to supply service at a low delivered cost. In fact, it may be the *density,* not the *size* of the installed base that is predictably related to cost of service calls. Part of the firm's position and its strategy should reflect this relationship. The measure, "geographic density of installed base" is not permissible because it has no relevance in other businesses. The specific exploration of this relationship and its clear articulation are not encouraged. (Emphasis in original).

While this is a parody of planning in multidivisional companies, the warning should be heeded. The methods and concepts of strategy analysis can serve only as a means to an end—which is clear thinking about the possibilities for gaining and sustaining advantage.

5. *Challenge the boundaries.* Planning methods help structure situations by placing boundaries around markets and organizational units. While this is an essential step, it can also cause myopia unless it is recognized that these are arbitrary lines

---

5. Carroll (1984).

drawn for convenience. Some of the biggest strategic payoffs come from stretching these boundaries—by entering new products or markets—or spanning boundaries to share skills and resources between business units. Indeed, diversified firms are only greater than the sum of their parts when these inter-dependencies are nourished.

Summary

Strategy analysis methods and concepts have many roles to play in support of the planning process. Yet, their benefits will be obtained only through informed usage that is sensitive to their possibilities and limitations. The objective of this book is to provide guidance on how to achieve their benefits while minimizing the costs. These methods are not for every situation; part of the art of strategy is in knowing when to use them to advantage.

Cost and Price Dynamics: The Effects of Scale and Experience[1]

Chapter 2

Competitive interactions create an ever-changing pattern of relationships between the costs of services, products, and their substitutes. When these cost changes are reflected in price changes, they shape the evolution of market demand. With markets becoming more competitive and the tempo of life cycles accelerating, a pressing need exists for better insights into whether and how cost advantages are gained and sustained. Cloudy understanding and poor judgments can be disastrous, as the story of RCA's videodisc failure in the following insert illustrates.

The experience curve speaks directly to the need for strategists to understand cost and price dynamics. Indeed, few strategy concepts have gained wider acceptance than the notion that unit costs (net of inflation) decline systematically with increases in cumulative volume. This idea is especially compelling because it applies to products as diverse as microprocessors, refrigerators, and Japanese beer. With every doubling in the number of units produced, the unit costs of these products will typically fall between 20 and 25 percent. The real value of the experience curve comes when it is applied to such problems as the size of the market leaders' cost advantage, forecasts of achievable costs, and shifts in the relative importance of individual cost elements.

The experience curve has spawned other strategy concepts and methods, notably the growth-share portfolio matrix. Many of the implications have been confirmed and extended by other approaches

---

1. This chapter is adapted from Day and Montgomery (1983).

RCA's Videodisc Failure: A Costly Lesson about Experience Effects

When RCA entered the videodisc market in 1981, the videocassette recorder already had a significant presence. Sales of VCRs had grown from 143,000 units in 1977 to 1.4 million in 1981, and the price had dropped from $1,300 to $800 in the same period. Nonetheless, RCA elected to proceed because of four key assumptions—each of which was found to be flawed.

The first assumption was that room could be made for both technologies, because the videodisc offered a sharper, clearer picture as well as better sound. Unfortunately, the magnitude of these advantages could not offset the inherent versatility of VCRs. VCRs not only could play prerecorded material but also could record TV programs off the air. Tapes were also reusable.

RCA's most serious error was to underestimate the ability of Japanese manufacturers to cut manufacturing costs. They had assumed the basic price of VCRs would not fall below $499. Instead, prices plunged to as low as $298 in 1984, which was roughly that of a videodisc player, and meant that a major anticipated basis of advantage had been completely eroded. How did the Japanese achieve such low costs? Three factors stand out:

- Economics of scale. By 1983 Japanese manufacturere were producing 18 million units a year.

- Simplifying design. By exploiting integrated circuit technology, the number of parts in a VCR was trimmed from 5,000 to 2,000.

- Automating production. On most assembly lines, 80 percent of the components were inserted by machine. The result was to eliminate most production workers.

Further gains will be much harder to achieve, for maximum economies of scale have been achieved, and the potential for savings from redesign is reduced.

Two further assumptions compounded RCA's problems. They did not believe in 1980 that the machinery needed to mass-produce pickup heads on tape recorders could be improved. Nonetheless, Japanese manufacturers were able to reduce their tolerances by 50 percent to a level that cannot be achieved by any U.S. manufacturer. Finally, RCA did not anticipate the rental market for movie tapes, which cut software costs for VCRs to well below the costs of prerecorded discs.

Source: Adapted from *Business Week* "The Anatomy of RCA's Videodisc Failure," (23 April 1984).

such as the PIMS model. An appreciation of the potential of these methods begins with a thorough grounding in the sources, strategic implications, and limitations of the experience curve. The objective of this chapter is to provide that perspective and build a foundation for the rest of the book.

The Concept of the Experience Curve

The experience curve was preceded by the production learning curve, first observed in the 1930s as a systematic decline in the number of labor hours required to produce an airplane.[2] In the late 1960s, the learning curve was extended by the Boston Consulting Group to encompass the behavior of all value-added costs and prices as cumulative volume or experience increases.[3]

A typical experience curve is plotted in Figure 2.1 for audio magnetic tape prices. Two sets of prices are shown: one in current dollars, the other in real or constant 1972 dollars using the government's final sales deflator for nondurable goods. The constant dollar curve shows that the industry was able to keep reducing prices while the current dollar price actually increased from 6.15¢ to 7.36¢ per square

Figure 2.1
Experience curve for audio magnetic tape

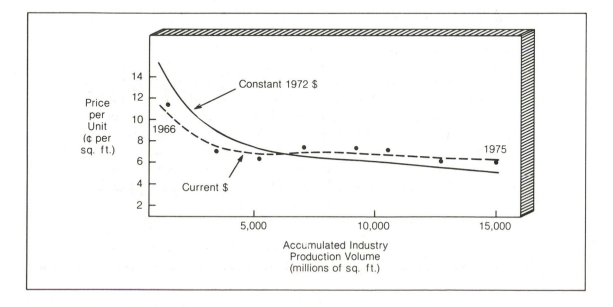

2. Yelle (1979).

3. Boston Consulting Group (1972).

foot between 1967 and 1972. Because we are mainly interested in what happens to prices and costs when accumulated experience doubles, these variables are usually plotted on log graphs. In this format equal percentage changes are always the same distance, no matter where we are on a log axis, and the experience curve becomes a straight line. The consequences of doubling experience are much clearer, as in Figure 2.2. However, progress down this curve was anything but even, with most of the decline in real prices occurring in just two years: 1968 and 1974. This makes it difficult to confidently forecast that prices will continue to decline at the same rate.

Accumulated industry experience refers to the total number of units delivered by all competitors since the beginning of production activity, and should not be confused with annual production rate. It also does not apply to calendar time. Experience will cumulate faster in calender time during periods of rapid growth.

Supporting Evidence.   Thousands of experience curves have been plotted during the past fifteen years by staff of the Boston Consulting Group.[4] They have looked at the direct costs of U.S. long-distance calls, integrated circuits, and life insurance policies, and the prices of bottle caps in Germany, refrigerators in Britain, and polystyrene molding resin in the United States. A typical example is the price

Figure 2.2
Experience curve for audio magnetic tape

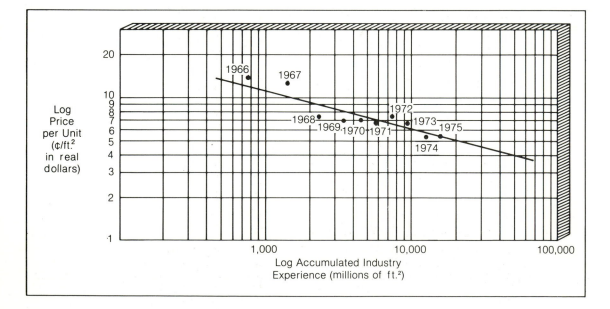

Log Price per Unit (¢/ft.^2 in real dollars)

Log Accumulated Industry Experience (millions of ft.²)

---

4. Henderson (1980).

Estimating the Experience Curve

The formula for the experience curve for costs is

$$C_q = C_n \frac{(q)^{-b}}{n}$$

where: q = total experience (cumulative output) to the present,
     n = experience (cumulative output) at some earlier point in time,
     C_q = the present cost of unit q (in real dollars),
     C_n = the prior cost of unit n (also in real dollars),
     $-b$ = a constant that reflects the elasticity of unit costs with respect to cumulative volume.

The two keys to reducing costs are the ratio q/n and the elasticity $-b$. A ratio of $q/n = 2$ implies that doubling experience from 100,000 to 200,000 units has the same percentage impact on costs as a doubling from 1,000 to 2,000 units. The percentage rate of cost decline when experience doubles is

$$1 - \frac{C_q}{C_n} = 1 - 2^{-b}$$

If $\frac{C_q}{C_n}$ = .80, then costs will fall by $(1 - .80)100 = 20$ percent as experience doubles. Then the experience curve is said to have an 80 percent slope. This slope will be observed only if the effects of inflation have been removed.

With the following table, we can translate the effect of different elasticities on the slope of the curve.

SLOPE	ELASTICITY
100%	0.000
95	.074
90	.152
85	.235
80	.322
75	.415
70	.515

Source: Abell and Hammond (1979).

experience curves for different sizes of Japanese motorcycles (see Figure 2.3), analyzed as part of a study of the British motorcycle industry.[5]

Sources of the Experience Curve Effect

Experience curves reflect the operation of three underlying factors: learning, technological advances, and scale effects. Unfortunately most experience curve applications confuse these three sources of cost declines.

Learning includes the increasing efficiency of labor as a result of practice, and the exercise of ingenuity, skill, and increased dexterity in repetitive activities. Learning includes the discovery of better ways to organize work via improved methods and work specialization (for example, doing half as much twice as often). Similarly, the performance of production equipment improves as personnel become better acquainted with their operation. For example, the capacity of a fluid catalytic cracking unit typically "grows" about 50 percent over a ten-year period as operators, engineers, and managers gain experience in operating the unit.[6] Similarly, learning by doing increased

Figure 2.3 Price experience curves for Japanese motorcycles (1959 to 1974)

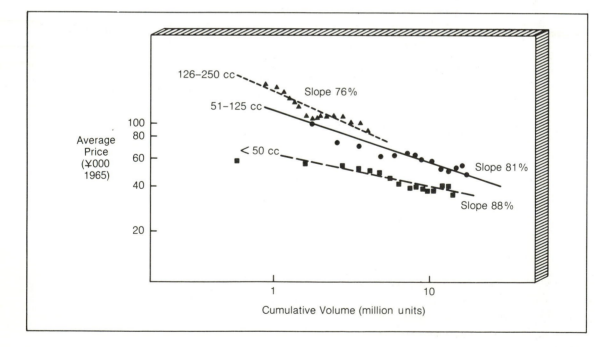

5. Boston Consulting Group (1975).

6. Hirschmann (1964).

the effective capacity of a particular piece of nuclear equipment by approximately 5 percent per year.[7] With experience, workers were more effective in using and maintaining the equipment and correcting technical "bugs."

Marketing activities also improve from learning. A recent survey of thirteen thousand new products launched by seven hundred companies found that cost of introduction of new products declined along a 71 percent slope.[8] Companies are constantly experimenting with new ways to organize and deploy sales forces and techniques such as telemarketing to reduce selling costs. This learning is certainly not cost-free; it requires an investment of time and money to acquire, apply, and adapt.

Learning is usually thought of as gains in productivity that are internal to the production process—the classic learning by doing. Another kind of learning, which comes through the application of products by users,[9] may also be important with technologically complex products or materials that have to perform in widely varying conditions. Learning by using generates two kinds of insights. One is feedback on the relationship of design features and performance, which can be used for subsequent design improvements. The stretching of aircraft, which contributed to a 50 percent reduction in operating energy costs per-seat mile of the DC-8, has been closely tied to a growing confidence in performance generated by learning by using. This knowledge may also lead to alterations in user practices that mean only minor modifications in hardware design but improve productivity by lengthening the useful life or reducing operating costs.

Technological improvements also contribute to the experience curve effect. New production processes, especially in capital-intensive industries, often contribute substantial saving. For example, Golden Wonder's introduction of continuous flow potato chip manufacture to replace the traditional batch frying yielded substantial economies in heating and quality control, and helped Golden Wonder achieve market share parity with the formerly dominant firm.[10] Changes in the resource mix, such as automation replacing labor, also contribute to the experience effect. Product standardization and redesign are also sources of the effect, as with the economies achieved in the automobile industry by modularization of the engine,

7. Joskow and Rozanski (1979).
8. Booz, Allen, and Hamilton (1982).
9. Rosenberg (1982).
10. Beevan (1974).

Table 2.1 Cost Reduction Changes on Office Equipment Machinery

	(JAPANESE YEN) SAVINGS IN MACHINE COST/UNIT		
CHANGE	BEFORE	AFTER	REDUCTION
1. Rod X: Carbon steel instead of stainless	Y 2870	Y 1830	Y 1040
2. Mounting Y: Sheet metal instead of diecast	Y 1695	Y 830	Y 865
3. Assembly Z: Much simpler shape; reduced weight	Y 649	Y 386	Y 263
4. Frame item T: Sheet metal instead of casting	Y 552	Y 190	Y 332

Source: Major Japanese manufacturer.

chassis, and transmission production. Substantial savings can be achieved with systematic "design to cost" approaches as we see in Table 2.1, which describes the experience of a Japanese office equipment manufacturer.

A graphic example of an experience curve dominated by technological breakthroughs is the plummeting cost of random access memories. This also shows how rapid growth can become self-reinforcing by pushing a product faster down the experience curve, which in turn makes the product more cost-competitive and opens up new applications so further volume increases are feasible. Per-bit prices of RAM chips have been dropping an average of 35 percent a year, and the world market has been growing 36 percent a year.[11]

Economies of scale, from the increased efficiency due to size, are the third source of the experience curve effect. These scale effects apply to the majority of investment and operating costs. Seldom does an increase in throughput require an equivalent increase in capital investment, size of sales force, or overhead functions. Scale effects are built into the familiar ".6 to .8" rule of thumb, used in many manufacturing and process industries. This heuristic says that if capacity is doubled, the investment required increases only 2^n with the exponent varying between .6 and .8. This corresponds to an

---

11. Business Week (2 April 1984).

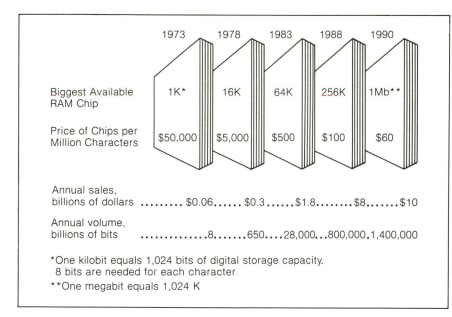

	1973	1978	1983	1988	1990
Biggest Available RAM Chip	1K*	16K	64K	256K	1Mb**
Price of Chips per Million Characters	$50,000	$5,000	$500	$100	$60

Annual sales, billions of dollars ....$0.06......$0.3......$1.8........$8.......$10

Annual volume, billions of bits ....8.......650....28,000...800,000.1,400,000

*One kilobit equals 1,024 bits of digital storage capacity.
 8 bits are needed for each character
**One megabit equals 1,024 K

Figure 2.4 Impact of cost declines of random access memory chips on market demand*

increase in investment of between 52 percent and 74 percent for a 100 percent increase in capacity. Similar effects are found with other cost elements; a supermarket chain with thirty stores in a trading area can spend far fewer dollars in advertising per store to achieve the same effect as a chain with only ten stores. These examples are of long-run economies of scale. Short-run economies of scale derive from a fuller utilization of existing investments such as processing plants, sales forces, or service organizations. In highly capital-intensive businesses, high-capacity utilization is critical if the low costs promised by larger-scale facilities are to be realized.

An increase in scale normally means a net increase in output. If total output does not increase, the new capacity must displace several smaller units that will no longer be required.[12] For an investment in larger scale capacity to result in a cost reduction, the total unit cost of the new facility, including return of capital and cost of capital, must be less than the operating cost alone of the displaced units.

Decomposing the Experience Curve

Experience curves capture the joint effects of learning, technological advances, and scale. For example, Sultan[13] found that costs per megawatt of output of steam turbine generators followed a steep

12. Henderson (1984).
13. Sultan (1974).

70 percent slope because of (1) practice in making units of each size (which followed an 87 percent slope), (2) scale economies by building larger units (six hundred megawatt rather than two hundred megawatt units), and (3) technological improvements in turbine bucket design, bearings, and high-strength steels for rotor shafts, which made possible the designs for larger units.

The separate contributions of scale, learning, and technology are hard to sort out, because the process of learning usually coincides with the expansion of scale.[14] Scale also creates the potential for vertical integration and division of labor, which in turn helps learning.

Implications for Strategy

The strategic messages from the experience curve are compelling in their logic and clarity. If costs per unit decrease predictably with cumulative output, then the largest competitor in the market has the potential for the lowest unit costs and highest profits.[15] The profit potential will not be realized if the dominant player is being outsegmented by more focused competitors or is doing a poor job of cost control.

Whether the smaller competitors are unprofitable depends on where the price has been set and the slope of the experience curve.

Figure 2.5 Cost experience for steam turbine generators

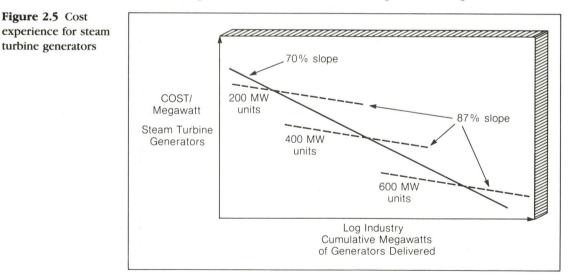

14. Some authors, such as Abell and Hammond (1979), prefer to keep scale effects separate from experience effects. Others, such as Pessemier (1977), prefer to distinguish static scale effects from dynamic scale effects, which are achieved over time.

15. Hedley (1976).

Smaller competitors face the situation in Figure 2.6, where Firm A leads both Firms B and C in experience and has a significant cost advantage. If the industry price is falling with experience, as Figure 2.6 suggests, then Firm A will have a substantial profit while Firm C will be suffering a loss. Firm A is definitely in control of the situation, for if it chose to cut prices as costs were reduced, it could possibly drive out the smaller competitors. However, if Firm A chose to maintain high margins, or reduced prices more slowly than costs, the resulting umbrella would protect the smaller competitors. The danger to the dominant competitor is that firms like B might then be encouraged to increase their experience base by building their market share.

The problems this scenario presents for the smaller competitors are acute. If smaller competitors are now profitable, they must continue to grow at least as fast as the leader and pursue cost reductions as effectively; otherwise, their profits will dwindle and eventually vanish. If share building is not feasible, or if the costs are excessive, their best course of action is to find an economically distinct market segment where they can sufficiently dominate the relevant experience base to achieve a viable overall cost position.

These implications focus on market position relative to competitors—and lead inexorably to the pursuit of dominance as a strategic imperative. A dominant position is best seized early in the game when experience doubles quickly. A further implication is that gains in experience are most easily achieved in fast-growing markets, by taking a disproportionate share of new sales.[16] This approach avoids a

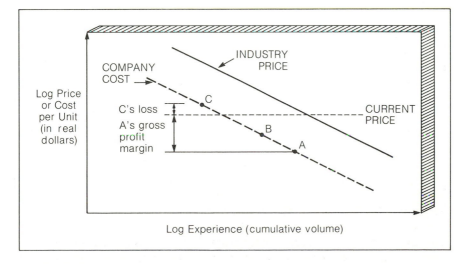

Figure 2.6
Profitability advantages of greater experience

---

16. Abell and Hammond (1979).

direct attack on the positions of the competitors. However, this strategy is also costly in the short run, for it requires investment in fixed assets and heavy expenditures on market development, promotion, and coverage at a time when margins may be reduced from lower prices. By the time growth slows, the firm with the largest market share will presumably have the greatest experience and will be able to use the cost advantage to resist competitive inroads. This strategy will succeed only if competitors are unwilling or unable to match the investment in large, efficient facilities. If they do feel compelled to match the investment, the result will be over-capacity and competitive gridlock rather than a cost advantage. This problem is acute in industries such as pulp and paper where new capacity increments are very large.

Experience effects that result from learning by doing or using, offer the most sustainable route to cost advantage. Even these gains will be quickly eroded unless the learning can be kept proprietary. This is especially difficult when basic design improvements can be revealed by reverse engineering or when the learning is vested in small groups of employees that can move to competitors. Proprietary learning can be partially protected by back integration. Japanese manufacturers often make their own machine tools and assembly equipment, which helps them protect specialized techniques.

Strategic Delusions?   In practice, these strategic signals can be elusive and are often misleading. They depend on assumptions that are often not satisfied. Specifically, the usual interpretation of Figure 2.6 requries that all competitors

- follow the same experience curve,
- realize the same price per unit,
- define their business the same way,
- share resources and experience with other parts of the corporation to the same extent, and
- operate at the same level of capacity utilization.

These assumptions are often unrealistic. The problem is to know when they do not hold true, and then adjust the interpretation. In the rest of this chapter, we address these issues and provide guidelines for adapting the experience curve to different settings.

The strategic relevance of the experience curve is also highly sensitive to the source of the observed cost reductions: Are they mainly attributable to scale, learning, or technological advances? Where the cost reductions are being achieved primarily from economies of scale through more efficient, automated facilities and vertical integration, then cumulative experience may be unimportant to the relative cost position.[17] In these situations, a new entrant may be more efficient than more experienced producers. If, however, experience effects are due to learning by doing or by using and can be kept proprietary, the leaders will maintain a cost advantage.

Finally, the experience curve will indeed be a delusion if cost declines are taken for granted. Cost reductions due to learning and technology are the result of continuous, planned efforts by management. Cumulative experience does not guarantee that costs will decline, but simply presents management with an opportunity to exploit.

Types of Experience Curves

Within a market environment a variety of experience curves can be found, depending on whether one is concerned with

- costs or prices,
- total costs or elements of cost,
- the effect of industry- or company-accumulated experience,
- dynamic (time-dependent) or static (cross-sectional) comparisons.

Three combinations of these variables are of particular interest, for they lead to experience curves with very different strategic insights. The first is the *company cost compression* curve, which relates changes in the company's costs to accumulated company experience. The second is the *competitive cost comparison* curve, which relates the current costs of all direct competitors to their cumulative experience. The third curve describes the behavior of *industry prices and average costs* as total industry experience cumulates. This last curve has a close relationship to the product life.

Company Cost Compression Curves

The company cost compression curve is the easiest to establish, for it comes from internal cost and production records. To be sure,

---

17. The distinction here is between cost declines that may occur at any point in time (due to scale effects) and cost declines that may occur over time (Amit and Fershtman 1985).

many hurdles must be overcome in establishing the cost corresponding to each level of company production experience with a specific product, service, or cost element. Short-term discontinuities may be present due to revisions to accounting procedures, to changes in the product, and to cost variances from fluctuations in capacity utilization. Nonetheless, it is usually possible to develop a meaningful company cost curve, which may be useful as a long-run cost control tool. Productivity goals can be set, based on continuing or improving past patterns of cost reductions with experience, and management can be held to these targets. Two major caveats must be observed before pursuing this application too enthusiastically. First, since short-run cost discontinuities often dominate long-run experience effects—especially in mature businesses with slow rates of experience accumulation—the curve's value for short-run cost control is dubious. Second, projecting cost improvements at historical rates assumes the same effects will be operating in the future. However, these effects are seldom well understood and are ultimately under the control of management. Not surprisingly, empirical studies have found large errors in predicting future costs (of the order of 25 percent variation) from past historical patterns.[18]

Competitive Cost Comparison Curves

Competitive cost comparison curves are cross-sectional experience curves that show the relative cost positions of the competitors in a market. This curve makes it possible to estimate the profitability of each of the competitors at the prevailing price. While potentially the most useful experience curve, it is also the most difficult to obtain.

We usually know the slope of our own cost curve and can reasonably estimate the cumulative experience of the relevant competitors from their market shares. Unfortunately, we cannot immediately jump to the next step and locate each competitor on our cost curve according to their relative experience. This will invariably overstate the cost differences. For example, the real price per unit of a split system central air conditioner (CAC) has been declining about 20 percent with each doubling of industry experience. Yet, a cross-sectional experience curve relating the costs of the major competitors has a 92 percent slope.[19] The slope of the cross-sectional curve is likely to be shallower than other experience curves for many reasons:

---

18. Dutton and Thomas (1984).
19. Biggadike (1977).

1. Followers into a market usually have lower initial costs than the pioneer:

   ■ The follower has an opportunity to learn from the pioneers' mistakes by hiring key personnel, conducting "teardown" analyses of the competitor's product, and conducting marketing research to learn the problems and unfulfilled expectations of customers and distributors.

   ■ A follower may "leapfrog" the pioneer by using more current technology or by building a plant with a larger current scale of operations.

   ■ Followers may have opportunities to achieve advantages on certain cost elements by sharing operations or functions with other parts of the company.

2. All competitors should benefit from cost reductions achieved by outside suppliers of components or production equipment. For example, in the spinning and weaving industry, most of the advances in technology come from textile machinery manufacturers who share these improvements with all their customers.

3. One competitor may have lower factor costs than another for reasons that are independent of experience, such as location advantages, the benefits of government subsidies, and reduced susceptibility to cost element inflation because of differences in cost structure.

   The comparison of competitors in global markets is enormously complicated by differences in the factor cost structures. For example, Japanese high-technology companies have low costs of equity because of low risk-free rates of interest and generally lower stock market premiums. In 1983 their cost of equity averaged 10.8 percent, which was half that of U.S. companies such as DEC and Prime. As a result, they can price to achieve only half as much profit as their U.S. competitors while still generating an acceptable rate of return.[20]

4. Cost comparisons will also be obscured by differences between overhead rates of competitors. A large multidivision company with heavy corporate overhead allocations to each strategic business unit may be at a disadvantage against a specialist producer with lean and

20. McLagan (1983).

efficient management. Whether there is net disadvantage depends on the ability of the diversified firm to exploit opportunities for shared experience gains through corporate coordination.

5. Finally, if significant changes have occurred in market position, current market shares may not be good measures of relative cumulative output.

The net effect of these factors is a cross-sectional experience curve with shallow slope, masking steeper company cost curves, which are often approximately parallel to one another as in Figure 2.7. There is no necessary reason for the various company cost curves to be parallel, since this implies equivalence in ability both to exploit cost reduction opportunities and to gain access to the necessary technology.

Narrowing of Competitive Cost Differentials. As markets mature and the forces acting on the cross-sectional experience curve continue to operate, competitive cost differences tend to narrow. Further narrowing of competitive cost differentials may be triggered by

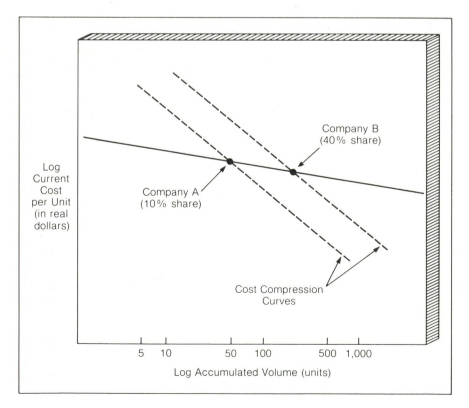

Figure 2.7
Competitive cost
comparison curves

changes in industry structure. In some industries, the full-line manufacturer is also a full-service manufacturer, with concomitant high
overheads and short production runs with many items in the product
line. But as markets mature, customers have less need for technical
service, engineering and lab support, and applications assistance.
Thus, the full-line, full-service manufacturers may be vulnerable to
competitors with less experience, but incurring fewer cost elements,
who are attacking specific segments. Indeed, the increasing fragmentation of markets during the maturity stage is a serious challenge to
the full-line manufacturer, for it creates a pressure for a proliferation
of products to satisfy the needs of different segments. The ensuing
costs may dissipate the advantages of experience.

Industry Price Experience Curves

The industry price experience curve relates the industry average
price to industry cumulative experience. A good example is in Figure
2.8, which shows price data for viscose rayon in the relatively self-
contained U.K. market. Since the time this analysis was done, the
synthetic fiber industry has become more European in scope and has
been battered by excess capacity and high raw material costs.

Price curves may be difficult to establish for two reasons. First,
what is the appropriate price? List prices are notoriously unrealistic
given the fluctuating discount structure (hidden and otherwise) used

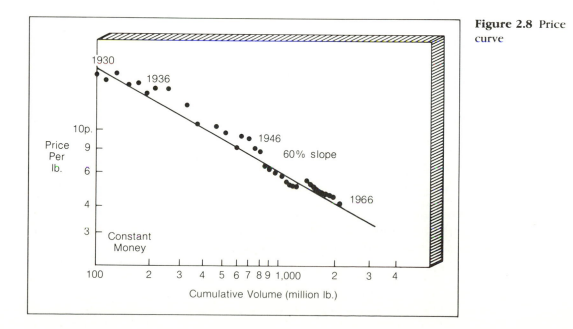

Figure 2.8 Price curve

to cope with changes in the demand.[21] A single price may be misleading if it requires averaging across disparate models, features, and accessories, or if different competitors use different marketing mixes. When some competitors are full-service, high-quality suppliers, and others provide minimal technical support or applications engineering while selling bare-bones components, there will be a high variance in observed prices. Always remember that the customer is paying for value-in-use. This value can be enhanced not only by a real price cut but also by adding benefits and services without corresponding price increases. The offer of a warehousing plan that permits customers to lower their component inventories is surely a price reduction.

A meaningful industry price curve also requires that we know the industry cumulative volume. This may be a problem simply because good industry data are unavailable or cannot be trusted. The problem is aggravated when different competitors use different strategies.

The Captive Manufacturing Issue.   In some component markets, the process of vertical integration is so far advanced that more than 50 percent of total output is "in-fed".[22] If this output is purely captive, ignoring it may be possible. This approach would be dangerous if the practice is to sell excess output on the open market to improve capacity utilization. If a beer company periodically sells 20 to 30 percent of their output of cans to other companies (especially during nonpeak periods), the long-run price patterns in the industry will eventually reflect the impact of these high-volume, low-cost producers.

Costs, Prices, and the Product Life Cycle

The average industry price curve frequently does not decline as fast as the cost curve in the early stages of the life cycle.[23] This widening gap is inherently unstable, so there is a sharp readjustment during a shakeout period before prices establish a stable margin relationship with costs. This pattern is juxtaposed on an idealized product life cycle in Figure 2.9.

Introductory Period.   During the introductory period, prices are held below current costs in expectation of lower costs in the future and to expand the market for the product by increasing the cross-

21. Burck (1972).
22. Hedley (1976).
23. Ibid.

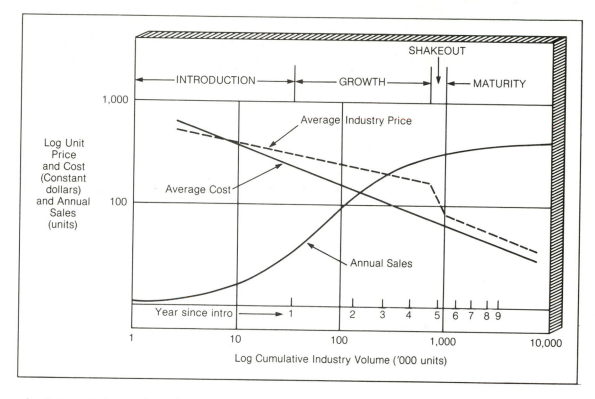

elasticity of demand with existing substitutes. A steep experience curve suggests a penetration price substantially below current costs.[24] Such a pricing strategy is even more attractive (1) when there is little prospect of creating and maintaining product superiority over competitors, (2) when there are few barriers to entry and expansion by competitors, or (3) when the lower price will significantly expand the current market. When, and if, the product takes off, the period of negative margins will eventually come to an end.

Growth Period: Building an Umbrella. The germanium transistor market is a good illustration of what can happen during the growth period. As demand surged, the overriding problem was obtaining product supply. Certainly there was no incentive to cut prices. However, the combination of rising average margins and rapid growth

Figure 2.9 Product life-cycle stages and the industry price experience curve

24. Robinson and Lakhani (1975) have shown that for a new product without direct competition and in the presence of imitative consumer demand, an optimal price policy would be a penetration price substantially below initial costs. The demand stimulus provided by this very low price coupled with experience-based cost declines were found to lead to profits several times greater than those generated by a myopic price policy that sets price to equate marginal revenue and marginal cost each period.

soon attracted a number of new entrants. These new entrants were able to survive profitably, because the price umbrella was still high enough to cover their high initial costs. Because of their narrow margins, these new entrants were motivated to gain share at the expense of the market leader and thereby reduce costs more rapidly than the leader.

During the growth period, the market leader who condones a high umbrella is trading long-run market share for current profits. There are many reasons for electing this choice. Current profits are often needed to fund the still rapid growth in capacity, working capital, R and D, and market development activity. The reward system often puts a premium on immediate profits. This also reduces the incentive to build capacity beyond short-run needs, since poor capacity utilization will penalize profit performance. But if market growth is underestimated, the market leader may be forced to give up further share because of capacity constraints.

Firms are increasingly questioning the virtues of holding a price umbrella. Nowhere are the consequences of this shift in strategy more evident than in the disarray among IBM's competitors described in the boxed insert.

The Shakeout Period.   The number of competitors attracted by the growth opportunities and high margins can be quite amazing. In industries such as housewares, with modest barriers to entry, it is not uncommon to find twenty to forty hopefuls entering during the

IBM Changes Strategy

For years IBM's strategy was fairly predictable. Products were sold for four or five years, and prices were kept stable until the end of the cycle. This strategy encouraged customers to lock themselves into long-term leases that assured IBM a reliable revenue stream. It also encouraged competitors to use newer and lower-cost technologies to sneak under the umbrella. If they followed IBM fairly closely, they could count on a few years of good profits.

In the late 1970s, IBM found that if it cut prices, demand increased faster than expected. This led to a push to sell rather than to lease equipment, and freed them to cut prices in line with cost reductions. They could also introduce new products sooner, without the worry of the premature return of machines out on lease. As a result, competitors had a smaller umbrella for protection and less time to make money.

Source: Uttal (1984).

growth period. Sooner or later the umbrella folds, for one or all the following reasons.

- Growth slows or declines because the market is close to saturation, a recession has intervened, or a new generation of technology is launched with superior cost performance.

- Aggressive late entrants buy into the market by cutting prices (a variant is the acquisition of an also-ran by a cash-rich outsider, which creates a competitor that can afford to invest in market share gains).

- The market leader attempts to stem the previous erosion of market share or regain previous share levels by cutting price.

- Retailers or wholesalers have limited space or capacity and decide to limit their offerings to the top three or four competitors that have a strong customer franchise.

The outcome is an abrupt break in the price trend. Meanwhile, expansion plans in the pipeline come into production during this period. The ensuing excess capacity puts further downward pressure on prices. The shakeout period becomes aptly named as marginal producers are eventually squeezed out of the market. In Chapter 4 the circumstances in which shakeouts are most likely to occur are examined.

Integrated circuit pricing is particularly susceptible to abrupt—but not entirely unexpected—price drops. Intel encounters this pattern regularly because of their practice of maintaining stable prices on one generation of products for as long as possible, while preparing to supersede it with a new generation. This practice may give them as much as a year of high profits before competition is able to copy and cut prices. This was the history of their 16K EPROM (erasable programmable-only memory chip). As Figure 2.10 shows, the price held stable through 1979, following the introduction in the first quarter of 1979 (1-79). Meanwhile, costs were declining along an 80 percent slope (these cost data are disguised and plotted on a different scale, so a direct comparison is not appropriate). In early 1980, prices began to decline down a 60 percent slope, in response to aggressive competition, until they had dropped to 15 percent of the original price by the end of 1981. At that point, Intel was ready with a 64K EPROM, and the action jumped to a new experience curve.

Toward Maturity and Beyond. Competitive cost differentials steadily narrow as the market matures. At the same time, the effect

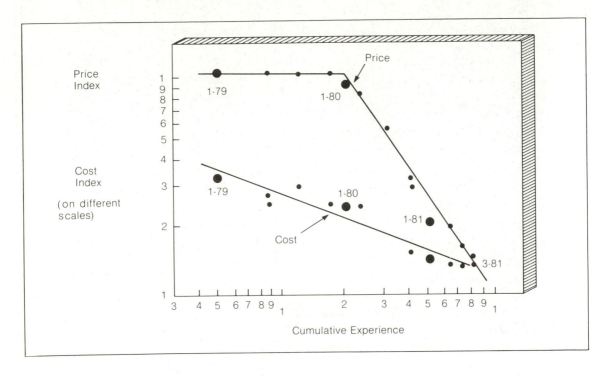

Figure 2.10 INTEL #2716—A 16K EPROM

of experience on real unit costs and prices becomes less evident. Doubling times are longer, so year-to-year cost reductions tend to be swamped by cost fluctuations caused by the economic climate, availability of materials, and so on.

Eventually, the product progresses into late maturity and decline, with unpredictable consequences for the experience curve. One manufacturer of industrial gases found that the cost curve for their bottled oxygen not only had flattened but also was turning up somewhat. This was not happening with either liquefied or pipelined oxygen. The two latter forms of oxygen supply were newer, and their success had pushed bottled oxygen into the decline stage of the life cycle. Despite the drop in industry sales, no competitors had dropped out, and everyone suffered reduced levels of capacity utilization and higher production costs.

Measurement and Interpretation Questions

The insights gained from the three types of experience curves depend on judgments about costs, inflation, shared experience, and the definition of the units of analysis. These judgments put further limitations on the strategic relevance of experience curves.

Which Costs?

Although the claim is that the experience effect applies to all costs, considering only total costs is misleading. Total costs decline from the effect of experience on the cost elements that combine to make up the product, including components, assembly, packaging, distribution, and so on. Only some of these costs can be influenced by management. Also, the amounts of experience accumulated in each cost element may be very different as a result of shared experience, and the slopes of the experience curves may also vary between elements.

Cost Component Analysis.   When the slopes of the experience curves of major cost elements are different, the relative importance of each component changes as experience with the total product accumulates. As Table 2.2 shows, this may also lead to a change in the slope of the overall experience curve. In this hypothetical example, Cost Component B with the shallowest cost curve rapidly becomes the most important cost component. While this is an extreme case, the same general effect is at work whenever the experience curves for major cost components have very different slopes. This distortion is accentuated when the company has extensive experience with one component. If they have already produced 200,000 units of Component B for other applications, the incremental volume from the new product will have little impact on the costs of this component. Fortunately, correcting for this problem is fairly easy.

Table 2.2 Changes in Cost Structure as Experience Cumulates

	COST PER COMPONENT AT EACH LEVEL OF CUMULATED EXPERIENCE		
	2,000 UNITS	8,000 UNITS	32,000 UNITS
Cost Component A (70% slope)	$1.00	$ .49	$ .24
Cost Component B (90% slope)	1.00	.81	.66
	$2.00	$1.30	$ .90
Average slope of total cost curve	80%	→	85%

Another consequence of the example in Table 2.2 is that products are likely to exhibit shallower total cost experience curves as they mature. The total cost curve is increasingly influenced by the cost element that is declining the slowest with each doubling of total experience. What often appears as a straight line on log-log paper may actually be a poor fit that obscures a gradual flattening of the experience curve.[25]

Value-added Costs.   The experience effect is largely felt on the costs that contribute to value-added. Inclusion of all costs—especially raw materials costs—may mask this effect. This problem arose during a study of the costs of insulated wire and cable. The total cost was dominated by raw materials, notably aluminum and copper, which are commodities subject to wide price swings. Only when these raw materials costs were excluded was any pattern evident. Whether cost elements outside of the value-added portion are included in the analysis depends on whether the company can influence the purchase price through scale and experience. For example, significant influence would be implied if a supplier dedicated most of the output of a component to a particular customer. When in doubt, breaking total costs into elements is always desirable.

Controllable Costs.   Process industries—such as chemicals and metal refining, which are subject to rigorous safety and environmental regulations—find that the costs of compliance behave like an unproductive add-on. As a result, the company cost compression curve has a dismaying habit of turning up, perhaps with a jump discontinuity as in Figure 2.11. It is less clear what impact a regulation has on relative cost positions within an industry, for regulatory burdens often fall most heavily on smaller producers. The cost of label changes in the food industry is proportionately greater for small volume packers.

Indentifying Relevant Costs.   Cost-accounting systems have to serve many purposes, so the resulting costs are often wildly inappropriate for experience curve analysis. The major problems are with the allocation of costs, the treatment of joint costs, and the deferred recognition of actual costs until revenue is realized. Cost allocations may be made to departments or profit centers rather than to specific products. Shared resources, such as a pooled sales force or central research and support staff, may be arbitrarily allocated as a percentage

---

25. Montgomery and Day (1984).

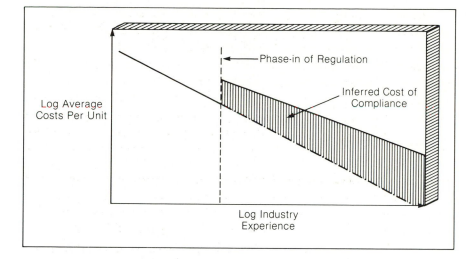

Figure 2.11
Discontinuities in the cost compression curve

of total sales accounted for by the product without reflecting the actual use of the resources.

Many problems can be avoided by using cash expenditures rather than accounting costs. However, annual cash expenditures include investments that are periodic and precede the revenue they eventually create. Thus, the ratio of cash flow to physical output will appear erratic from one year to the next. A better approach is to measure the experience curve as the rate of change in the cumulative cash input (always in constant dollars) divided by the cumulative physical output.[26] Because both the numerator and the denominator are cumulative, the ratio between them is exponentially smoothed. The result is a relevant average cost.

Choosing the Unit of Analysis.   When costs are averaged across a broad product line, a change in the total cost may be observed simply as a result of a change in the sales mix. For example, refrigerator manufacturers have been producing larger units on average. Here the solution is to define the product as a cubic foot of usable refrigeration space and observe the evolution of costs on this basis. This will only partially control for a shift in the mix of sizes, as the cost of a cubic foot is cheaper in a larger refrigerator. A related problem is the treatment of product variations and modifications—especially where the aim is to enhance the value of the product to the customer. At the extreme, the product may have changed so much it no longer resembles the original.

---

26. Henderson (1984).

Which Deflator?

There is no single rate of inflation.[27] For example, during 1980, when the GNP deflator was 9 percent and the implicit price deflator for producers' durable equipment was 6.5 percent, the following industry inflation rates were observed.

Textile Machinery	10.2% per year
Underground Mining Machinery	2.5% per year
Accounting Machines and Calculators	.6% per year

On balance, the GNP deflator is a poor representation of inflation in any particular industry, although it may be adequate to evaluate long-term shifts in strategy. For shorter-term cost analysis, a better approach is to choose a deflator that reflects the inflation of factor costs within the industry. However, care must be taken that the deflator is not so closely allied with the specific industry that the slope is defined away.

What About Shared Experience?

Cost differences between competitors are often less than we would expect from our knowledge of relative market shares and the slope of the company cost compression curve. A major reason is the effect of *shared experience* between two or more products using a common resource. The experience gained with one of the products can be applied to a reduction of the costs of related products.

For example, suppose Company A and Company B both produce Product X using the same three production steps. While Company A produces only Product X with these three steps, Company B makes two other products using the same first two steps as Product X. Company B gains an advantage by applying the volume from these other products to its cumulative experience in the first two steps. If Companies A and B then have similar cumulative experience with Product X, Company B would have lower costs on the first two steps and lower costs and higher profits on Product X.

Shared experience comes in many guises:

- Manufacturers of semiconductor components for calculators utilize many of the same capabilities to produce random access memories.
- Textile fiber manufacturers use similar polymerization and spinning processes for polyesters and nylon.

---

27. Wilson (1982).

- The same assembly operation may produce high-torque motors for oil exploration and low-torque motors for conveyers.
- Major appliance manufacturers use the same sales and service organization for a variety of products.
- Procter and Gamble was able to overcome a lack of experience in manufacturing paper products by being far along the experience curve in selling packaged consumer products when it entered the disposable diaper market.

Shared experience is best treated as an increment to the accumulated output of the specific product or processes of which the product is comprised. The hypothetical example in Table 2.3 helps illustrate this point. Here, the cost position of Company B is weakened by the lack of transferable experience with related products.

As illustrated in Table 2.3, the assessment of a competitor's shared experience as well as the company's own shared experience is important to understanding the relative economics of the various competitors. A textile producer found that since most competitors in the textile industry produce several fibers, it was necessary to estimate the unique, shared experience base of each competitor in order to understand relative cost positions. This company claims this approach has been used successfully on several occasions and has produced insights into competitive positions that would otherwise have eluded them.

How can the amount of the carry-over from shared experience be estimated? As with the basic experience effect, shared experience merely presents an opportunity to reduce costs, but does not guarantee it will happen. If a company has two plants making identical products, which were constructed independently, and the plants do not exchange cost reduction information, then the shared experience

Table 2.3 Effect of Shared Experience

	ACCUMULATED EXPERIENCE WITH PRODUCT X	SHARED EXPERIENCE FROM PRODUCTION OF RELATED PRODUCTS	TOTAL ACCUMULATED EXPERIENCE
Company A	1,000,000 units	600,000 units	1,600,000 units
Company B	600,000	—	600,000
Company C	200,000	350,000	550,000

effect will be negligible. To assess whether experience has been shared, it is usually necessary to apply expert judgment to each cost element. For example, manufacturing personnel can be asked to estimate where cost reduction projects for individual products have originated in the past. Similar approaches can be used to determine the effect on sales and distribution costs of a pooled sales force and warehousing facility. This kind of analysis represents a formidable amount of work.

Which Product-Market?

Few issues create more uncertainty than the choice of product-market boundary for the experience curve analysis. Published evidence suggests that industrywide cost compression effects are most evident when a broad, product-market definition is used:

- Kilowat hours of electricity generated
- Silicon transistors
- Gallons of beer
- Pounds of viscose rayon

Such broad definitions work because they are able to encompass most sources of shared experience. Yet, a definition that is too broad may mean that an opportunity for cost leadership in a specialized market may be overlooked:

> [T]he grinding wheel industry produces hundreds of thousands of different kinds of wheels, each particularly suited for certain industrial applications. Production of a given type of wheel requires development and control of a "recipe" consisting of quantity, type and size of abrasives, bonding agents, filters, wetting agents, etc. the timing of adding these to the "mix," baking times and temperatures; finishing techniques and so on. Likewise a firm can gain important experience advantages in the selling and servicing of wheels to a particular application.
>
> Experience advantages on a given type of wheel can yield important cost advantages. Here the unit of analysis should be the type of wheel on the application; if it were simply "grinding wheels" significant cost advantages due to specialization would be missed.[28]

The dilemma of the breadth of product and market boundaries may be resolved if segments can be found such that cost sharing

---

28. Abell and Hammond (1979).

between segments is less important than competitive cost differentials that depend on the relative position within the segment. This will yield a useful definition if most competitors approach the market in the same way. However, there are many situations in which different competitors define their business very differently. Laboratory ovens, for example, can be manufactured and sold by oven specialists or by laboratory equipment specialists. Whether laboratory ovens constitute a distinct segment depends on whether manufacturing or selling and servicing have the greater influence on total costs. When in doubt, it may be necessary to repeat the experience curve analysis using several different definitions of both products and markets.

A recurring problem is the treatment of new technologies. For example, should there be a single experience curve for tire cord, or separate curves for rayon and nylon tire cord? In general, if the consequence of the new technology is primarily to reduce product costs without a change in the functions provided to customers, a new curve is not necessary. However, if the new technology offers significant new functions, as happened when cash registers became electronic, then a separate curve is necessary. The same problems are encountered when undertaking product life-cycle analysis, so we will look at them in more detail in the next chapter.

Assessing Strategic Relevance

The logic of the experience curve is appealing, the empirical support seems persuasive, and the strategic implications are often profound. Yet, despite these advantages, acceptance of the concept is waning. The diminished enthusiasm is traceable to both the numerous pitfalls in applications and the irrelevance of the basic experience curve notion to many situations.

The most successful applications have been within high-value-added continuous processing capital-intensive industries that are usually highly concentrated. Here we expect to find steeply sloped cost curves and a significant relationship between market share and profitability.

By contrast, there is little point in looking for experience effects in custom industries such as tool and die making, which have traditionally been fragmented (although numerical control machine tools are slowly changing that situation). Service industries have been especially resistant to experience analysis. According to one study, the effect of learning on total costs has never been demonstrated in a service situation.[29] In fact, a negative association of return on assets and market share was found among French private commercial banks.[30] This may not hold true in the United States with the advent of new banking services, such as automated teller systems or daily interest checking accounts, utilizing capital-intensive computer systems.

Even when experience effects appear pervasive in an industry, the implications can be misleading if one forgets that no two competitors are likely to define their business in the same way. Viable competitors must achieve an experience advantage on the particular cost elements that are important to serving a distinct segment. However, these critical cost elements may differ significantly between segments. This is why specialists can prosper in the shadow of broadline competitors who serve all segments. To survive they must find cost elements the leader has to provide to all segments, but that some segments do not want, or alternatively where the leader cannot afford to offer all segments the particular feature or benefit. However, neither specialists nor broadline competitors can be complacent about a seemingly secure position, for the other lesson to remember is that the relative importance of cost elements is constantly changing as they proceed down experience curves with different slopes.

Specialists may also prosper when their competitors fail to recognize segments in which costs behave differently. When costs are simply averaged across products or buyer groups, the prices on some products to some buyers will be excessive relative to the true costs. This provides an umbrella which protects a specialist that only competes in the overpriced segment. For example, white wine is cheaper to produce than red wine because it requires less aging. However, if the prices do not recognize this cost difference, the price of white wine will subsidize the price of red wine.

Experience effects have the greatest relevance during the early stages of the product life cycle when the rate of doubling of cumulative output is very rapid. For example, both optical fibers and vacuum cleaners follow experience curves of 60 percent to 65 percent.[31] Currently it takes less than two years to double fiber optics output, so costs decline as much as 20 percent a year. By contrast the mature vacuum cleaner market requires nearly 20 years to double output, and so the cost savings are in the range of 2 percent per

29. Carman and Langeard (1980).
30. Larréché (1980).
31. Ghemawat (1985).

year. This means that nearly all the practicable, experience-related cost reductions have been taken. Success now requires finding new sources of advantage. Cost leaders in mature industries may not have the most experience. In the steel industry the lowest costs are achieved by smaller, focused competitors with modern facilities.

Hazards in the Pursuit of Cost Reduction

All-out dedication to cost reduction requires maximizing the scale of operations, and relentlessly pursuing opportunities for specialization of work force, production processes, and organizational arrangements. This has a number of advantages, as smaller competitors will quickly attest. Unfortunately, the necessary single-mindedness also breeds problems and bad habits that can immobilize the business.[32] The rigidities of highly specialized processes and systems, along with strategies of verticial integration to capture all the margins in the value-added chain, reduce the ability of the business to respond to technological opportunities or changes in market requirements. Ford recently had to close a large, supposedly efficient engine plant because it could not be converted to making new energy-efficient engines. American automakers were slow to move to disc brakes because of their huge investment in automating the production of cast-iron brake drums.

A more subtle risk of experience curve strategies is a "definition of the business" distorted by an excessive commitment to a particular technology rather than to satisfying customer needs. One becomes preoccupied with competitors who make products with similar functions, materials, and so on, and loses sensitivity to threats from other technologies that satisfy the same customer needs. The paper industry, for example, was slow to recognize the threat to paper grocery bags from plastics. Now that a plastic grocery bag is cost-competitive, with the bonus of greater strength and reusability, the paper grocery bag is experiencing a competitive setback.

Slavish devotion to the experience curve—and the resultant mind-set—may have other unintended consequences. As one chief executive noted, "We act as if cost—and thus price—is the only variable available these days. In our hell bent rush to get costs down, we have given all too short shrift to quality and service. So we wake up, at best, with a great share and a lousy product. It's almost always a precarious position that cannot be sustained."[33] Low-cost strategies

---

32. Abernathy and Wayne (1974).
33. Quoted in Peters (1984).

are simply one route to profitability, and may not be the best route to take if attractive revenue enhancement opportunities for differentiation and niche exploitation are available.

Summary

The simplistic market share dominance prescriptions that marked the early experience curve applications have been replaced with a growing sensitivity to the complexities of this concept. While its appeal as an organizing framework remains high, there is a realization that the experience curve effect is itself a product of underlying scale, technology, and learning effects. Whether the experience curve is strategically relevant depends initially on whether these three effects are influential features of the strategic environment. Beyond this there is a growing recognition that there is a family of experience curves, each addressing different strategic issues, from cost component analyses to price forecasting to competitive cost comparisons. One consequence is that the earlier broad generalizations have been replaced with focused applications, where experience curve analysis plays a supportive role as one of a number of analytical methods.

Dynamic Analysis of Products and Markets

Chapter 3

All products and markets are in a constant state of evolution. In some markets the pace is so measured and predictable that change can be accommodated easily. In others the rapidity of change creates a competitive climate that can be likened to a video game. The target constantly moves, and new opponents zoom in from various sectors. Focusing solely on one target may mean losing the game to an unforeseen development. In these volatile markets, the greatest rewards frequently go to the first firms to capitalize on these changes. In an era of rapid technological, social, and economic change, an increasing number of markets are having to adjust to a more rapid tempo. This puts a premium on understanding the processes underlying the evolution of products and markets, and formulating strategies that can exploit these changes.

The rewards that come from understanding market dynamics can be handsome. Certainly this has been true for Merrill Lynch as a result of their introduction of cash-management accounts. These accounts are primarily a computer-driven repackaging of existing financial services. Cash balances of brokerage clients are automatically deposited into a money fund. Other securities—stocks, bonds, and so on—are added to this money fund holding to create an asset base, against which the investor/depositor can write checks. The result, however, is an array of financial services well suited to the needs of its chosen market. Merrill Lynch has built a commanding lead over the other brokers in this market by being first, with capacity to meet rapidly growing demand.

The penalties for misjudging the requirements of fast-moving markets are equally significant:

■ Black and Decker was forced to divest its McCulloch chain saw business in the wake of a severe and sudden drop in demand for gas-powered chain saws. When U.S. shipments rose from 1.8 million units in 1976 to a peak of nearly 3 million in 1979, McCulloch built a major new plant while others expanded existing facilities. By 1982 the market dropped to 1.5 million units, because of both the recession and the stability of energy prices, which reduced the interest in cutting firewood for home heating. All the manufacturers failed to recognize the severity of the downturn, but as one competitor noted, "McCulloch missed it worse than everyone else."[1]

■ Sony experienced the opposite problem in 1983, when it misread the demand for the Watchman, a take-along television set with a two-inch screen. Management evidently considered the handheld unit little more than a gimmick, and never planned to put it into high-volume production. They started with a facility designed to produce two thousand units a month, but soon found they could not come close to meeting demand. After six months they redesigned and relaunched with a facility capable of producing ten times as many units. Their competitors learned from this mistake and moved directly into mass production with even smaller and more distinctive products, thus taking the initiative from Sony.[2]

These successes and failures are being repeated daily, although their genesis is usually found in events or trends initiated many months earlier. What managers need are robust frameworks to organize the myriad forces at work in their markets and to help identify the most powerful influences. The objective of this chapter is to assess the ability of the product life-cycle concept to meet this challenge. Description and prediction are not sufficient, for managers also want to use their insights about market dynamics to assess the risks and rewards of alternative strategies. But teasing out strategic implications is far more difficult. Life cycles are not inevitable, for they not only shape strategy but also are shaped by the actions of the competitors in the market. Chapter 4 builds on this chapter and develops the strategic issues encountered when entering, building, holding, or exiting markets with differing growth prospects.

1. *Business Week* "Black and Decker Saws Off a Loser," (8 November 1982).
2. *Business Week* "Big Times for Tiny TV's," (18 April 1983).

The Product Life-Cycle Concept

Products have lives, and they pass through discernible cycles; that much is indisputable. The product life-cycle concept goes further to describe distinct stages in the sales history of the product. Each stage poses different threats and opportunities that dictate changes in the appropriate strategy. Most representations of life cycles share the following features.

- Products have a limited life.

- Their sales history follows an S curve until annual sales flatten, when penetration of the potential market is achieved, and eventually decline.

- The inflection points in the sales history identify the stages known as introduction, growth, maturity, and decline. Some life cycles add more stages, including a period of shakeout or competitive turbulence once growth begins to slow.

- The life of the product may be extended by finding new uses or new users, or getting present users to increase their consumption.

- The average profitability per unit rises and then falls as products move sequentially and inevitably through the stages (this follows directly from the presumed correspondence of the life cycle with the experience curve for average industry prices).

The life story of a typical, successful product looks like Figure 3.1.

An Evolutionary Perspective

The concept of the product life cycle has an enduring appeal because of the intuitive logic of the sequence from birth to growth to maturity to decline. The problem with this simple biological analogy is that many products do not behave this way; they seem to skip some stages while lingering in other stages, and may be revitalized after a period of decline. These seemingly unpredictable patterns have led to well-aimed criticisms of the product life-cycle concept as a *predictive* model for anticipating when one stage will succeed another, or as a *prescriptive* model of the appropriate strategies to follow at each stage. It often seems that little progress has been in the twenty years since Levitt observed, "The concept of the product

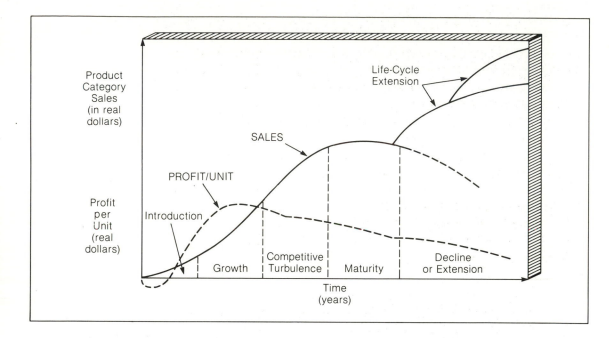

Figure 3.1 Life cycle of a typical product

life cycle is today at about the stage that the Copernican view of the universe was 300 years ago; a lot of people knew about it, but hardly anybody seemed to use it in any effective or productive way."[3] In fact, progress has been made toward establishing strategic relevance. The key is found in a broader view of life cycles as evolutionary processes reflecting the outcome of numerous market, technology, and competitive forces present in the market, each force acting in concert with others to facilitate or inhibit the rate of product sales growth or decline.[4]

An evolutionary perspective is at odds with prevailing beliefs about life cycles as deterministic models. First, this perspective suggests that there is no necessary reason why stages should follow each other in a predetermined sequence or that sales patterns will conform to any particular shape. Second, while the evolution of product sales proceeds within the dimension of time, the process is not time-dependent. In other words, stages do not last for predictable periods of time; rather, they are stretched or compressed as a consequence

---

3. Levitt (1965).

4. This notion is developed in Tellis and Crawford (1981). The biological analogies to technological, market, and competitive forces are respectively: the genetic system, which is the source of promising variations; the environment, which operates as a selective force favoring those variations best equipped to survive; and human intervention, which acts as a mediative force.

of changes in the motivating forces. Finally, it contradicts the notion that strategies must always be tailored to fit the particular life-cycle stage. A more realistic perspective is that strategic changes will themselves contribute to the pattern of growth, just as the response of a species to environmental change determines whether it will grow, proliferate, stagnate, or decline.

The most persuasive support for an evolutionary versus a deterministic process comes from past attempts to validate the existence of life cycles.[5] These studies have uncovered many shapes, durations, and sequences, only a few of which resemble the classic shape. Some commentators have seized on these findings to argue that we should "forget the life cycle."[6] Such advice is ill-advised if it distracts us from understanding the interplay of market, technological, and competitive forces that is the basis for informed forecasting and strategy development.

What is a Product?

The question of the appropriate level of analysis has probably caused more confusion than any other issue. Life cycles have been constructed for all levels of the hierarchial product structure in Figure 3.2, ranging from the generic product class and industry, to the product type and form, and even down to variants and individual brands. But any concept that is equally applicable to all these levels would be so general and abstract as to be meaningless for any specific application. What is needed are guidelines for identifying the level at which the evolutionary concept of life cycles is most applicable.

The relevant question is, which level best captures the consequences of the underlying forces for change? However, there are many dimensions along which a product can change. When is a change sufficiently distinct to justify a separate life-cycle analysis? One useful answer is that a product is the application of a distinct *technology* to the provision of a particular *function* for a specific customer *group*.[7] Only when a change occurs along one or more of these dimensions, which involves a sharp departure from the present

5. Buzzell (1966), Cox (1967), Polli and Cook (1969), and Rink and Swan (1979).

6. Dhalla and Yuspeh (1976).

7. See Chapter 4 of the first volume in this series (Day 1984) for further discussion of this approach to product definition.

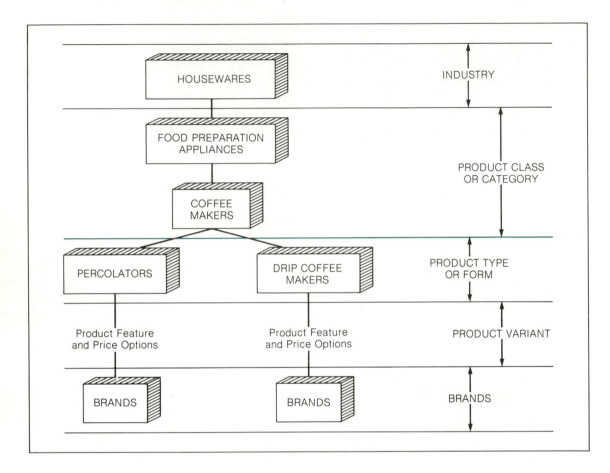

Figure 3.2
Product-market
hierarchies

strategies of participating competitors, is a separate life cycle necessary. Applying this guideline to the housewares example in Figure 3.2 leads us to choose coffee makers as the appropriate level. All coffee makers—whether drip or percolator type—perform the same function, with only minor variation in the basic technology, and are sold to similar customers through the same channels. Following the same argument, electronic mail services have a distinct life cycle from overnight courier services, because the technology is completely different and the functions provided are different, although the market is the same.

The advantage of this heuristic for defining products can be seen from its application to problem situations that have fueled enduring doubts about the life cycle:

■ The timeless consumer product. Was the chairman of Procter and Gamble justified in saying they do not believe in the product life cycle by citing the case of Tide synthetic laundry detergent, which was introduced in 1947 and still growing in 1976? During the twenty-nine year lifetime, Tide had undergone fifty-five significant modifications in response to changes in consumer preferences, laundry habits, washing machines, and fabrics. Clearly, Procter and Gamble has successfully adapted this product to extended maturity without significantly changing either function, technology, or customer.

- The multiple function material. Is there a meaningful life cycle for a material such as nylon, which is subsequently processed further to be suitable for different applications such as carpeting, tire cord, and hosiery?[8] The answer is certainly no, for each application requires an entirely different strategy. Indeed, it would be more meaningful to construct a life cycle for synthetic carpet fibers, for example.

- Technological substitution processes. Until the mid-sixties, beverage cans were almost exclusively three-piece steel/tin combinations, until two-piece aluminum cans began to replace them. Then in the mid-seventies, two-piece steel cans were developed to recapture the position of steel.[9] But during this period, neither the functions nor the customers of metal cans were changed. Thus, a new product life cycle was not necessary.

- Sequentially unfolding segments. Some life cycles are a composite of the sequential introduction and development of a basic function/technology within a series of related customer segments. Figure 3.3 shows how a specialized communications system was first accepted for process control applications and then extended to security applications within the same adopting firms.[10] After two years, a new segment for combined security and process applications was identified.

As each of these examples demonstrates, product life cycles summarize the effects of many concurrent changes. While these influences

---

8. Levitt (1965).

9. Machnic (1980).

10. Cardozo (1979).

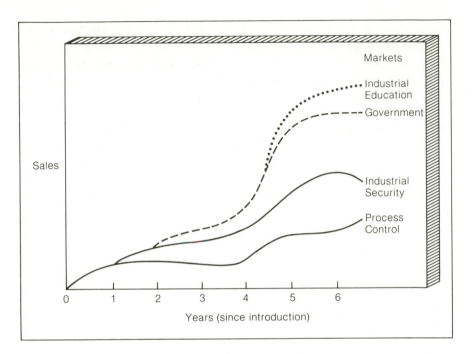

Figure 3.3
Sequential market
entry

must be understood, they may not dictate an entirely new product
life cycle.

Product Class or Product Type?   Properly defined product types
or forms within a class are substitutes that perform the same function.
As such, they are not the relevant level of analysis. Each new type
attracts a portion of the volume in the product class, by displacing
an existing type, and later may be displaced by another type: Bonnet
hair dryers were replaced by salon dryers, which were replaced by
styling dryers, and in turn these were replaced by the pistol dryer.
This product form or type substitution process is driven by significantly different variables than those influencing the life cycle for hair
dryers and must be treated as such.

While the product class level best captures the interplay of market,
technology, and competitive forces that underlie the life cycle, it is
also useful to develop separate sales curves to understand the rate
of substitution of one product type by another. The family of curves
will then capture all the significant environmental forces.

What About Brands?   Some have argued that since managers cannot directly control product types or classes, the analysis should be
confined to the brand level. This argument is a basic misunderstanding of life cycles, because the plot of the sales history of a brand

reflects both environmental forces and the strategy of the business. The life-cycle concept deals solely with the underlying forces for change that inhibit or facilitate total sales of a product class. This should not be confused with the different question of how well an individual brand is performing within this environment.

Product Class and Industry. A product class is usually—although not always—narrower than its industry. For example, there is a housewares industry made up of all firms manufacturing housewares. Some are full-line, completely integrated companies, while others are limited-line specialists that are primarily assemblers of components. This industry spans a large number of product classes, from toaster ovens to irons to blenders and hair dryers. Many of the same environmental forces encountered at the product class level also shape the evolution of the industry. However, the effects are more diffuse, and other influences such as materials cost and supply, the relative power of distributors, threats from offshore producers, and so forth may be more salient. Thus, there is a distinct difference between the analysis that is undertaken for specific nylon products such as tire cord or hosiery, and the analysis of the evolution of the nylon or synthetic fibers industry.

The Introductory Stage of the Life Cycle: Emerging and Uncertain Markets

Most life cycles are initiated in response to a market need.[11] Entrepreneurial firms—frequently small, start-up situations—take existing technologies and knowledge and combine them in novel ways. A smaller proportion of major product innovations are technology driven and emerge more directly as a product of research and development efforts.

Rate of Diffusion

The length of time new products spend in the introductory stage varies greatly. Some diffuse very slowly into their potential market and exhibit a virtually flat sales curve for many years. Others may

---

11. Some studies (Sherwin and Isenson 1967, Utterback 1974) suggest this proportion may be as high as 80 percent of all new products.

almost bypass this stage. The determinants of the rate of diffusion include the following:[12]

- The perceived comparative advantage of the new product relative to the best available alternative. The greater the perceived advantage, whether in terms of higher profitability, reliability, ease of operation, savings of time and effort, or immediacy of benefits, the more quickly the new product will be adopted.

- The perceived risk or the subjective estimate by a prospective buyer of the probability of a negative outcome.[13] This risk is a joint function of the financial exposure in the event of failure coupled with uncertainty as to the outcome. This uncertainty has many origins, including an unpredictable rate of technical obsolescence, the uneven quality of early production runs, or a lack of product standardization. Thus, potential videodisc buyers waited to see whether grooved or grooveless capacitance systems would dominate solid-state laser systems, since the discs are incompatible.

- Barriers to adoption (such as commitment to existing facilities or incompatibility with existing values) will slow acceptance even when other factors are supportive. Products such as computerized process controls that require major changes in manufacturing facilities and processes generally diffuse very slowly.

- Information and availability. Not only must the product be readily available (for purchase and servicing), but also the buyer must be aware of the product and informed of the benefits. Products that lend themselves to trial applications or demonstrations will be accepted more quickly.

Influencing the Rate of Diffusion.   Research on diffusion of innovations emphasizes information variables and the capacity of formal and informal sources to reduce perceived risk. The relevance of this work is compromised by taking the comparative advantages of the product as fixed. In reality these advantages can be influenced by the strategic decisions of both the pioneer firm and the followers. Thus, manufacturers can invest in promotion and distribution coverage to increase awareness, expand sales activity to induce trial,

12. Zaltman and Stiff (1973) and Rogers (1983).
13. Webster (1969).

reduce risk by providing technical service, warranties, and after-sales service support, and enhance the comparative advantage by reducing the delivered price or by adding new features.

Experience effects are very significant during this stage. Reduced costs should eventually lead to lowered prices, which in turn will improve the comparative advantage of the new product. The effect is highly interactive, for an increased comparative advantage should accelerate the rate of acceptance and hence the rate of accumulation of experience. Whether this acceleration of demand will materialize depends on the initial pricing strategies and the persistence of the remaining barriers to diffusion.

Other Exogenous Factors.   The early history of many new products is shaped by factors beyond the immediate industry and the potential substitutes. Among these factors are changes in the position of complementary products and changes in government regulations and policies. For example, the demand for electronic home entertainment products such as television and videodiscs was or is dependent on the growth of broadcast capabilities and programming. Similarly, the growth of a new computer-based office services depends on the availability of software.

The impact of government policies can be especially dramatic, for they frequently are abrupt events. Consider the impact on demand for automatic teller machines of a ruling that these machines are not considered branches in states where branch banking is not permitted. Who would have believed very far in advance of the legislation that every heavy truck would be required to have electronic antiskid devices, or that in one year cars would have seat belt interlocks— and that requirements would be discontinued the next year?

Coping with Uncertainty

The most pervasive feature of emerging markets is uncertainty with respect to the underlying forces in the market. Early entrants have to absorb the ensuing risks. Their principal consolation is that some potential entrants will be deterred by these uncertainties, or will be at a disadvantage when they finally enter.

Technological Uncertainty.   Here some of the key questions are: Will the technology function as expected when placed into volume production? For example, Thomson-CSF in France has been pursuing low-cost flat screen displays as an alternative to the usual cathode ray tube for low-cost data processing terminals. There are growing doubts that acceptable cost levels can be achieved.

Which technology will be dominant? This is a particular problem with dramatic technological changes, such as local area networks. These are data communication networks that enable word processing, data processing, and communications equipment to interact with, or "talk to," each other in a limited physical environment such as an office building. This would be a major step forward in achieving office automation. Unfortunately, major differences exist among vendors as to whether the best technology has a digital, single-channel or analog, multichannel capability. Each has performance advantages, so it is highly uncertain which technology will eventually prevail.

Uncertain Customer Acceptance.   The rate of customer acceptance will be slowed by lack of product standardization, perceived likelihood of technological obsolescence, and the unpredictable quality of the products first into the market. If these problems are significant, most prospective buyers are likely to adopt a "wait and see" attitude. This tendency in turn reinforces the inertia that comes from satisfaction with existing alternatives and reluctance to change established behavior patterns. These problems have created a significant barrier to the large-scale acceptance of assembly-line robots, which often require a complete redesign of manufacturing processes before they can be effectively utilized.

Uncertain Costs.   Despite the ubiquity of the experience curve, doubts are always present as to whether high initial costs can be offset by sharp drops in the costs of critical components. Without these cost declines, the relative attractiveness of the new product will be seriously diminished. However, strong demand may create its own problems if shortages of essential components such as microprocessors result in high prices.

Competitive Uncertainty.   During the introductory stage, the structure of competition is in flux. Both present and prospective entrants face major questions:

- What protective actions will be taken by the products that are being supplanted?
- What is the commitment and resources of other entrants?
- Who are the potential direct competitors, and what entry strategies might they employ?
- What about other emerging technologies that can provide similar functions? Both pay TV and videotape recorders have had a big impact on the acceptance of videodiscs in major applications.

To this daunting array of uncertainties, the manager of a new product must also consider the variability of the economic climate and the position of the government and regulatory agencies. Not surprisingly, many companies wait until the situation has clarified before entering a new market.

The Transition to Rapid Growth

The first sign of arrival of the rapid growth stage is a sudden upturn in sales. If the product offers obviously significant advantages and the barriers to adoption are not great, this takeoff may be steep. As experience with the new product is gained, uncertainty is further reduced, and the growth process gains an increasing capacity to sustain itself. Previously reluctant buyers and competitors are more eager to participate in the action. Other facilitating factors, such as repeat buying, which were latent during the period when the initial uncertainties were being resolved, assume greater importance.

Reduction of Uncertainty: Buyer Experience

Low levels of buyer experience with a new and unfamiliar product result in tentative behaviors that impede acceptance:[14]

- Buying patterns are marked by experimental purchases, pilot tests, and ad hoc evaluation procedures. This is especially true for complex and innovative high-technology products with numerous types of applications, such as microcomputers. The conflicts among data processing, communications, and word processing departments over who should control microcomputer acquisition and usage lead to confusing and inhibiting buying patterns.

- Product usage is tentative. The new product is frequently underutilized, or confined to lead users who may or may not share their experiences. During the introductory stage for microwave ovens, usage was often limited to warming coffee and reheating leftovers.

- A paucity of information exists. Even advertising and salesperson communications provide little comparative performance and operating information, since neither

---

14. This section is adapted from Cady (1983).

vendors nor users have agreed on product standards. Consequently, buyers have great difficulty discriminating among vendors.

As customers gain experience, these inhibiting behaviors are replaced with more informed and confident usage, and broader usage then follows. Often the inhibitions and uncertainties are overcome by conscious efforts of vendors to make the product usable. Microwave ovens were underutilized and unappealing until industry vendors supplied microwave cookbooks, cooking schools, and specially designed microwave cookware.

Reduction of Uncertainty: Emergence of a Dominant Design

A significant milestone—often reached early in the rapid growth stage—is the emergence of a dominant design synthesized from all the experimental forerunners.[15] The dominant design has two consequences. First, it enforces standardization so that production economies can be gained. Second, the consensus around a dominant design reduces this source of uncertainty for both manufacturers and buyers, and helps lower a major barrier to wholehearted acceptance.

Often a dominant design emerges when a leading firm decides there is more to be gained by concentrating on one design and starting down the cost experience curve at a faster rate than can be gained through continued experimentation. The experience curve of a dominant design may also have a steeper slope because both learning and scale effects are more concentrated.

Unless standardization exists, it may not even be possible to shift from a small-scale job shop to a more rationalized system able to produce enough volume to meet market needs. However, this move is risky if the firm prematurely drives for volume with a design that is not clearly dominant. Texas Instruments paid a high price when they took the plunge and made the LED watch in volume, rather than waiting for the LCD technology to be perfected.

The presence of a dominant design can have a powerful, galvanizing effect on a confused market. The IBM PC has played this role in the microcomputer market.[16] This computer represented a reasonably advanced design by incorporating the powerful sixteen-bit

---

15. Abernathy and Utterback (1978).

16. *Business Week* "Personal Computers: And the Winner is IBM", (3 October 1983).

microprocessor made by Intel. Until then, nearly all personal computers processed only eight bits of data at a time. Equally important was the timing of introduction of the PC just as the market was shifting from hobbyists to professional users. Faced with a hundred brands of unknown manufacturers to choose from, business customers suffered "computer shock" and opted for the security of the computer giant. This tendency accelerated when dealers lost their interest in lesser-known brands and emphasized a few brands that would be a surefire success.

Facilitating Factors

A number of new factors come into play under the impetus of accelerating growth and evidence of wider acceptance.

Changes in the Relationships with Substitute Products.   The improved ability of the new product to capture sales from the substitute reflects improvements in the price/performance ratio as experience accumulates, designs are improved, new features are added, and the real price declines. This will determine how quickly the new product will replace the substitute and how much of the volume will be replaced. Substitution will also be triggered by large jumps in the price of the substitute, as happened during the period 1974–75 when powdered soft drinks mixes grew rapidly at the expense of canned fruit juices, which had to absorb large sugar price increases.

Differences in Innovativeness.   Most buyers of a new product go through roughly the same *adoption process,*[17] beginning with (1) awareness followed by (2) intermediate stages of interest and evaluation of the suitability of the innovation, culminating in (3) a small-scale trial, and then (4) adoption of the innovation on a full and continuing basis. However, individuals and companies differ greatly in the speed at which they begin and end this process. The earliest adopters are innovators who are willing to try new ideas, even at some risk, because they see significant benefits. Later adopters are more risk-averse and usually wait for evidence that the innovation worked for someone else. Often this evidence is communicated by word of mouth, coupled with some social influence. These effects tend to feed on themselves, generating a process that resembles the cumulative spreading of an epidemic. Thus, the typical curve describing the timing of an adoption is similar to Figure 3.4. The elapsed time from the first trial purchase to complete saturation may be a few

---

17. Rogers and Shoemaker (1971) and Rogers (1983).

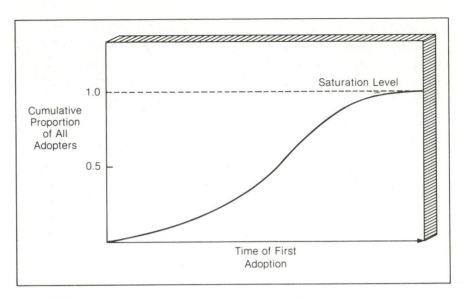

Figure 3.4
Cumulative adoption
process

months for supermarket products to more than a decade for some
capital goods.

Competitive Entry Strategies.   In many product-markets, the strategic window seems to open at roughly the same time for most
potential entrants. First, the initial acceptance of the product helps
reduce the uncertainties that clouded the early prospects. These
uncertainties may also have encouraged experimentation with alternative process technologies, designs, and marketing strategies. The
results of these experiments and ongoing marketing research reduce
the uncertainty to a level that is tolerable for larger firms with lower
risk profiles—witness recreational vehicles, video games, and solar
heating.[18] A second incentive is the widespread belief that it is easier
to gain share in high growth markets. The combined impact of many
competitors, each aggressively spending to gain a sustainable market
position, may create significant acceleration in the rate of growth.

The Influence of Repeat and Replacement Buying.   Sooner or later,
a significant proportion of the total volume of a product category
will consist of repeat purchases (if the product is a nondurable such
as consumable food product) or replacement purchases. The size of
this proportion will depend on the number who were satisfied with
their first purchase or do not have any other product they could
switch to for the same function. Other influences are the product's
useful life (before it breaks, fails, or becomes obsolete) and the prac-

---

18. Porter (1980).

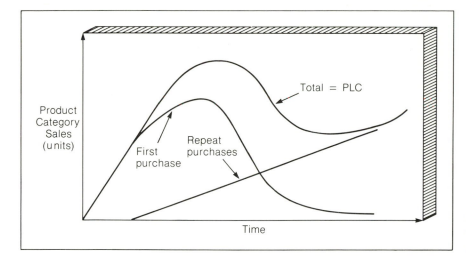

Figure 3.5
Components of the product life cycle

ticality of repair versus replacement. In some categories, the useful life is highly unpredictable, as this can be influenced by the owner. But during the rapid growth stage, the combination of a continuing level of first purchases overlaid with replacement or repeat purchases can give the product sales curve a real boost. Figure 3.5 shows this additive pattern in the sales of a new food product.[19]

Does Growth Induce Growth?   As the market expands, there are new opportunities for segmentation and the adaptation of the product or service to better fit the needs of customer groups whose requirements were previously too modest to be served with a tailored offering. These niches make the rapidly growing market even more attractive to prospective entrants.

Supporting the possibilities for increasingly differentiated treatment of customer segments are technological improvements that open up new possibilities for variation in product design and reduce the costs of producing these variations. Thus, market growth creates its own momentum, drawing more and more new buyers to the product until the potential for further growth is exhausted.

Evolution to Maturity

As the cumulative sales penetration approaches the ultimate market capacity and the growth rate slows, the dominant factor becomes

19. Harrell and Taylor (1981).

the replacement rate. However, this is not a period of stability, for the ultimate potential is an elusive target and new forces come into play.

Expanding Market Potential

While the market capacity for use or consumption may be stable on a per capita basis, there could still be expansion from demographic changes that cause the target market to expand or shrink. At the same time, changes in social or economic trends influencing underlying needs—such as protection against property theft, or energy conservation—will affect consumers' demands for end products such as security devices and energy-saving products, which filters back to component suppliers.

Buyer Experience

In a maturing market, most buyers have considerable usage experience and may have made a number of repeat purchases. As products approach a familiar—perhaps even commodity—status, buyers become more price and service sensitive. This puts added pressure on costs and may force competitors to acquire more modern facilities and equipment. At the same time, buyers are less responsive to advertising and promotion efforts either by the industry or by individual competitors.[20]

Competitive Turbulence

In many markets, there is a distinct period of competitive turmoil, immediately before maturity.[21] During this period, the slowdown in the growth rate that signals impending maturity reveals excess capacity and triggers a competitive battle for market share. This will be accentuated if the rate of capacity addition does not slow down to adjust the slower market growth. Because capacity increments are planned long in advance of their availability—and are justified by forecasts of continued growth—the amount of capacity usually overshoots the demand. Overshooting leads to even more excess capacity and price cutting as firms search for volume to keep the plant operating above break-even capacity. The consequences of overshooting capacity are especially severe in capital-intensive industries, such as chemicals, where efficient capacity increments are large.

---

20. Erickson and Montgomery (1980).
21. Wasson (1978).

Competition for Share

When demand is stable or growing slowly, any significant sales gains by one firm come at the expense of the competitors' capacity utilization. As this will immediately and adversely impact competitors' cost structure, the losses will be aggressively resisted. The result is an uneasy equilibrium. Further stability comes because the established firms and distributors have a vested interest in current products and processes. At the same time, new products and applications are more difficult to find—the more obvious candidates being exploited first. These pressures against major strategic change shift the emphasis to superior execution. In the fast-food business, this means building up the breakfast and dinner business, achieving greater efficiencies in existing outlets, and introducing new menu items that will attract a broader spectrum of consumers. These moves have to be supported by increased advertising and promotional budgets and programs to maintain the visibility of the chain in a media environment occupied by other chains trying to achieve the same ends.

The Onset of Decline

One recent analysis of declining industries observed that there had been virtually no attempt to sort out the factors that influence the strategic choices managers face during a decline.[22] This study found that some declining environments were much more hospitable than others in terms of long-run sales, profitability, and price stability. The least hospitable environments were the result of fashion or demographic changes because they were much less predictable than declines created by technological change. Another reason some declining markets were more hospitable than others was pockets of enduring demand, which could be protected from incursions by displaced competitors.

Forecasting Life Cycles

The strategic relevance of product life-cycle analyses is frequently compromised by elusive boundaries between stages. This ambiguity may be a realistic reflection of the uncertainties about the evolution of the product and its market. However, until the present stage is established, it is not possible to adapt the marketing strategy to the threats and opportunities presented by the next stage.

---

22. Harrigan (1980).

Some boundary identification problems stem from the sensitivity of life-cycle analyses to the choice of measures.[23] Should one use unit volume, current or constant dollar total revenue, or per capita consumption to measure sales? What adjustments should be made to eliminate the effects of economic conditions? Consumer durables and industrial materials are especially susceptible to changes in economic activity that can cloud the interpretation of the prospects for the product.

Further complicating the identification of boundaries is the variety of possible life-cycle patterns. This makes it unlikely that a product's position in its life cycle can be established simply by observing changes in the past sales pattern. The implications of the difference between a temporary or even an extended pause in sales growth versus a true topping out of growth are profound. Thus, the future sales path of the product must be forecast if sensible judgments about the present life-cycle position are to be made.

The Potential for Acceptable Forecasts

The ability of a forecasting model to account for the facilitating and inhibiting forces that move the product through its life cycle will generally determine the accuracy of the forecasts. Some idea of the implications of this requirement can be gathered from Figure 3.6

Figure 3.6
Life-cycle forecasts

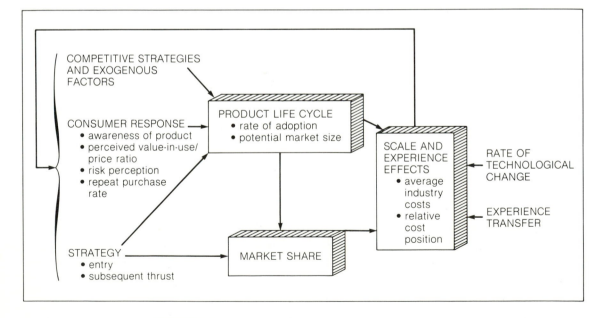

23. Wind (1981).

which illustrates the relationships among the forces operating during the introductory and growth stages. One immediate difficulty is the need to account for the feedback effect of declining real costs—due to scale and experience effects—on the comparative advantage of the new product. The enhanced value-in-use of the product relative to the competitive alternatives interacts in turn with the reduction in perceived risk as key market and technological uncertainties are resolved. Further complex and unpredictable interactions are introduced by exogenous factors and competitive entries into the new product category.

In light of the growing complexity of the forecasting task as products mature, it is not surprising that efforts to forecast the rate of first purchases have been more successful than the forecasting of the late growth and maturity stages. These first purchase diffusion models are described in the Appendix to this chapter. Some progress has also been made in understanding how and when different shapes and patterns are likely to occur, and in forecasting individual component parts of the life cycle, such as the rate of technological change.

Determinants of Life-Cycle Shape and Duration

Few product life cycles follow the idealized squashed bell shape found in textbooks. Judging by the empirical evidence, it is more likely that a product will follow some other pattern such as a cycle-recycle or camelback, stable, maturity, innovative maturity, growth to decline to plateau, or rapid penetration.[24] Even within a single industry such as housewares, there are at least three distinct shapes, as shown in Figure 3.7. Products such as radios, which offer a high degree of functionality and can be highly differentiated (e.g., clock radios, portables, and component systems with different levels of performance, plus styling differences), come closest to the classic shape. On the other hand, a highly useful single-function product, such as a steam iron, has an initial large lump of sales reflecting original purchases that saturate the available market, followed by a lower plateau of sales from replacements plus gifts or purchases by new family formations. However, a major product improvement such as the lightweight no-spot iron can accelerate the replacement rate and lead to a significant hump in the sales plateau. Finally, a fad item such as a single-patty hamburger cooker has a short life, because most of the sales are gift purchases made during one or two years. Because

---

24. Midgley (1981).

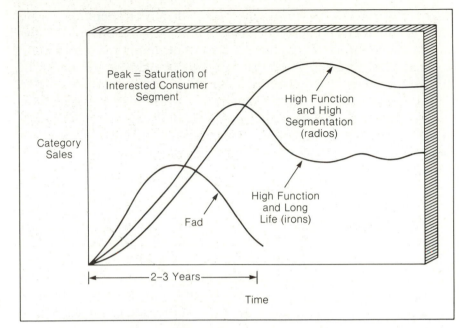

Figure 3.7
Housewares product
life cycles

of the limited functionality of these products, they tend not to be replaced.

The diversity of observed life-cycle shapes and durations is attributed to five underlying factors:

- Repeat purchase rate
- Stage of industry life cycle
- Intensity of competitive activity
- Potential for life extension
- Derived and reciprocal demand effects

Not all these determinants are relevant in every situation. Taken together, however, they give a good picture of the variables that need to be considered to ensure an acceptable forecast.

Repeat Purchase Rate and Volume. Product life cycles represent the combined results of initial adoptions plus repeat or replacement purchases. In mature product categories, the replacement rate is the dominant factor, but this variable is even more difficult to forecast than initial purchases. It is necessary to account not only for the product's consumption frequency or useful life (time from purchase to failure, breakage, or obsolescence) but also for the proportion of buyers who make a repeat or replacement purchase. In most markets, buyers have the option of postponing their repeat purchase or switching to a competitive product that is a functional substitute.

The difficulty of forecasting the repeat or replacement rate does not diminish its influence on the shape of the life cycle. Evidence of its importance comes from simulation studies that vary the ratio of the average time of adoption to the average interpurchase time.[25] Ratios between .5:1 and 5:1 were able to replicate almost all the empirically observed shapes. As the diffusion process becomes longer relative to the period between the first and replacement purchases, the pronounced peak in the life cycle disappears and the shape begins to look like the familiar bell-shaped curve.

Stage of Industry Life Cycle.   New industries are constantly emerging; recent entrants include solar heating, robotics, biotechnologies such as gene splicing and cloning, fiber optics, personal computers, and data communications networks. The life cycles of these industries as they mature will represent the sum of the life cycles of the product classes that constitute the industry.

When the industry is in its embryonic or formative stages, the product class and industry definitions are synonymous. In this environment, diffusion rates tend to be gradual, for not only is there great uncertainty about the product, but also the rudiments of the supporting distribution, delivery, and service infrastructure are not yet in place. Indeed, the essential characteristic of an embryonic industry is that there are no rules to the game—they all have to be developed.

As the industry structure develops further, the introduction of new product classes becomes easier. Penetration rates are more rapid, because consumers are more knowledgeable, the distribution and service network is better established, financing institutions are more comfortable with the potential of the industry, and sales and promotion efforts are more effective. By the time the industry reaches maturity, the infrastructure is capable of quickly introducing new products. However, as Figure 3.8 shows, rapid acceptance of a new product is likely to be followed by equally rapid flattening. First, other competitors in the industry will observe the success and follow quickly, and in the process of jockeying for position will invest heavily to accelerate acceptance of the product. At the same time, the established products in the industry that are being replaced will make adjustments to protect their declining position. As a result, the rate of substitution may slow quickly.

Intensity of Competitive Activity.   Direct competition for sales of a new product class is most aggressive in mature industries. However,

25. Ibid.

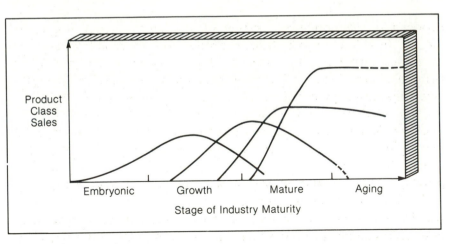

Figure 3.8
The shape of the
product life cycle as
the industry matures

the relative aggressiveness of competitors also depends on the attractiveness of the market, the anticipated growth rate, the barriers
to entry into the specific market, and the numbers of competitors
within the industry who could muster the capabilities to enter the
market for the new product. The effect of numerous aggressive competitors is to accelerate the rate of acceptance of the new product:[26]

- Prices are likely to erode sharply as competitors anticipate
  experience curve economies. This expands the potential
  market for the product and encourages quicker adoption.

- Distribution coverage improves as each additional
  competitor brings a specific channel strength to the market.

- There may be increased product availability resulting from
  competitor's inventory building to support product launches.

- Aggressive advertising, promotion, and selling efforts
  designed to secure a strong long-run position in the market
  build awareness quickly and reduce lingering uncertainty.

Derived Demand Effects.   Some products do not have a "life" of
their own. Instead, their future is dictated by larger forces to which
they can only react but not control. This is the nature of derived
demand, in which the sales of a product are tied to developments
in the industries that use all the output. Machine toolmakers have
always suffered or benefited from the fortunes of their customers.
This is most evident in the recent surge of orders for equipment to
make semiconductors.[27] There are three types of equipment: wafer

---

26. Harrell and Taylor (1981).
27. Dumaine (1983).

processing, assembling, and testing, of which wafer processing is the largest. In this complex stage of production, incredibly fine-tuned machines turn chips the size of a baby's finger into miniaturized printed circuits. The evolution of these machines has made progressive chip shrinkage possible; while the best-selling chip in 1983 was the 64K RAM, by 1986 it is likely to be the 256K RAM, which contains over 256,000 memory circuits. Ultimately, the demand for these chip-making machines will depend on the demand for the chips, which in turn is a function of consumer spending for cars, personal computers, appliances, and other products that contain semiconductors.

Derived demand is not necessarily a one-way street. Over the long run, there is often a reciprocal relationship, such as is occurring with new chip-making machines that provide new capabilities that enhance the cost/performance ratio of chips and thus encourage wider usage.

Derived demand can also work against a new product when a supporting product is not available in sufficient quantities or quality. This is most evident with software such as the programming needed to convert a television set into a functioning entertainment product. In the early days of television, there simply were not enough interesting programs being broadcast to make it worthwhile to own a TV set. More recently, the demand for videodisc players has been impeded by the relative paucity of popular movie titles available in disc format and distributed widely for easy rental or purchase.[28] Generally, there is a lag in the provision of related software, including computer programs, so when the hardware requires this software, the result is to shift the life-cycle curve to the right and cause it to peak earlier.

Forecasting life cycles when demand is largely derived is complicated by the volatility of these markets.[29] Some of this volatility is due to the *acceleration* effect, which is most obvious with capital equipment. Suppose unit demand for a product such as shower stalls is flat for two years then jumps by 10 percent. This will have little or no impact on the demand for shower stall molding equipment so long as excess molding capacity is available. When this is absorbed, there will be a sudden surge of demand for molding equipment that may represent a 50 to 60 percent increase in annual sales. This kind of volatility is exacerbated by the behavior of purchasing agents who slow purchases in anticipation of a downturn—and excess capacity,

---

28. *Business Week* "Videodisc Markets Make an Amazing About-Face", (20 September 1982).

29. Bishop, Graham, and Jones (1984).

which results in lower prices—but will speed up purchases in a prospective upturn.

Indicators of Maturity

One commentary on the state of strategic planning concluded that "probably the area in which strategic planning has performed the poorest is with the well established product line that has only average growth . . . what has created disaster for the planners is the difficulty in accurately determining the maturity of a product, particularly when outside forces can change that designation almost overnight."[30] No single reason for the poor forecasting performance has been isolated, other than the general inability of sales forecasting models to incorporate the underlying forces that determine whether a product will stagnate, decline, or revive. A number of variables have been hypothesized to behave as leading indicators of the top-out point, at which product sales growth slows to approximately the GNP rate:[31]

- Evidence of saturation (as evidenced by a declining proportion of new trier versus replacement sales)
- Increasing rate of decline in real prices and profit margins
- Industry overcapacity levels that cannot be accounted for by short-run economic fluctuations
- Appearance of substitute technologies and related products
- Changes in the ratio of exports and imports,[32] due to growing off-shore sourcing and production
- Declining responsiveness of sales to advertising, promotion, and sales efforts, in conjunction with increasing price sensitivity
- Increasing reluctance of buyers to pay for technical services
- Decreasing profitability and reduced risks of backward integration by customers

Unfortunately, there has been no systematic study of the predictive validity of these leading indicators, and many of them are appropriate only in specific industry contexts. For this reason, several different indicators must be used simultaneously, for when the same

---

30. *Business Week* "The New Planning", (18 December 1978).
31. Patel and Younger (1978) and Wilson (1969).
32. Ayal (1981).

signal is given by two or three indicators, it is much more likely to be meaningful.

Two recently proposed variables are worth discussing in detail, for they indicate the potential payoff from finding the right leading indicator in a given situation.

Declining Price Premiums.   Analysts at DuPont have found that prices of products in capital-intensive industries, such as chemicals and plastics, have two distinct components: (1) the commodity or base price for the product class that is subject to the forces of supply and demand and (2) the premium price differential, gained by a high-quality supplier, which often remains fairly stable amid the month-to-month turbulence of the commodity price. As the product matures, and customers have less need for supporting technical services and other product augmentation, the size of the price premium achievable by the superior quality competitor begins to decline. The start of this decline signals that maturity is impending and the product is moving into a commodity status where lowest delivered cost is the important determinant of profitability. Figure 3.9 shows how this pricing pattern typically unfolds as the market evolves toward maturity.

Technological Life Cycles.   The development of a technology follows an S-shaped curve, beginning with the onset of investigation

Figure 3.9
Pricing in capital-intensive industries

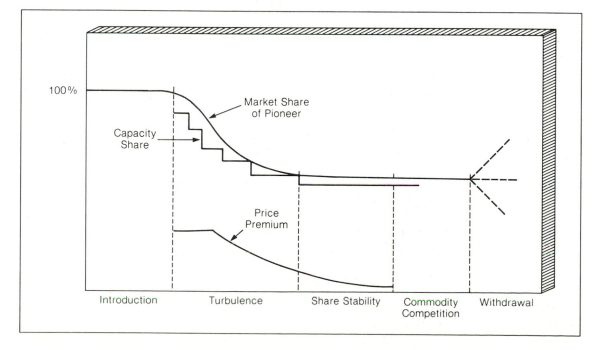

into the possibilities and culminating in the full achievement of performance potential. This level is achieved when the technology has either bumped up against a natural limit or is being supplanted by a new and better technology. At this point, the returns on R and D devoted to the technology are likely to be poor, and resources should be shifted to the next generation of technologies, which provide the basis for a new product life cycle.

Mature technologies are usually readily available to all competitors, so they are no longer a competitive advantage. This detracts further from the returns on R and D investments in these technologies. Indeed, once the rate of improvement begins to slow, it is a clear signal that thinking about a move to a new technology should begin. This is not easy, for it is probably just at this point that products using this technology are most profitable. Yet, the risks of misreading the transition point and staying with the mature technology for too long can be crippling:[33]

> Viewing tire cords in terms of S-curves illustrates the strategic importance of knowing what the limits of varying technologies are. The cords, which add strength, resilience, and blowout protection to tires, were made first from cotton, then rayon, then nylon, and finally polyester. Each succeeding technology outperformed its predecessor, but those who championed the earlier ones lost market leadership to the newcomers. During the late stages of nylon cord development, for example, when the polyester version was being developed, the return on R&D for the latter was some 4.5 times greater than for the former. Polyester has proved itself superior, enabling Celanese Corp. to get far more for its research dollar than could DuPont Co. No company can

Figure 3.10
Technological life cycles

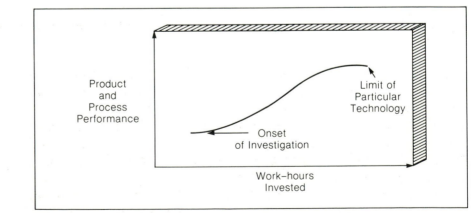

---

33. Foster (1982).

support that level of cost disadvantage for long. Clearly, in technology, the economics of attack are frequently superior to those of defense.

The problem is to know when a technology is approaching the limits of development. A number of plausible indicators have been suggested, which could be used with broader-based indicators of product life-cycle maturity:

- A trend toward missed R and D deadlines, because effectiveness is becoming more difficult to achieve.

- A shift in emphasis toward process rather than product improvement. Typically, as limits are reached, process improvements are easier to attain, and these are often facilitated by experience curve effects.

- A perceived loss of R and D creativity and consequent disharmony among the R and D staff.

- Loss of market position by industry leaders to small specialist competitors.

- Little difference in returns despite spending substantially more or less than competitors over a period of several years. In part, this comes about because the technology developments diffuse quickly through the industry.

None of these indicators is conclusive in isolation from others, but when the cumulative signals from several indicators are considered, the evidence should suggest that the point of diminishing returns has been reached.

Summary

The product life cycle has considerable *descriptive* value as a systematic framework for explaining the evolution of markets that are subject to the complex and uncertain interplay of customers, competitors, and technologies. This concept has a more limited value as a *predictive* model, although some promising results have been obtained in forecasting life cycles in special circumstances. Such successes depend on the ability of the forecasting model to incorporate the specific facilitating and inhibiting forces that are operating in the market. Many of these forces are a consequence of strategic actions by present and prospective competitors. Their collective willingness to invest in market development, improve the perceived value of the product by reducing the price, or introduce features that better meet the needs of the potential market can significantly accelerate (or delay) the evolution of the market. As we will see in the next chapter, this perspective has profound consequences for the strategic relevance of the product life-cycle concept.

First Purchase Diffusion Models *Appendix*

The most popular of first purchase diffusion models was developed and tested by Bass.[34] The basic notion is that in every time period, there will be both innovators and initators buying the new product. Innovators are not influenced by the number of persons who have already bought, but may be influenced by promotional activity. As the diffusion process continues, the relative number of innovators diminishes. This tendency is offset by the imitators who are influenced by the number of previous buyers and thus become increasingly important as time passes. The structure of the model combines these two components:

$$Q_t = p\,(Q - Q_T) + r\,(Q - Q_T)$$

where: Q_t = number of adopters at time t,
Q = saturation levels (ultimate number of adopters),
Q_T = cumulative number of adopters to date,
r = effect of each adopter on each nonadopter (imitation rate),
p = individual conversion rate in the absence of adopters' influence (innovation rate).

The Bass model, and its numerous variants, share four distinctive features:

- They are applicable only to infrequently purchased products when repeat purchases are negligible.
- The diffusion curve is S-shaped and constrained to grow within a level of saturation that is assumed constant over time.
- Diffusion is considered to be only a function of time, and there is no explicit consideration of marketing decision variables such as price or advertising.
- The population of adopters is assumed to be homogenous.

Reasonable forecasts can be achieved when these assumptions are not unduly limiting and there is sufficient prior sales data to obtain stable parameter estimates.[35] More often, little actual data are available, which calls for calibration using analogies from similar products. Also, the assumptions are often limiting and difficult to overcome.

34. Bass (1969).
35. Heeler and Hustad (1980).

Consider the problems that had to be overcome in applying the Bass model to forecasting the acceptance of optical scanners for super-markets.[36]

Supermarket scanners are complex systems that often cost as much as $250,000 per store. The first scanner was installed in 1974, but few sales were made during the next three years, as most chains elected to experiment with one or two units. By the end of 1979, acceptance was gowing rapidly and there was no evidence that a peak in sales was approaching. Clearly, there was a high payoff to accurate forecasting, to avoid overoptimistic sales projections, production schedules, and market development programs. The first problem to overcome in preparing the forecast was to decide whether the adopting unit was the store chain or the store itself. The latter was chosen because scanners are produced in store unit modules, and the great disparity in chain sizes would seriously distort the results. The next problem was to assess total market potential in order to calibrate the model. There was great variance in the estimates made by industry participants, reflecting their uncertainty about future prices of systems, the minimum size of store that could benefit from the system, and the likelihood that the majority of new stores would have scanners installed before they were opened.

The forecasting results were fairly typical of other studies using first purchase diffusion models. There was a high degree of inaccuracy in forecasts of scanner purchases and instability of model parameters until sixteen quarters of data were available from the time that rapid growth actually began. But just as the model was beginning to deliver accurate forecasts of the next year's sales, interest rates took a big jump. Many chains responded by stretching out their store conversion programs, and actual scanner sales dropped unexpectedly.

Improvements to the forecasting accuracy of first purchase models have been sought mainly through the addition of decision variables such as advertising levels or price trends,[37] or relaxing some of the more onerous assumptions. However, progress has been only piece-meal, as the extensions have usually incorporated only one decision variable at a time.[38]

---

36. Tigert and Farivar (1981).
37. Bass (1980), Dolan and Jeuland (1981), Horsky and Simon (1983), Lillien (1980), and Robinson and Lakhani (1975).
38. Mahajan and Muller (1979).

Strategic Issues in Life-Cycle Management

Chapter 4

Successful market strategies are forward-looking—constantly shifting to exploit or accommodate the relentless evolution of markets, technologies, and competitors. An inability to adapt is a problem that ven "excellent" companies encounter. A recent follow-up analysis of the forty-three companies highlighted by the authors of *In Search of Excellence* found that fourteen had stumbled in the three years since the book was written.[1] Moreover, twelve of the fourteen were judged to be inept in adapting to their market.[2] The overall conclusion was that strict adherence to the eight well-known attributes of excellence—which do not emphasize adapting to shifts in the trends underlying the industry and product life cycle—can be damaging to a company.

> Delta Air Lines, which had flourished by maintaining a low debt and exploiting a close-knit culture to keep costs low, failed to see that deregulation had changed its world. The Atlanta-based carrier was slow in recognizing the importance of computers to keep tabs on ticket prices in different markets. Consequently, Delta first failed to meet competitors' lower prices. Then it overreacted. The result: an $86.7 million loss in its fiscal year ended June, 1983, and a brand-new computer system.
>
> Staying close to the customer can backfire on a company when a market shifts dramatically, leaving the company close to the wrong customer. This is what happened to Avon Products Inc. and to Dart & Draft's Tupperware unit when the housewives to whom

1. Peters and Waterman (1982).
2. *Business Week*, "Who's Excellent Now" (5 November 1984).

Table 4.1   Typical strategic implications of life-cycle stages

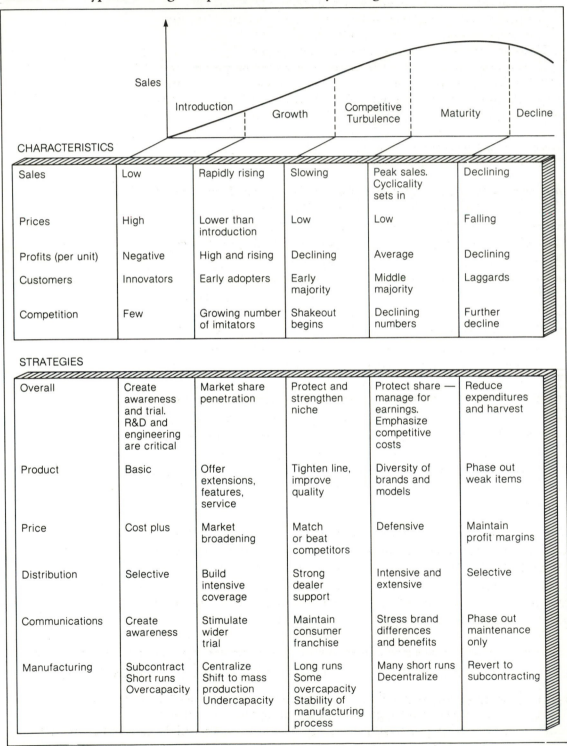

CHARACTERISTICS	Introduction	Growth	Competitive Turbulence	Maturity	Decline
Sales	Low	Rapidly rising	Slowing	Peak sales. Cyclicality sets in	Declining
Prices	High	Lower than introduction	Low	Low	Falling
Profits (per unit)	Negative	High and rising	Declining	Average	Declining
Customers	Innovators	Early adopters	Early majority	Middle majority	Laggards
Competition	Few	Growing number of imitators	Shakeout begins	Declining numbers	Further decline

STRATEGIES	Introduction	Growth	Competitive Turbulence	Maturity	Decline
Overall	Create awareness and trial. R&D and engineering are critical	Market share penetration	Protect and strengthen niche	Protect share — manage for earnings. Emphasize competitive costs	Reduce expenditures and harvest
Product	Basic	Offer extensions, features, service	Tighten line, improve quality	Diversity of brands and models	Phase out weak items
Price	Cost plus	Market broadening	Match or beat competitors	Defensive	Maintain profit margins
Distribution	Selective	Build intensive coverage	Strong dealer support	Intensive and extensive	Selective
Communications	Create awareness	Stimulate wider trial	Maintain consumer franchise	Stress brand differences and benefits	Phase out maintenance only
Manufacturing	Subcontract Short runs Overcapacity	Centralize Shift to mass production Undercapacity	Long runs Some overcapacity Stability of manufacturing process	Many short runs Decentralize	Revert to subcontracting

they catered began to pursue careers. Similarly, DEC and HP—companies run by engineers—have stumbled in trying to sell to customers without a technical background.

   Hewlett-Packard's famed innovative culture and decentralization spawned such enormously successful products as its 3000 minicomputer, the handheld scientific calculator, and the new ThinkJet nonimpact printer. But when a new climate required its fiercely autonomous divisions to cooperate in product development and marketing, HP's passionate devotion to the "autonomy and entrepreneurship" that Peters and Waterman advocate became a hindrance.

Strategic Guidelines.   What managers need are "handrails" that help focus their thinking on the strategic changes dictated by shifts in their markets. They are more likely to find rather vague prescriptions for the appropriate strategic moves at each stage of the "typical" life-cycle pattern. A composite of these prescriptions is provided for illustration in Table 4.1.

   These guidelines are not without virtue. They are usually comprehensive and internally consistent. By characterizing the major challenges at each stage of the life cycle, they may be helpful in identifying the strategic issues a firm should consider at each stage.

   Ultimately, any such generic guidelines will be misleading, for they rest on the erroneous assumption that life cycles are immutable and inevitable. The sole determinant of strategic choices is the product's stage in its life cycle, while critical differences among types of products, competitive structures, and relative business position are ignored. A recurring theme of the previous chapter is that there is no empirical or theoretical support for this position. At best, descriptions of "typical" strategies can be viewed only as plausible hypotheses.

Strategic Issues.   A further danger with life-cycle strategy prescriptions is that they may myopically narrow the perceptions of what is strategically feasible. To broaden one's perspective, it is necessary to shift the focus to the basic strategic issues posed by an evolutionary perspective on product life cycles. These issues are summarized in the following boxed insert.

Strategic Issues in Product Life-Cycle Management

1. *Timing* of entry: whether to be a pioneer, fast follower, or late entrant.
2. Choice of *entry strategy* in light of the consequences for rate of market acceptance. A penetration strategy by the pioneer will force quicker growth and preempt or discourage potential followers, but is inherently riskier

---

Strategic Issues in Product Life-Cycle Management—cont'd

given the uncertainties of the introduction and growth stage of the life cycle.

3. Management of *product modifications* and enhancements to extend the life cycle by creating more frequent usage among current users, new uses, or new users.
4. Exploiting *growth segments* within mature markets.
5. Maintaining, harvesting, or divesting a position in a declining market.

Pervading these issues is the fundamental question of the relative attractiveness of fast-growing versus mature markets. The next section addresses this question directly, and provides the specific context for two further sections on market entry and timing strategies and the management of mature and declining markets.

Competitive Risks in High-Growth Markets[3]

A market is neither inherently attractive or unattractive because it promises rapid future growth. The real question is whether the business can exploit the opportunities presented by high growth to establish a competitive advantage. The answer lies in the validity of the following premises used to make the case that firms should participate early in growth markets.

- Gaining share is easier.
- Share gains are worth more.
- Less price pressure exists.
- Early participation in a growth market is necessary to ensure access to the technology.
- An aggressive early entry will deter subsequent entrants.

Each of these premises may be valid in general but seriously misleading in a particular situation. By understanding the limitations of these premises and the conditions under which they are unlikely

---

3. This section is adapted from Aaker and Day (1985).

to hold, we will be in a better position to formulate a growth market strategy.

Gaining Share in Growth Markets Is Easier

Two arguments support the premise that gaining share is easier. The first is that growth markets offer more opportunities for new users entering the product category. As these new users have no established brand loyalties or supplier commitments, they are easier to attract than buyers in mature markets. Second, it is widely felt that competitors are less likely to react aggressively to market share erosion, so long as their sales are growing at a satisfactory rate.

The argument that new users do not have entrenched loyalties to overcome has both point and weight. Yet, it is still necessary to attract these new users to an unfamiliar product—a task that is both difficult and costly. They have to be informed of the advantages, persuaded that the benefits are greater than the risks, and educated in the use of the new product. Formidable investments were made to overcome the barriers to acceptance of such products as freeze-dried coffee, microwave ovens, industrial robots, personal computers, and automatic teller machines.

The argument that competitors are less likely to react to share losses so long as revenues grow at a satisfactory rate is more dubious, for it overlooks their expectations. The critical distinction is between the competitor's expectations of future sales—which dictate their resource commitments and capacity additions—and their actual sales level.[4] Competitors may react just as aggressively if their expectations are not achieved, whether they are in a slow or a rapid growth situation. If the growth area is important to the competitor's future, because of its profit potential or because of its impact on their other business units, then the competitor's expectations are likely to be high. The realism of these expectations depends on whether competitors have the financial and managerial resources to expand with the rest of the industry.[5]

Share Gains in Growth Markets Are Worth More

The argument here is that a market share point earned in a growth market will return dividends through time that will grow as the market grows. The same share point earned in a mature market is

---

4. Wensley (1981).
5. Porter (1980).

presumed to yield a profit stream that will not grow. An implicit assumption that merits close scrutiny is that market share can be held during the subsequent growth phase. Customers once earned should be relatively easy to retain, and the market momentum should allow the firm to obtain its share of new customers.

This premise contains a number of potential problems:

■ The ability to hold share depends first upon how it is obtained. If the share increase was the consequence of new channels, as in the case of L'Eggs hosiery, it may be quite feasible to sustain a share position. However, if share was obtained from dealer promotions or short-term pricing actions that can readily be matched by competition and may tarnish the brand image, then such market share positions may be vulnerable.

■ As a market grows, the key success factors may change. For example, during the early growth stage of the CT scanner market, the key success factor was technology, and the industry could support many firms. As this market matured, a service capability became necessary, which was difficult for some smaller firms to obtain. As the industry matures still further, it seems clear that a key success factor will be to have synergies with components, computer technologies, software technologies, and instrumentation. The firms that ultimately survive will likely be the large diversified electronics firms like GE, Hitachi, Phillips, and Siemens. Thus, the assumption that an early market share position in this industry could be retained would be faulty unless the firm was in a position to compete when the nature of the industry and its key success factors also changes.

■ As a market expands, it may fragment into numerous small segments, each characterized by specialized products, channels, or service needs. As a result, the market in which the firm is able to compete, effectively shrinks as segment after segment is splintered away.

■ Competition can be more intense than anticipated. Often, firms that may not be very visible or may be completely unknown are preparing to enter the market. If the barriers to entry are low, new competitors may be attracted.

■ The business may not be able or willing to manage or finance the rate of growth required to maintain share. High rates of growth impose heavy cash flow requirements from additional working capital and plant and equipment needs.

The consistent theme of each of these potential problems is that market positions gained during the high-growth period will not be retained unless there is a sustainable competitive advantage. Although Texas Instruments was a vigorous early entrant in the digital watch market, it was forced to exit in mid-1981 because it had no advantage in consumer marketing. Similarly, the systems houses that sell turnkey computer systems for general business applications are vulnerable to competition from computer makers and computer services companies. Their problem is that the expertise required to adapt software to specific applications is not proprietary, and they lack visibility relative to these new competitors, who also have more resources to devote to marketing. The survivors will be those with distinct market specializations—chromatography systems, for example—that are too small to be attractive to the big computer companies.

Arguments for participating in high-growth markets that are based on an experience curve rationale are superficially appealing. After all, if one can enter the market early and gain a competitive cost advantage (which can be converted into low prices), then potential competitors may be discouraged. However, as we saw in the previous chapter, the experience curve is neither certain nor automatic. Worse, it may deflect attention from the possibility that followers into a market will usually be able to start farther down the experience curve, by learning from the pioneer's mistakes or by leapfrogging by using the latest technology or building a plant with a larger scale of operations.

Growth Markets Have Less Price Pressure

In markets experiencing vigorous growth, demand often exceeds supply and therefore no pressure is exerted on prices; in fact, the excess demand may support premium prices. Thus, early participation in growth markets provides a unique opportunity to recover the start-up investment. Industries that are highly capital-extensive, such as plastics and textiles, also present the early entrant with an opportunity to command a significant premium above the average commodity price. Later entrants usually have quality problems and less reliable delivery performance as they struggle to start up complex, integrated facilities. At the same time, customers of the new product are usually willing to pay extra for technical service and applications support as they learn how to use the product. As both customers and competitors gain experience, the premium that can be achieved without loss of share slowly shrinks.[6] Indeed, it may eventually disappear if buyers no longer perceive a meaningful value difference among competitors.[7]

Two problems arise when attempting to achieve price premiums during the growth phase. First, attractive margins serve to attract competition, which in the long run may cause profits to be weaker. Second, a few firms may well be pricing low, perhaps below their costs. They may be attempting to apply the experience curve logic or may simply feel they have no other competitive option in a market they regard as important.

Early Participation Provides Technological Expertise

Participants in high-technology markets often argue that early involvement in the technology is important to staying current. Experience with the first-generation technology and the customer applications of that equipment can lead to superior second-generation technology. A late entry, lacking customer contact, production experience, and an established R and D capability, will be at a disadvantage.

However, an early commitment to a technology may later turn out to be a disadvantage or even a liability as alternate technologies emerge. Once a commitment is made to one technology, adapting to a new technology is frequently difficult. Management must be certain that present customers are not left in vulnerable positions. They are naturally reluctant to withdraw too quickly from mature technologies that are highly profitable.[8] Thus, Medtronic's leadership position in the cardiac pacemaker market was eroded when it waited too long to switch to a new lithium-based technology. An outside firm, without the constraint of the established technology, was able to exploit this delay and successfully enter the market.

A commitment to one technology may also make it difficult for businesses, and even entire industries, to properly assess emerging technologies. Old-line toy companies were generally slow to recognize the impact of "intelligent" electronics on the toy and game industry. In retrospect, those that did not commit to this market are

---

6. The phenomenon of shrinking price premium is discussed previous in the chapter as a leading indicator of maturity.

7. Gross (1979).

8. Yip (1980).

probably pleased that they avoided the collapse of the electronic game market.

Early Aggressive Entry Will Deter Later Entrants

When a firm makes a major commitment to a business area, it may sacrifice flexibility, but it does send a strong signal to competitors. It is in business for the duration and will spend whatever is necessary to preserve and expand its position. If one or more films send such signals, the market will look less appealing no matter how attractive the growth rate. Further, the early entrant can generate substantial barriers to entry by establishing a strong brand image, by preempting a distribution channel, or by other similar action.

The validity of this premise will depend upon the context. Some markets will be considered "must" areas for certain firms. If the market offers important long-term synergies to the firm or is so important in terms of growth and size that it cannot be bypassed, then the firm will not likely be discouraged. For example, it was inevitable that IBM would eventually enter the personal computer market. IBM wanted to wait until the market was large enough to support business that was worthwhile relative to the size of the IBM organization, but it was not going to be preempted. Similarly, Ford and General Motors introduced small diesel trucks in 1982, although IVECO had launched such a product two years earlier through International Harvester channels. Clearly, they were not going to let a major diesel market develop without their participation.[9]

The ability of early entrants to discourage competitive firms from entering will depend on the nature and size of the barriers to entry that they are capable of building. If the product lines and associated marketing and production efforts do not yield a competitive advantage that can be sustained, then competitive firms may actually be encouraged to enter the market.

Assessing the Risks of a Shakeout

Growth markets are especially unattractive when a surplus of competitors enters with unrealistic market share expectations. Such an unstable situation will eventually lead to a wrenching shakeout. Look at the plight of the thirteen participants in Japan's $200 million facsimile transmission market. Although this market is growing at a

9. *Business Week,* IVECO: A Brash Attempt to Exploit Its Harvester Connection" (17 May 1982).

35 percent annual rate, this still provides less than $20 million revenue to the average participant—well below the amount required to justify investments in new digital technologies and extensive sales and service networks.[10] The personal computer market is a more extreme candidate for a shakeout. At the end of 1982, an estimated 150 manufacturers of microcomputers, plus another 300 or so firms dealing with add-on products, software, service, sales, and support, were involved. Most of these will not survive as independents; indeed, it is forecast that by 1986 only a dozen manufacturers will still be in the market.[11] The losers will be those unable to achieve low-cost production or offer a wide range of software.

The risks of a shakeout are greatest when the premises used to justify entry are superficially valid but ultimately misleading. This leads us to the following high-risk conditions.

- The industry and its growth rate has high visibility. As a result, strategists in related firms are encouraged to seriously consider the industry and may fear the consequences of turning their backs on an obvious growth direction.

- There is very high forecast and actual growth in the early stages. This is pointed to as evidence confirming high industry growth as a proven phenomenon.

- Limits to the growth potential are not considered or are discounted. Little exists to dampen the enthusiasm surrounding the industry. The enthusiasm may be contagious when venture capitalists and stock analysts become advocates.

- Few initial barriers to entry exist to prevent firms from entering the market.

- Products employ an existing technology rather than a risky or protected technology. Technology sometimes provides a more obvious and formidable barrier than, for example, a finance or marketing barrier. The true significance of a marketing barrier to entry, such as limited retail space, may be evident only after the market is overcrowded.

- Some potential entrants have low visibility, and their intentions are unknown or uncertain. Thus, the number and commitment of competitors are likely to be underestimated.

---

10. Ohmae (1982).

11. *Business Week*, "The Coming Shake-Out in Personal Computers" (22 November 1982).

The shakeout itself may occur within a relatively short period of time. The duration will depend on whether the trigger is (1) an unanticipated slowing of market growth, either because the market is close to saturation or because a recession has intervened; (2) aggressive late entrants buying their way into the market by cutting prices; (3) the market leader attempting to stem the previous erosion of market position with aggressive product and price retaliation; or (4) a change in the key success factors as a consequence of technological change, perhaps raising the minimum scale of operations, or there is a shift in the value-added structure as cost elements that are resistant to experience effects assume greater importance. Each of these possible triggering events introduces further sources of risk.

Market Entry and Timing Strategies

The product life-cycle concept poses a number of questions to managers assessing their strategy for an emerging industry or product class:

When should we enter?

- As one of the pioneers?
- As a fast follower?
- As a late entrant?

How should we enter?

- What approach: internal development, acquisition, or joint venture?
- Magnitude of participation: small toehold entry versus an aggressive drive for leadership?
- Basis of competitive advantage?

What actions should be taken to preempt potential competitors or respond to later entrants?

This section focuses on the strategic choices for pioneers and fast followers, shown schematically in Figure 4.1. Each of these choices has major consequences for the resources and skills needed to succeed and the risks to be taken.

Strategies for Pioneers

Although pioneers take the greatest risks—and are shaken out in the greatest numbers—those that survive are well rewarded. One

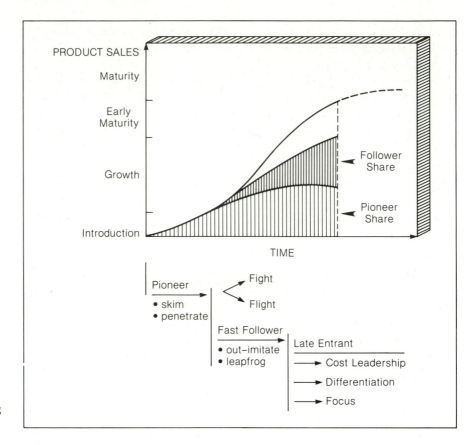

Figure 4.1   Timing of entry

study of a broad cross section of mature industrial businesses found that the average market share at maturity for pioneers was 30 percent, for followers 21 percent, and for late entrants market shares were 15 percent.[12] The pioneers in the fluorescent lamp, nickel, aluminum, and plain paper copier markets have been leaders for years. This finding is comforting for managers of pioneering firms that have survived, for it confirms the wisdom of their strategy. It also accounts for some of the allure of new markets to those preparing to take the plunge. The challenge, then, is to improve the odds of success by entering when the circumstances are appropriate.

Early entrants must be prepared to bear the costs of pioneering and the risks that conditions will change. These are the potentially unattractive features of high-growth markets examined earlier in this chapter. Fortunately there are offsetting benefits for the firms that are willing to accept the uncertainties. Most of these benefits are derived from the opportunity pioneers have to define the rules of

12. Robinson (1984).

competition to their advantage. The potential cost or differentiation advantages come from the following opportunities.

Preemption of Competition.   A pioneer can develop and position products for the largest and most lucrative market segments while leaving smaller and less desirable ones to the later entrants. Stouffers effectively captured a position for its frozen entrées as gourmet meals for busy people rather than as quick, filling meals for the family. This required significant investments in product development, including menu selection and sauce technology, and product quality, to achieve dishes with consistently attractive appearance and taste. These investments were reinforced with heavy spending on consumer advertising and sales force coverage to ensure attractive retail shelf displays and rapid restocking.

Early entrants with a viable product usually have the pick of the best brokers, distributors, and retailers. The followers have the thankless task of persuading the pioneer's distributors to shift or divide their commitment. Failing this the followers have to find a new channel or settle for less desirable channel members. The problems this creates for followers are acute in the personal computer market where the scarcest resource is the shelf space controlled by the large chains of computer retailers such as Computerland.

Leadership Reputation.   The first company in a market naturally has a unique position, which also confers a potential leadership image that is not available to followers. Whether this advantageous reputation has more than temporary value depends on the credibility of the firm and its capacity to invest in marketing. Small firms have often introduced innovations to the industrial battery market, but have not been able to capitalize on them because they are viewed as high-risk suppliers.

Customer Loyalty.   A customer may be forced to be loyal to the first supplier in the market because switching costs are high. These are one-time costs the buyer absorbs when switching suppliers, associated with employee retraining, new ancillary equipment, the need for technical assistance and product redesign, and the time required to test and qualify a new source. For example, hospital management contracts are costly to change, because of the disruption caused by a new administrator, a new computer system, and budgeting and operating procedures.

Proprietary Experience Effects.   A pioneer gains an initial cost advantage when learning through cumulative experience is an important contributor to cost reductions. Whether it is sustainable depends on how difficult the learning is to imitate, and whether it will be nullified by a competing technology. Of course, the best protection against imitation is a strong patent position, but even this advantage must be vigorously policed.

Access to Scarce Resources.   The pioneer may gain a long-term advantage by acquiring the best sites (for retail stores) or the richest ore bodies that are close to major markets. The pioneer may be able to negotiate favorable deals from suppliers who are eager for new business or who do not appreciate the size of the opportunity for their raw materials or component parts. There may be an offsetting cost, if the early sources of supply are operating at a small scale with uncertain quality or reliability of delivery.

Sustainable Lead in Technology.   Such a lead will result if the competitors are unable to duplicate the technology, or the firm innovates at a faster rate than the competition so followers are never able to catch up. DuPont was forced to abandon the consumer color film market when Kodak announced a major advance in their film. DuPont was preparing to launch the previous generation of technology which has poorer color and image resolution.

A technological lead is likely to be sustainable under the following conditions:

1. The technology has been developed largely within the industry. If the source of technology is external sources such as suppliers of machinery or components, or construction engineering firms that design production processes, the latest advances will be available to all present or potential competitors. Indeed the last entrant will be the greatest beneficiary by having access to the latest technology.

2. The rate of diffusion of the technology is slow, because the advances are difficult to copy. But when design improvements can be readily revealed by reverse engineering, the advances are communicated in scientific proceedings, or are carried outside by mobile personnel, then the cost or differentiation advantages will be transitory.

3. The firm has a relative cost advantage or greater effectiveness in continuous technology development. Three factors contribute to this area of advantage. One is

economies of scale in R and D. The largest firm can have the largest budget, but still not incur a cost penalty because their R and D spending as a percent of sales will be lower than their direct competitors. Second, distinct learning effects have been observed in the development and launching of new products. Each new feature and improvement costs less than prior changes because of the accumulated stock of skills and experience. Of course, if there is a major shift in technology then this hard-earned base of knowledge may be more of an impediment than an advantage, especially if the personnel are strongly committed to the old technology.

Designing Entry and Response Strategies

The creation of barriers to entry, that deter some potential entrants and prevent or dampen the success of those who enter, is a major consideration when designing an entry strategy. The basic choices are usually between a skimming and a penetration strategy. The merits of a penetration price to drive for rapid market development, especially when there is a steep experience curve, are described in Chapter 2. This strategy is inherently risky but makes sense in large markets, where there is strong potential competition and most potential buying segments are price-sensitive.

A skimming strategy, designed to recover as much gross profit per unit as possible, is more often chosen. This strategy not only is more flexible—as it is much easier to cut prices than to raise them substantially—but also usually means the initial investment is recovered more rapidly. The risk is that short-run profits are purchased at the expense of long-run share losses to competitors attracted by the fat margins. This strategy makes most sense in niche markets, where there are price-insensitive segments and where potential competition is not imminent. A skimming strategy is often employed when market development costs are high and substantial gross margins are required to support technical service, customer, and distributor education, and awareness-building communications programs. Among the masters of this strategy is 3M. According to one manager, "We hit fast, price high (full economic value of the product to the user) and get the heck out when the me-too products pour in." The new niches pioneered by 3M are generally small ones of $10 million to $50 million and may be dominated only for five years or so. By then, it is time to launch the next generation of abrasives or tape products that will supplant the highly competitive product.

Responding to Competition: Fight or Flight?   3M represents one response to inevitability of competition. What sets them apart from many pioneers is that they know it is coming and are fully prepared to suffer some loss of share. Their preferred option is *flight,* which means either launching a new generation of technology to perform the basic function or creating new markets with the technology. If this is not viable, then they stay and *fight* to try and maintain dominance.

The *flight* option is attractive in an era of shortening life cycles and low-cost global competition. The key success factors dictated by this option are not so easily satisfied by most pioneering organizations, since they require the following:

■ The ability to identify and develop primary demand in narrowly defined market niches.

■ A capability for continuous innovation.

■ An organization with a high degree of flexibility that translates into quick, effective product development.

■ A willingness to cannibalize their own product rather than have the competitor do it. Thus, NCR decided that rather than making incremental changes to upgrade their electronic bank teller, they should launch an entirely new, programmable machine.[13]

Timing the flight option is critical. Osborne Computer's failure was a direct consequence of premature announcement. They successfully pioneered the portable computer. When competition emerged, they tried to protect their position by announcing a second-generation portable long before it was ready to ship. The dealers' response was to stop buying the first machine and wait for the advanced version. This created a serious cash flow problem, which was compounded when the machine did not live up to the early promises.

The decision to *fight* to retain dominance requires a very different set of skills and resources, which are often out of the pioneer's reach. To succeed in a competitive market, pioneers must do the following:

■ Shift from the development of primary demand to creating competitive advantages in chosen market segments, and then effectively communicate these advantages.

■ Learn to get close to customers who are not early adopters.

---

13. Fraker (1984).

As we saw in the previous chapter, these behave very differently and are far more segmented in their requirements.

■ Have access to substantial financial and organizational resources to build capacity *in advance* of market growth at 25 to 50 percent per year. As markets move into the growth stage, the achievable market share is often constrained by the share of available production, distribution, and service capacity.

Both the fight and flight options view competitors as threats to be deterred or avoided. There are circumstances in which a more productive response is to *encourage* competitors through offers of licensing or other technology-sharing arrangements. When these competitors arrive, they help share the burden of developing an embryonic market and may also participate in advancing the technology. Here the appropriate focus is not on direct competitors but on the suppliers of substitute products that are already meeting the needs of the market. Small firms that pioneer a new product or service are often at a disadvantage because they lack credibility. New entrants that are respected factors in related markets help overcome this barrier.

Strategies for Fast Followers

Fast followers converge on a market when product sales show clear signs of takeoff. Otherwise, they are content to let the pioneers resolve the uncertainties of early development. For fast followers, the critical decisions are whether to simply out-imitate the pioneer or try to leapfrog by launching a new product or by entering a previously untapped market. The question of how fast is fast is answered by the length of the introductory period of the life cycle. The window for a fast follower may be open for only a few months for microprocessors but several years for new machining systems.

Out-imitating. Out-imitating usually means serving the present market segments with a product that is demonstrably superior on a key attribute. The success of this approach means consciously sacrificing leadership in introducing an unproven technology and waiting until there is a version that better meets the customer's needs. These needs may take some time to come into focus, but by then it is also clear where the pioneers are making mistakes. A variant of this strategy is to identify market segments whose needs are only partially satisfied with the early versions, and target them specifically with a new product.

The execution of this strategy requires the following:

- Insightful market and competitor monitoring in order to accurately sense the takeoff and anticipate changing customer requirements and competitive strategies
- Strong developmental R and D, with a definite tilt toward applications engineering and process improvements rather than searching for basic advances in technology
- An ability to respond quickly, through purposeful design of organizations and manufacturing systems
- A willingness to out-invest the pioneers and force them to fly or to fail in flight

The cost of poor performance on any one of these critical success factors can be staggering. Texas Instruments was forced to exit the home computer business in late 1983 after absorbing a loss of $660 million because it did not keep a close eye on the investment strategies and costs of its rivals. Apparently, the company mistakenly assumed it could make the 99/4A home computer at a competitive cost.[14] One former executive believes, "It thought it could withstand the price pressure because its costs were competitive.... It was wrong. You don't get into a price battle, particularly one where you bet on capturing enormous volume, with a competitor like Commodore who has significantly lower costs."

Changes in customer requirements as the market evolves present significant opportunities to fast followers. Until recently, Japanese manufacturers of chip-making machinery could not keep up with the rate of technology change in the successive generations of aligners, etchers, and other processing gear. This confined them to their home market, where they served captive customers with superior reliability and short setup times. Two trends underlying the evolution of products in this market are now working in their favor.[15] First, advances in wafer processing technology seem to be nearing the point of diminishing returns. Instead, chip makers are emphasizing automation to improve yields. While U.S. suppliers excel in the software needed to link processing machinery into an automated system, the Japanese have an edge in electromechanical technology for handling

14. Ibid.
15. Uttal (1984).

wafers. What really matters in automation, however, is ensuring that the system works reliably.

Leapfrogging.   Where the imitator adopts and refines the pioneer's product or process technology and design and market strategy, the leapfrogging entrant looks to advances in technology or preempts a previously unserved segment in order to gain a competitive advantage. Matsushita uses this route to enter attractive markets with superior, lower-cost products. Although their VCR format (VHS) trailed Sony's Betamax by a year, they still managed to move their format to account for 70 percent of worldwide sales by 1982 and retain the dominant share of those sales.[16]

Successful leapfrogging on the product dimension is difficult because one must out-innovate the pioneers. The best circumstances are found when the pioneer is either committed to realizing a return on an older, higher-cost technology or lacks the resources to respond.

Managing the Transition to Maturity

The inevitable transition to maturity signals a major shift in the planning agenda. The dominant feature of the planning horizon is no longer market growth. With relative stability of market size, competition, and technology, and increasingly sophisticated buyers, the focus of strategy shifts toward market position: how to gain or protect share. The basis of competitive advantage also shifts toward a greater emphasis on cost position, quality, and service support. This may require a dramatic change in the way of life if the business has been used to competing on other grounds. New skills and capital commitments will be required to support the needed change in functional activities. The underlying changes have two further effects, which put serious constraints on the ability of the business to adapt. The first problem is that emerging competitive forces, coupled with experienced buyers and increasingly standardized products, work to reduce average industry profits from the previously heady levels seen when the market could absorb all the available output. The same problems also impact the distribution channels, with the consequence that distributor and retailer margins fall, and the marginal ones drop out. This makes it increasingly difficult to find qualified

---

16. *Business Week*, "Matsushita: Seeking Industrial Markets While Staying Strong in Home Products" (17 May 1982).

dealers, and enhances the power of those that remain. A major aspect of the new competitive environment is the difficulty of maintaining market coverage.

Product life-cycle analysis that is relevant to strategies in maturing or declining environments must be coupled with a broad-based assessment of competitive position. This notion is one of the dominant themes in coming chapters on PIMS and portfolio analysis. However, there are two issues that life-cycle analysis can usefully illuminate. The remainder of this section deals with the potential for life-cycle extension and the assessment of threats and opportunities in declining markets.

Potential for Life-Cycle Extension

Many products suffer from premature identification of maturity. This creates a self-fulfilling prophecy in which the established competitors collectively decide their best action is to reduce the marketing and R and D investments to the level necessary to defend their share positions. This will free up cash flow for investment in growth opportunities in emerging markets. But if product class sales are sensitive to market development activity (as in the case of engineered plastics) or advertising expenditures (as is the case with powdered breakfast drinks) and these budgets are reduced by the dominant firms, the product growth rate will begin to slow as everyone expected.

Consider alternately the opportunities found in one of the oldest industries, clothing. Designer blue jeans, active sportswear, and pantyhose have each grown dramatically in recent years. These volume increases are on a much larger scale than is found in emerging markets that are still small and undeveloped. Most seemingly mature products can be infused with new life by enhancing them to create

- more frequent usage among current users,
- more varied usage among current users,
- new users, or
- a combination of these.

The possibilities suggested by these life-stretching activities remind us that a life cycle is not a *fait accompli* that can only be reacted to, but is instead a consequence of management actions. Products are not static entities, and future augmentations, enhancements, and improvements will have a significant bearing on the duration of the life cycle.

The following examples further illustrate the potential for life extension:

■ In 1979 a slow-growth popcorn popper market was revived by the introduction of hot air poppers, in which corn is added into a chamber where hot air is blown over the kernels and they pop without oil. The added convenience made this a more attractive gift item, and the absence of oil opened up a new segment of diet watchers and cholesterol counters who previously avoided the product.

■ The continuing growth of automated teller machines has been facilitated by the introduction of cash dispensers. These are stripped-down single-function machines that can handle only cash transactions. However, these account for 60 percent to 70 percent of all ATM transactions. The low cost of these ATMs has permitted banks to install more, which encourages more frequent usage, and their simplicity of operation has evidently attracted some new users.

■ The previous chapter mentioned the problems Sony had encountered by misreading the initial demand for small-screen TV sets. Now growth forecasts are being raised even further to reflect previously unthought of possibilities for this product—including uses in combination with miniature cameras for home security systems, and portable television and computer models with the addition of a keyboard, memory, and telecommunications capability.

Look for Growth Opportunities.　The sheer size of mature markets offers numerous possibilities for segmentation. Each segment has its own rate of growth and decline, with some offering considerable growth potential.[17] Examples are elsewhere: low-tar cigarettes, health cereals, gourmet entrées in frozen foods, super-premium beer, or the Southwest for many services. Heublein recognized early the trend toward light liquors due in part to the increased consumption by women and younger people during the late 1960s and 1970s. As a result, Heublein invested in its Smirnoff vodka brand and promoted bottled mixed drinks such as Screwdrivers and Bloody Marys. In doing so, it established a solid position in this submarket.

Opportunities for competitive growth in seemingly mature markets may also come from rapid changes in industry structure. The sweeteners market is unquestionably mature, yet events have pre-

---

17. Hearne (1982).

sented some competitors and entrants from outside the industry with strategic windows. First was the saccharin scare and the development of new artificial sweeteners. Then high-fructose corn syrup entered the picture. Meanwhile, international politics and U.S. budget deficits lead to changes in U.S. agricultural support prices for sugar and a decline in industry profitability. Further changes will be felt when a granular high-fructose corn syrup is developed. There will be winners and losers as a result of each of these changes.

Further openings will be available if most of the established competitors behave maturely. One company went from nothing to $400 million in revenue within the seemingly stagnant athletic footwear market, by meeting the unsatisfied market demand for better engineering and better styling. Previous industry participants had ignored these market needs, because they were either complacent or distracted by other problems.

Managing in Declining Markets

Managers first confronted with obviously declining market demand will likely try to harvest the business, by eliminating investment, maximizing cash flow, and eventually divesting. This strategy may be sensible; indeed, it may be the only option if the rate of decline is precipitous or the competitive position is already tenuous. Usually a careful second look at such markets is more appropriate. A myopic focus on a harvest strategy may lead to a self-fulfilling prophecy that could have been avoided. Instead, some astute survivors are profiting from declining markets by following strategies that are normally prescribed for growth situations. What they have found is that some declining environments are more hospitable than others.

Assessing the Declining Market

Even though sales are shrinking, some markets remain highly profitable while in others the profits evaporate much faster than sales. The extent to which profits erode depends on how readily industry participants pull out and how fiercely the survivors try to contain the shrinkage in sales. Four structural factors have to be considered in this assessment:[18]

---

18. Harrigan and Porter (1983).

1. *Rate and pattern of decline.* Here we have to determine the underlying causes of decline, whether it is substitution, a shrinking customer group, or changes in life-styles, for this will determine the speed and certainty of decline. In general, the slower the better.

2. *Structure of remaining demand pockets.* In many declining markets, profitable niches remain that are resistant to the industry pattern. In the cigar industry, the branded premium-quality segment has been more stable and has not seen much price erosion. Upholstery leathers are a profitable segment in a slumping leather market.

3. *Exit barriers.* Competitors are locked into unprofitable situations for many reasons. They may have specialized assets that cannot be liquidated, or may face large fixed costs of exit due to labor settlements, commitments to provide spare parts to customers, or cancellation penalties in long-term contracts. Further exit barriers are raised if the

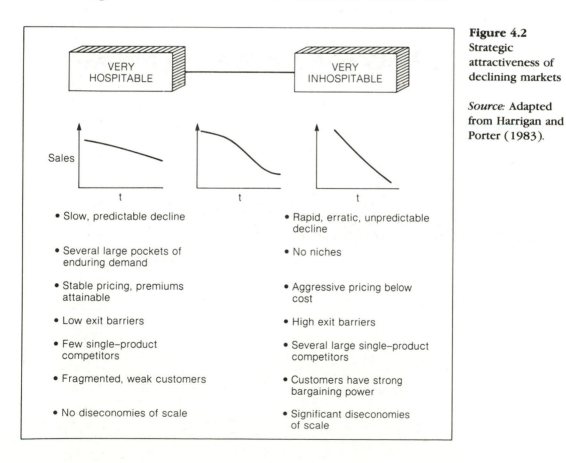

Figure 4.2
Strategic attractiveness of declining markets

Source: Adapted from Harrigan and Porter (1983).

declining product shares resources with other parts of the company, or government social policy puts a high premium on protecting jobs.

4. *Intensity of competitive rivalry.* A declining industry may continue to be profitable if the customers are not powerful bargainers or if there are no disecononomies of scale. If there are many aggressive competitors facing high exit barriers, the prospects for profitability are poor.

Declining markets can be located on a continuum reflecting varying degrees of long-run hospitality for the surviving competitors.

Choosing and Implementing the Appropriate Strategy

Once the market environment has been assessed for strategic attractiveness, two further questions become pivotal:

■ How well do the company's strengths fit the requirements of the remaining pockets of demand? Companies that try to cut back to achieve profitability without having definite strengths usually collapse. Once service or market coverage deteriorates or prices are raised, the customers quickly shift their business.

■ Does the corporate strategy support the decision to remain in the declining market? Cash flow requirements may dictate a harvest or early sale regardless of the forecast attractiveness.

Where the declining market is attractive and the business can compete in the remaining pockets of demand, it may even be desirable to achieve leadership before switching to a controlled harvest.[19] The premise here is that the leader can then achieve greater profitability on the way out by avoiding unrewarding price competition. A leadership position can be achieved by forcing others out of the market by taking aggressive price or marketing actions, or by reducing competitors' exit barriers by acquiring their product lines at prices above the going rate and then retiring them. To reinforce the competitors' perceptions that decline is inevitable, it may be desirable to develop and disclose credible marketing research on substitution effects, changing buying patterns, and the like.

---

19. Harrigan (1980).

Once a harvest strategy is put in motion, the biggest risk is that insufficient support will be provided to maintain a viable presence in the market. Then the business will be forced to exit much earlier than necessary while forgoing significant cash flow on the way out. The following boxed insert describes what not to do.

Mismanaging a Harvest Strategy

In the late seventies, there was no doubt in the minds of Timex managers that sales of mechanical windup watches would decline in the face of aggressive pricing of electronic watches. The only question was how quickly. To manage the shrinkage properly and harvest mechanical watches for profits, the trick was to keep reducing production capacity just below the level of potential sales. As for slowing the rate of decline with advertising and product upgrading, that should have gone without saying. Instead, all spending to support sales was cut off. "We started treating the mechanical as if it only had hours to live," said an internal company memo in 1981. As a result, one former employee added, "We allowed our *only* product to die." Meanwhile, management spent heavily to promote digitals and other new ventures. By the end of 1978, mechanical watch sales were below the break-even point. In 1979, a loss of $4.7 million was reported on sales of $600 million.

Source: Magnet (1983).

Summary

The derivation of generalized strategy *prescriptions* for each stage of the life cycle is often dubious and may be counterproductive. Such prescriptions are bound to be misleading, for they assume a single role for the life cycle as a determinant of strategy, structure, and performance. Unfortunately, this role is implicitly endorsed by a majority of marketing textbooks through an emphasis on strategic guidelines appropriate to the various stages. A more realistic view is that life-cycle analysis serves several different roles in the formulation of strategy, such as an enabling condition, a moderating variable, or a consequence of strategic decisions.

The life cycle serves as an *enabling condition* in the sense that the underlying forces that inhibit or facilitate growth create opportunities and threats having strategic implications. Market growth—

or the expectation of growth—enables competitors to enter the market and creates opportunities for offerings directed to segments previously uneconomic to serve. The stage of the life cycle also acts as a *moderating variable* through its influence on the value of market share position and the profitability consequences of strategic decisions. Finally, a product life-cycle forecast is not a *fait accompli* that can only be reacted to, but instead is only one of several scenarios that are shaped by competitive actions.

The Analysis of Pooled Business Experience: the PIMS Program

Chapter 5

The PIMS approach to strategy analysis seeks guidance from the collective experience of a diverse sample of successful and unsuccessful businesses.[1] In 1985 this sample represented over 2,800 businesses contributed by more than 250 corporations.

Within the sample are many stellar performers; 12 percent of the businesses reported pretax returns on investment of more than 50 percent. Another 13 percent are real losers, having posted losses in each of the preceding four years. PIMS looks behind these outcomes to ask what features of the business and its environment account for the spread in profitability and cash flow. Three sets of factors are persistently influential, regardless of industry, country, or economic climate. One set describes the *competitive position* of a business and includes market share and relative product quality. The second describes the *production structure,* including investment intensity and productivity of operations, and the third reflects the relative *attractiveness of the served market,* market growth rate, and customer characteristics. Together these variables account for 65 to 70 percent of the variability in profitability in the sample.

The intent of the PIMS Program is to apply what has been learned about these profitability determinants to answer specific strategic questions about individual businesses, such as the following:

■ What rate of profit and cash flow is "normal" or PAR for this type of business, considering its market environment, competitive position, and strategy being pursued (and assuming average luck and operating effectiveness)?

---

1. PIMS stands for the Profit Impact of Market Strategies.

■ If the business continues on its present track, what operating performance could be expected in the future?

■ How will this performance be affected by a change in the strategy employed?

The PIMS project has done much to advance our basic understanding of the determinants of strategic performance. However, as a management tool its record has been decidedly mixed. Managers and planners tend to be skeptical about the underlying premises of the PIMS Program, and their uneasiness is compounded by the necessary rigidities of the data and the complex analyses needed to extract useful insights from these data.

The purpose of this chapter is to put PIMS into perspective. Our basic position is that PIMS is best used in a supportive role in the planning process, but even here it can be dangerous unless the built-in limitations are appreciated. The departure point for the chapter is a discussion of the conceptual framework and the sample. This discussion will provide a basis for describing the feasible applications of the PIMS model to situation assessment, competitive analysis, evaluation of strategic options, and validity testing. Before the general results or specific applications can be appreciated, however, one must understand the guiding premise of the PIMS Program.

Why Investigate Strategic Peers?

The basic premise is that a business can learn as much from the experiences of *strategy peers,* conducting a large series of strategy experiments from a similar position, as it can learn from *industry peers* who participate in the same industry but face different strategic situations.[2]

PIMS advocates agree that the details of the specific market situation will dominate the choice of strategy. They also argue that simply looking at each business on its own will be incomplete or even misleading.[3] A business that is a weak number three in an industry would be ill-advised to emulate the strategies of a market leader. Better guidance may come from studying how other weak number three businesses have coped with the problem, and observing the profit outcomes of these strategic moves. At a minimum, the insights from the experience of broad classes of businesses will certainly help managers to avoid mistakes.

---

2. Collier (1980).
3. Gale (1978).

The use of strategy peers has been likened to the diagnostic procedures used by doctors. While doctors appreciate that each patient is unique, they will nonetheless focus on characteristics that are common to all individuals, such as pulse rate, blood pressure, body temperature, and weight relative to height. This is the frame of reference within which problems can be identified.

The Structure of the PIMS Program

The genesis of the PIMS Program was a project within the General Electric Company begun in 1960. The impetus was a recurring need to evaluate and compare the strategic options proposed by operating departments from many different industries. While early results were provocative, the question was whether they were limited to the businesses General Electric was in, or could be applied more broadly. The project was broadened and moved in 1972 to the Marketing Science Institute, a research organization then affiliated with the Harvard Business School. By 1975 the data base had been expanded to almost six hundred businesses and generally verified the basic GE findings.[4] However, this growth created an urgent need to give the member companies more consulting assistance so they could get more effective use from the research program. To meet this need, the Strategic Planning Institute was established in 1975 and continues to manage both the research program and the consulting activities.

The Sample of PIMS Businesses

By 1985 the PIMS data base contained information about 2,800 businesses. This sample continues to reflect the origins of PIMS within GE, and the wider diffusion of the basic concept within the manufacturing sector. As a consequence, the service and distribution sectors are seriously under-represented. The representativeness of the sample is further influenced by the nature of the participating companies; they are likely to be large—about 20 percent of the Fortune 500 are members—profitable, and innovative. These companies also tend to submit their more successful and established businesses for PIMS analysis. The net effect is that the average PIMS business is likely to be in a mature market, and have a higher product quality and price and a stronger market share position than the average of

---

4. Schoeffler, Buzzell, and Heany (1974), and Buzzell, Gale, and Sultan (1975).

Table 5.1 Composition of the PIMS Sample

INDUSTRY CLASSIFICATION	% OF SAMPLE
Consumer products	26%
Capital equipment	19%
Raw materials	10%
Components	28%
Industrial supplies	10%
Service and distribution	7%
	100%

Total businesses in sample = 2,800

GEOGRAPHIC LOCATION	SIZE OF CORPORATION (TOTAL SALES)	
	OVER $100MM	UNDER $100MM
North American based	55%	35%
Foreign	10%	0%
	65%	35%

the other competitors in the same served markets.[5] One encouraging development is the increasing proportion of international businesses in the data base, with 19 percent of the sample now coming in approximately equal numbers from the United Kingdom, Europe, and South America. Apparently, no major differences exist between the results obtained in the North American and International data bases.

What are the Determinants of Profitability and Cash Flow?

The basic structure of the PIMS profitability model is shown in Figure 5.1. The key distinctions are between those variables that establish the *relative attractiveness* of the market versus those that reveal the *strength* of the business within that market. The sign beside each variable in Figure 5.1 indicates whether it has a positive or a negative influence in profitability.

Market attractiveness is established by the average level of profitability of the market relative to all other markets in the data base. The variables used here capture most of the forces that contribute

5. For example, the average PIMS business secures a price 3.7 percent higher than others in the same market and has a market share that is 62 percent of the combined shares of the top three competitors.

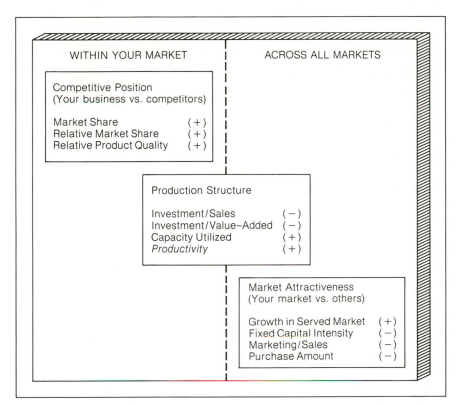

Figure 5.1
Determinants of
profitability

to the intensity of industry competition.[6] Business strength variables measure relative profitability; here the question is how much the profits of each competitor differ from the average profit level of the industry. The production structure variables play a dual role, since investment intensity (dollars of investment in fixed and working capital per dollar of sales) is largely determined by the type of industry, but can be offset by strategic decisions of the business to use less working capital or manage for higher capacity utilization rates.

The notion of relative profitability is amplified in Figure 5.2, which makes three crucial distinctions:

- How the business is strategically positioned to achieve a competitive advantage,
- The consequences of the strategic position for the relative price and cost position and relative rate of turnover of capital, and
- The accounting measures of profitability as a consequence of margins and turnover ratios

---

6. Porter (1979), (1980).

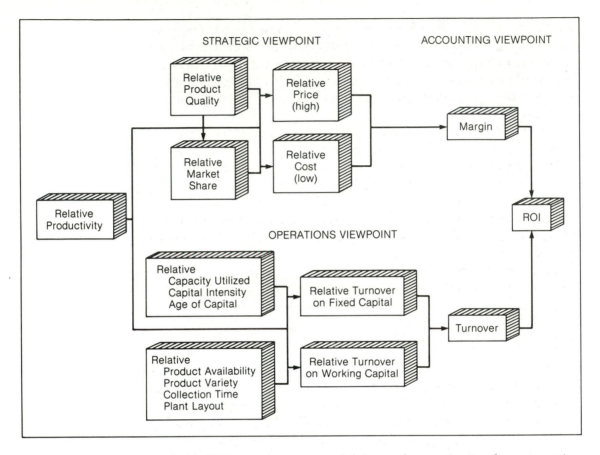

STRATEGIC VIEWPOINT

ACCOUNTING VIEWPOINT

Relative Product Quality

Relative Price (high)

Relative Market Share

Relative Cost (low)

Margin

Relative Productivity

ROI

OPERATIONS VIEWPOINT

Relative
Capacity Utilized
Capital Intensity
Age of Capital

Relative Turnover on Fixed Capital

Turnover

Relative
Product Availability
Product Variety
Collection Time
Plant Layout

Relative Turnover on Working Capital

Figure 5.2 Business strength: what variables account for relative profitability?

A multiple regression model is used to estimate the respective contribution of each of the variables to overall profitability. One of the appealing features of this regression model is that the adverse impact of weak performance on one variable can be offset with a strong showing on another variable. Many businesses achieve acceptable profitability, despite a small market share, by compensating with high quality or superior use of assets. No single variable— whether it be market share or quality—is the key to strategic success. Reality and the PIMS model are more complex. What matters is superior performance on sets of variables that can be used as the basis for a competitive advantage, while not overlooking the need to perform adequately on all business functions.

Measures of Key Variables

The information submitted to the PIMS data base is exceedingly sensitive. In recognition of the need to preserve confidentiality, there is no explicit description of the particular industry or product on the data forms. The only identification is a numerical business code number so that the data for the particular business can be retrieved. For further protection, there is a capability to multiply all absolute numbers, such as sales and investment levels, by a disguise constant. This capability precludes direct comparisons of size-related variables but does not affect ratios such as market share and return on investment.

The PIMS profitability models require as input more than one hundred separate variables ranging from balance sheet and other accounting ratios to measures of competitive position and the market environment. (The operating definitions of the key variables are summarized in a glossary at the end of this chapter.) Most variables are straightforward in concept and measurement, and require little discussion. However, the definition of the business and the served market and the measurement of relative product quality are notoriously tricky, so an understanding of the judgments required by these variables is critical to informed usage of the data base.

Defining the Business and Served Market.   A PIMS business is an operating unit selling a distinct set of products or services to an identifiable group of customers, in competition with a well-defined set of competitors. The difficulties of actually identifying business units are legion—especially when there are shared resources, global markets, and competitors who define their businesses differently or vary in extent of vertical integration. Some guidelines for dealing with these problems are provided in a companion volume.[7]

The served market definition is equally difficult and even more controversial. Originally, the instructions were to define served markets narrowly, as shown in Figure 5.3. According to the PIMS Data Manual, "A served market is usually smaller than the total market . . . . Serving a market means that the business develops, manufactures, distributes and/or services products appropriate to that segment of the total market. It addresses its sales efforts, direct or indirect, to particular customers . . . a business may focus its marketing effort on customers in a distinct geographic area . . . customers with one national purchasing office . . . customers capable of servicing products without further support from their vendors."

Whether such a narrow definition is appropriate will depend on whether competitors can gain major cost advantages by serving segments that the business does not care to pursue.[8] This is the kind of

7. See Appendix to Chapter 2 of Day (1984).

8. Ideally, this problem would be resolved with a compound share model that combines broadly defined markets to capture relative cost positions, with narrowly defined markets based on a demand perspective. For further discussion of this issue see Chapter 4 of Day (1984).

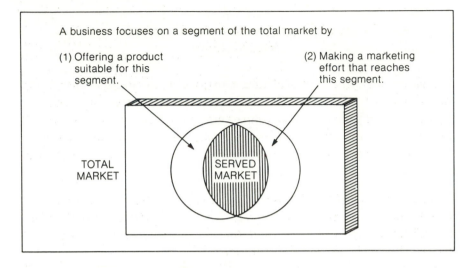

A business focuses on a segment of the total market by

(1) Offering a product suitable for this segment.

(2) Making a marketing effort that reaches this segment.

TOTAL MARKET

SERVED MARKET

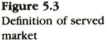

Figure 5.3
Definition of served market

question faced by passenger tire manufacturers who serve the replacement market through large retailers and do not sell anything to the original equipment companies.

Assessing the Relative Quality Position.   The myriad of noncomparable approaches used by PIMS businesses to measure their quality position has been a persistent problem. What is needed are customer perceptions of the relative quality of the product and all associated services, for this determines the ability of the business to obtain premium price differentials. The difficulty is that many businesses lack this information because their view of quality is dominated by internal considerations of conformance to design specifications and defect rates. Consequently, many relative quality indexes in the data base reflect only rough management judgments of the proportion of sales from products that are superior to competitors versus the proportion of sales from inferior products. Experience with this index indicates that suppliers' opinions often do not match customers' perceptions.

The recommended procedure is to use customer judgments to first identify and assign weights to product and service attributes, and then rate the augmented product and those of the top three competitors on each attribute. An overall quality index for the business would be computed as

Percentage of weights from attributes
ranked superior

minus

Percentage of weights from attributes
ranked inferior.

If customers rate a brand of tires as superior in riding comfort and durability but inferior in road noise and ease of mounting, and the first two attributes are more important to consumers, the brand will rate well on this index.[9] Where the business sells multiple products, the quality index is based on a weighted average of the indexes of individual products.

Indicators of Profitability and Cash Flow.   The basic measure of profitability is derived from standard accounting data, but is modified to highlight those elements of return on investment within the control of the business unit management:

$$ROI = \frac{Earnings\ (BIT)}{Average\ Investment}$$

Earnings are after deduction of corporate expenses but before interest charges and taxes. The exclusions are made on the grounds that interest charges and tax rates reflect the corporate debt policy and tax situation.

Investment is working capital plus fixed capital (at book value), usually averaged over a four-year period. The use of book values is a matter of concern because it biases the measure toward businesses with fully depreciated fixed assets. Unfortunately, the difficulties of using replacement costs have been too great to overcome.

The emphasis on ROI is often criticized because of recurring evidence that this measure inhibits long-run goal attainment. For better or worse, ROI remains one of the most widely used measures of the financial performance of business units.[10] In any event, PIMS models are available for a variety of other business objectives including cash flow/investment, ten-year discounted earnings, and ten-year discounted cash flow. (Here cash flow is defined as cash generated by after-tax earnings *minus* cash used within the business.)

Although member companies tend to submit only their more successful businesses, large differences are present among reported

9. Gale and Klavans (1983).
10. Reece and Cool (1978).

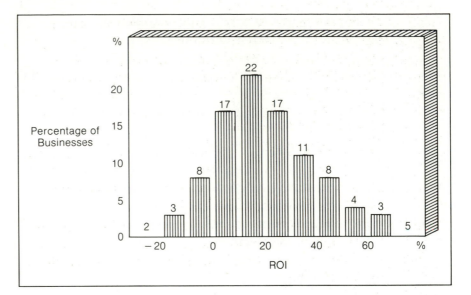

Figure 5.4
Dispersion of
profitability in the
data base

ROIs. As Figure 5.4 shows, the mean ROI (before interest and taxes)
for the sample is 22 percent. However, 13 percent of the businesses
actually lost money. As we turn to the task of extracting useful insights
from PIMS, this mean ROI will prove useful as a performance benchmark.

Applications of PIMS to the Planning Process: Situation Assessment

The concept of PIMS is inherently complex. To understand it on
its own terms, we need to see it in action. Otherwise, it is not possible
to appreciate how it supports strategic thinking and management
decision making. Experience with PIMS also reveals why the generalized insights will invariably be dominated by the details of the
situation. As always, the question is which details are worth attention.
Here PIMS provides a framework for focusing attention on important
issues.

A standard progression of PIMS analyses roughly follows the planning process:

Step 1: Describe the situation using the standardized data
forms.

Step 2: Assess the current performance and strategic potential
of the business with a PAR Model. This model

compares actual ROI and cash flow with the normal profitability for this type of business.

Step 3: Use the Analysis of Look-Alikes to select the ten or fifteen businesses in the data set most like the one being studied. A comparison can be made between the similar businesses that were successful and those that were not.

Step 4: Assess the strengths and weaknesses of the competitors using the Limited Information Model (LIM). This model is a stripped-down version of the PAR Model and is used when data collection is difficult.

Step 5: Test the profitability consequences of feasible changes in strategy with the Strategic Analysis Model. This is a simulation model based on experience of similar firms in the data base.

Each of these steps was used by the management team of a PIMS client company as they wrestled with the problem of financing a rapidly growing division. Although the situation described in the boxed insert is disguised, it gives a good flavor of the urgency of the problem.

Within the company there was little consensus on how best to cope with the continuing cash demands. Corporate management was seriously divided over whether the division should be sold to someone with enough resources to support growth. The opposing camp argued that the best move was to keep the division but conserve cash by postponing any new expansion. Meanwhile, the division general manager and his team strongly advocated continuing investment as the best way to exploit an attractive situation and assure long-run profitability. These investments would be used to capitalize on previous R and D work that showed how capital productivity could be greatly improved. Unfortunately, there was not much productivity in the strategic dialogue, for no one was sure whether the business would yield a long-run return on investment that would meet or exceed the corporate goal of 35 percent, or whether this was a reasonable target for this type of business. Our purpose here is not to resolve these questions but to demonstrate the benefits and limitations of the PIMS approach in guiding the search for insights.

Situation Description

The PIMS data forms contain questions on more than one hundred aspects of the business and its environment. For many management

Managing Growth: The Indal Division of Magnusson Industries

Until the mid-seventies, the Indal Division was a small factor in the market for passive electronic components such as resistors, capacitors, and inductors. Fortunately, management had recognized the opportunities created by the integrated circuit revolution in electronic circuiting. Initially, this revolution eliminated many passive components, and so existing suppliers lost their interest in the market. However, ICs could not perform all the electronic functions of passive components, such as inductance, high or precise resistance, circuit trimming, or tuning and interconnection. These segments began to grow rapidly relative to the total market, and Indal was well positioned with a new range of products to satisfy this market.

Indal's served market had grown from $60 million in 1977 to $100 million in 1980. Demand was forecast to grow at a compounded rate of 22 percent per year, of which 10 percent represented price increases. After 1985 growth was expected to be 18 percent, of which 6 percent would be from price increases.

By 1980 the Indal Division was modestly profitable with sales of $27 million and pretax ROI of 16 percent. Market share had grown from 16 percent in 1977 to 27 percent as Indal took advantage of the new product line. Component products were sold directly to manufacturers who numbered approximately one thousand in total. About fifty of these companies provided 50 percent of Indal's sales. Most gains in share had come at the expense of the major competitor in the market, whose share had declined from 43 percent in 1977 to 36 percent in 1980. This competitor had experienced difficulty in meeting the high quality requirements of the IC circuit designers, and was also believed to be suffering from internal management problems.

The Indal Division produced passive components in medium-sized batches in a nonunion facility in Ohio. Total employment in the division was three hundred. There was little finished goods inventory and a reasonable level of backlog. However, the plant was operating close to peak capacity, and a decision to expand the plant would have to be made shortly if the business were to continue to build market share. The cash flow implications of this particular decision forced to the surface the strategic choices of grow versus maintain or harvest.

SUMMARY OF DIVISIONAL SITUATION

	1977	1978	1979	1980
Sales	$9,424	$12,900	$18,362	$26,600
Sales Deflated	7,363	9,699	13,116	16,943
(1973 = 100)	(128)	(133)	(140)	(157)
Profits, Pretax	622	448	2,206	1,734
Cash Flow (After-tax)		(946)	(950)	(1,659)

Investment	5,075	6,245	8,298	10,824
ROS, Pretax (%)	7	3	12	7
ROI, Pretax (%)	12	7	27	16
Market Share	16	19	23	27
Share—Three Top Competitors	65	63	59	56
Relative Market Share	25	30	39	48
Relative Product Quality	30	35	40	50
Capacity Utilization (%)	72	90	83	89

PROFIT AND LOSS STATEMENT
(PERCENTAGE OF SALES)

	1977	1978	1979	1980
Sales	100%	100%	100%	100%
Purchases	41	42	40	45
Value-Added	59	58	60	55
Manufacturing, Distribution, & Depreciation	23	26	22	26
Gross Margin	37	32	38	29
R&D	9	8	5	5
Marketing	16	16	16	12
Other	4	5	5	5
Profit (Pretax)	7	3	12	7

BALANCE SHEET SUMMARY
(PERCENTAGE OF SALES)

	1977	1978	1979	1980
Cash	2	2	2	1
Receivables	18	17	18	17
Inventories (Finished Goods)	9	8	12	7
Inventories (Work in Process)	11	11	11	14
Current Assets	40	38	43	39
Gross Book Value of Plant and Equipment	52	45	34	29
Net Book Value of Plant and Equipment	29	24	17	15
Other Assets	1	1	0	0
Total Assets	70	63	60	54
Current Liabilities	16	14	15	13
Average Investment	54	49	45	41
Working Capital	24	24	28	26

Source: Data and background description based on material provided by courtesy of Joe Patten of the Strategic Planning Institute.

teams, the completion of the forms is their first opportunity to systematically discuss the strategic situation of their business, with everyone using the same language. PIMS thus becomes a useful vehicle for focusing the initial situation analysis activity toward the important issues where critical data may be lacking.

Analysis of Past Performance: The PAR Report

The first question a PAR analysis asks is, What ROI and cash flow/investment are normal for this type of business, given its market environment, market share position, degree of differentiation, production structure, budget allocation, and the historical pattern of strategic moves? The benchmark is the average for all businesses in the PIMS sample—which currently is 21.5 percent for pretax ROI and 2 percent for cash flow/investment. The PAR report shows by how much, higher or lower, the business is expected to deviate from this global average, given its circumstances and past strategy. PAR ROI is the return normally expected from an average management team with average luck. The difference between the average ROI for all businesses and the PAR ROI is attributable to the impact of the key strategy factors. Each of the thirty-two factors used as independent variables in the PAR regression model can have an impact.

In the case of the Indal Division, the major influences on the PAR estimate of ROI were as follows:

POSITIVE FACTORS

- Good market share
- High relative product quality
- High capacity utilization
- Absence of a union
- High labor productivity
- High receivables/investment ratio

NEGATIVE FACTORS

- High marketing/sales ratio
- Large purchases by immediate customers

Tables 5.2 to 5.4 show the details of a PAR analysis for this business (code number 992). What is particularly striking is the increase in PAR ROI from 10 percent in 1977 to 36 percent in 1980, reflecting a higher market share, more effective use of investment, increased labor productivity, and greater research support.

Interpreting the ROI—Influencing Factors. It is tempting to compare the individual factors by the size of their impact on the PAR ROI. By this rule of thumb, capacity utilization has the greatest impact, as it contributes a net 3.6 percent to the PAR ROI. This is because the Indal Division is operating at 89 percent of full capacity,

Table 5.2 PAR Versus Actual ROI

PAR Return on Investment (1980-1980) . . . 36%

PAR ROI is an estimate of the pretax return on investment normal for businesses similar to this business with respect to their market attractiveness and competitive strength. These factors are measured using thirty factors that have exhibited a consistent and strong relationship with return on investment over a wide range of business types and time periods.

Actual Return on Investment (1980-1980) . . . 16%

Actual ROI performance has two components: PAR ROI and the deviation from PAR. The deviation between PAR and actual ROI can often be explained by data errors, errors in business definition, or other factors outside the model.

If, however, such factors are not found to be present, PAR may be used as a benchmark for profit performance over a four-year time span; the PAR deviation measures the operating effectiveness in managing this strategic position.

Deviation from PAR = Actual ROI − PAR ROI
−20%   =   16%   −   36%

Note that the choice of time span can affect the deviation, especially if key PAR determinants are changing over time. The object of averaging is to smooth out the short-term impacts of such changes. Different time spans give the following results.

	1977		1978		1979		1980
One-Year PAR	10%		21%		24%		36%
One-Year Actual	12%		7%		27%		16%
One-Year Deviation	2%		−14%		3%		−20%
Two-Year Par		16%		22%		30%	
Two-Year Actual		9%		18%		21%	
Two-Year Deviation		−7%		−4%		−9%	
Three-Year PAR			19%		28%		
Three-Year Actual			17%		17%		
Three-Year Deviation			−2%		−11%		
Four-Year PAR				24%			
Four-Year Actual				16%			
Four-Year Deviation				−8%			

Source: Strategic Planning Institute (1980).

compared with an average of 75.6 percent for all businesses in the data base. This factor also has fairly high leverage relative to the factors such as investment intensity and market share. The analysis of leverage is based on the two right-hand columns of Table 5-4, which show the effect of changing each factor by a small amount

Table 5.3 Key Strategic Factors for This Business

The impact of each factor in the PAR ROI depends on
■ Its overall importance in influencing ROI.
■ Its value for this business relative to other PIMS businesses.
■ The levels of other, interacting factors.

The key factors are those that actually or potentially have the greatest impact on ROI for this business. The current impact of each factor on PAR ROI is shown in Column 1. Column 2 shows how the impact would be changed by a small increase in the factor. The combined magnitude of these numbers represents the importance of the factor to this business. A detailed tabulation of all factors and their impacts is given on Table 5.4. The term numbers correspond to the order of terms on Table 5.4.

NO.	KEY STRATEGIC FACTOR	IMPACT ON PAR ROI	CHANGE IN IMPACT*
24	Capacity Utilization	3.6	0.9
20	Investment Intensity Index	2.2	−1.9
4	Relative Product Quality	3.0	0.8
23	Log Labor Productivity	2.2	1.3
1	Market Share Index	1.5	1.9
10	Unionization (%)	2.0	−0.2
31	Receivables/Investment	1.4	0.7
11	New Products (% of Sales)	0.8	0.6
15	Purchase Amount: Immed. Cust.	−3.5	−0.4
14	Marketing/Sales	−1.6	−0.8
	Sum of impacts of key strategic factors	11.6	
	Sum of impacts of other factors	2.5	
	Total sum of impacts	14.1	
	PIMS base ROI	21.5	
	PAR Return of Investment	35.6	

Source: Strategic Planning Institute (1980).

*This is the effect on PAR ROI corresponding to a factor increment of approximately one-fifth of a standard deviation. Table 5.4 for details.

(specifically, an increment of one-fifth of a standard deviation). For example, if capacity utilization can be increased from 89 percent to 92.6 percent, the PAR ROI will go up .9 percent. Is this more feasible than an increase in market share from 26.6 percent to 30.6 percent, which would increase PAR ROI by 1.9 percent?

Attempts to answer such questions as the desirability of improving performance on one factor rather than another are compromised by two problems. The first is the quality of the data. Measurement prob-

Table 5.4 Impacts of ROI-Influencing Factors: A Diagnosis of Strategic Strengths and Weaknesses

	PIMS MEAN	THIS BUSINESS	IMPACT	SENSITIVITY A DATA CHANGE OF	ALTERS IMPACT BY
COMPETITIVE POSITION			5.2		
1 Market Share Index			1.5		1.9
2 Market Share	23.4	26.6		4.0	
3 Relative Market Share	62.1	47.5		10.0	
4 Relative Product Quality	25.8	50.0	3.0	6.0	0.8
5 Relative Price	103.7	103.0	−0.1	1.0	0.1
6 Relative Direct Cost	101.8	100.0	0.8	1.0	−0.4
7 Patents re Process or Products	0.4	0.0	−0.0	0.1	−0.1
8 Rel. Range of Customer Sizes		Same	0.1		
STAGE OF LIFE CYCLE			3.2		
9 Real Market Growth, Long-Run	4.2	10.0	0.8	2.0	0.3
10 Unionization (%)	43.0	0.0	2.0	7.0	−0.2
11 New Products (% of Sales)	10.3	4.0	0.8	3.0	0.6
12 Research & Development/ Sales	2.2	4.6	−0.5	0.5	0.1
13 Selling-price Growth Rate	7.6	8.6	0.0	1.0	0.3
MARKETING ENVIRONMENT			−4.5		
14 Marketing/Sales	9.3	12.4	−1.6	1.0	−0.8
15 Purchase Amount: Immed. Cust.		$.1MM $1MM	−3.5		
16 % of All End User's Purchases		.25% 1%	−0.3		
17 No. Customers = 50% of Sales	337.2	29.7	0.4	100.0	−0.2
18 Products Produced to Order?		No	0.2		
19 Industry Concentration	57.5	60.0M	0.3	5.0	0.2
CAPITAL & PRODUCTION STRUCTURE			10.2		
20 Investment Intensity Index			2.2		−1.9
21 Investment/Sales	52.8	40.7		5.0	

Continued on next page

Table 5.4—*Continued*

	PIMS MEAN	THIS BUSINESS	IMPACT	SENSITIVITY A DATA CHANGE OF	ALTERS IMPACT BY
CAPITAL & PRODUCTION STRUCTURE—cont'd					
22 Investment/ Value-Added	96.0	74.7		8.0	
23 Labor Productivity	100.0	109.5	2.2	6.0	1.3
24 Capacity Utilization	75.6	89.0	3.6	3.0	0.9
25 G.B.V. of P&E/Investment	89.1	70.9	0.6	10.0	0.0
26 Vertical Integration	56.0	54.5	−0.1	3.0	0.2
27 Investment per Employee	29.8	23.5	0.1	6.0	−0.0
28 Relative Employee Compensation	100.7	100.0	0.0	1.0	0.0
29 Shared Production Facilities		<10%	0.3		
30 Accounting Convention		FIFO	0.2		
31 Receivables/Investment	32.7	40.9	1.4	4.0	0.7
32 Raw Matls. & W-in-P./ Val.-Added	21.5	26.2	−0.3	3.0	−0.2

Source: Strategic Planning Institute (1980).

lems or changes in assumptions may mean the margin of error is as much as the change increment in Table 5-4. One's confidence in the strategic relevance of a particular factor such as market share is a direct reflection of one's confidence in the input data. What would happen, for instance, if the served market definition was expanded and Indal's market share dropped as a result? Where this is a possibility, a good idea is to test the sensitivity of the results to changes in assumptions.

The second interpretation problem is due to an unfortunate condition of the data base, called multicollinearity. This condition stems from the correlation of strategic factors with each other as well as with ROI. When severe, multicollinearity can make an important factor appear inconsequential. Even when mild, it blurs the relative impact of different factors. For example, if high market share helps profitability, and low relative costs also help profitability—but share and costs are highly correlated—then it is difficult to determine how much each contributes to profitability. We then cannot say that the observed impact of market share on PAR ROI shown in Figure 5.4 is due to that factor alone, with all other factors held constant. Fortunately, the extent of multicollinearity in the PIMS data base is fairly mild; only 2 percent of all possible pairs of factors have intercorrelations above .3.[11] The problem has been further minimized by grouping the factors into four major categories, which are almost completely independent of each other. Thus, the overall impact of the factors making up competitive position is separate from the profit impact of capital and production structure.[12]

Understanding Deviations from PAR.   The second basic question a PAR analysis asks is, How well is this business performing relative to what could reasonably be expected? The benchmark here is the PAR ROI, and the relevant comparison is with the actual ROI. Differences of 3 percent or less are not worth specific attention. In the case of the Indal Division, this difference is 20 percent and has been widening with the increases in PAR value. Clearly, this difference must be understood, for the problem with Indal is not the profit potential of the business but the ability of management to take advantage of the opportunities inherent in this position.

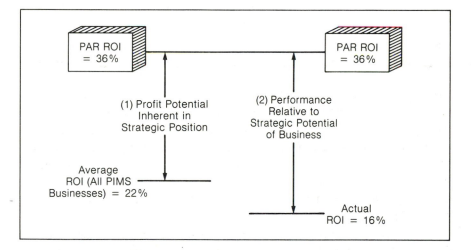

A 20 percent difference between PAR and actual ROI is large but not unusual. The distribution of the following deviations shows that

11. Chussil (1984).

12. Schoeffler (1977) also describes the presence of interaction terms in the ROI model that further complicate interpretation of the factors. For example, the relationship of market share with ROI is specified to depend on the level of other variables, such as number of customers.

30 percent of all businesses have deviations from PAR that are more than 15 percent above or below.[13]

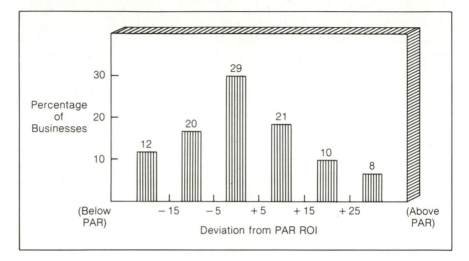

There is some possibility that a particular deviation may be due to an erroneous estimate of PAR, stemming from a poorly defined market, inappropriate allocation of investments, or some other measurement problem. More likely, the difference is real for one or other of the following reasons.

■ Transitory events such as strikes, unusual weather, unanticipated moves by competitors, technological problems or breakthroughs, and economic cycle effects may create an environment that is very different from that encountered normally—or likely to be encountered.

■ Lagged effects of prior strategic moves, such as major investments in process redesign to improve productivity or build market position. The costs may be incurred in one unusual year, with the benefits to be taken later.

■ Operating efficiency, derived from managements' ability to get superior (or inferior) labor utilization, working capital usage, marketing program impact, and the like. These are the day-in and day-out tactical moves that can reliably get superior results from the same resources as everyone else in the industry.

■ The beneficial effects of synergies or shared resources with several other businesses in the corporate portfolio.

---

13. Branch (1981).

As time passes, large deviations tend to shrink, and the actual profitability moves toward the PAR level that reflects the fundamentals of the market environment and business position. This includes the impact of lag effects—especially the payoff from prior strategic moves—and the likelihood that transitory good or bad fortune is likely to be balanced by a run of luck in the opposite direction. This leaves operating effectiveness and synergies as the most durable reasons for continuing deviations.

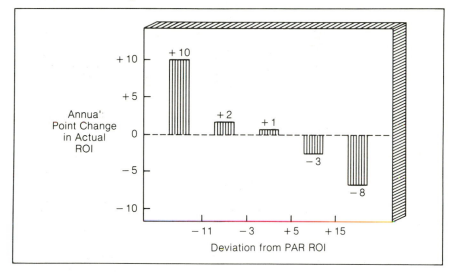

The Benefits of Synergies.   Evidence on the profitability benefits came from a study of companies that have ten or more businesses in the data base. Businesses that were a part of marketing-intensive or R and D intensive companies outperformed PAR by an average of 1.6 to 3.8 percent. Extensive use of shared marketing programs, or company-owned distribution outlets when they were available, was associated with an average deviation of PAR of 4 percent. As with operating effectiveness, this is an enduring advantage for the business that permits it to consistently outperform its competitors.

Cash Flow PAR Analysis.   The cash flow PAR model is similar to the ROI model but asks the question, What cash flow can we reasonably expect from this business? The interpretation of the model is also the same. The benchmark is the average cash flow/investment for all businesses, which in 1980 was a positive cash generation of 2 percent of the investment base.[14] From Tables 5.5 and 5.6 we see that the

---

14. Cash flow as computed in this model does not include deductions for corporate dividend assessments or repayments to corporate. These must be deducted separately to assess net cash flow.

Table 5.5 Cash Flow PAR Report

```
        CASH FLOW/INVESTMENT 1978-1980          DEVIATION
           Actual  -  14.0%  PAR  -  5.7           FROM
                                                 PAR -8.3%


      Impact by category: cash flow/invest-
        ment

        Decision use of cash                      -9.7
        Change in investment/sales                -0.9
        Forced use of cash                         -2.1
        Strength of competitive position          -0.5
        Differentiation from competitors           0.7
        Capital and production structure           4.8

        Sum of impacts                            -7.7
        Average cash flow/investment               2.0

      PAR cash flow/investment                    -5.7%
```

```
                         CASH FLOW PAR MATRIX


                  I- - I- - I- - I- - I- - I- - I- - I- - I- - I- - I
       HIGH PAR   I                   :         :                   I
          15  - I                     :         :                   I
                I                     :         :                   I
          10  - I                     :         :                   I
                I                     :         :                   I
           5  - I                     :         :                   I
PAR             I- - - - - - - - - - -- - -- - -+- - - -- - - - - -- - I
CASH       0  - I                     :         :                   I
FLOW            I- - - - -- - - - - - -+- - -- - -+- - - - - - - - - - I
          -5  - I                     :         :                   I
                I                     :         :                   I
         -10  - I              *      :         :                   I
                I                     :         :                   I
         -15  - I                     :         :                   I
       LOW PAR   I                    :         :                   I
                  I- - I- - I- - I- - I- - I- - I- - I- - I- - I- - I
                  -16  -12   -8   -4    0    4    8   12   16
                  BELOW PAR                         ABOVE PAR
                         DEVIATION FROM PAR
```

Source: Strategic Planning Institute (1980).

Table 5.6 Cash Flow PAR Report

	PIMS MEAN	THIS BUSINESS	IMPACT	SENSITIVITY CHANGE OF	CHANGES IMPACT BY
DECISION USE OF CASH			−9.7		
1 Market Share Growth Rate	3.2	18.3	−7.5	2.00	−0.98
2 Marketing Expense Growth Rate	10.3	25.1	−1.6	2.00	−0.22
3 New Product Sales/ Total Sales	13.1	5.7	1.2	5.00	−0.83
4 R&D Expense/Sales	2.4	5.5	−0.6	0.50	−0.07
5 Marketing Expense/ Sales	10.3	14.4	−1.2	2.00	−0.45
CHANGE IN INVESTMENT/SALES			−0.9		
6 Point Change Invest- ment/Sales	−4.7	−3.9	−0.9	2.00	−2.55
FORCED USE OF CASH			−2.1		
7 Real Market Growth, Short-Run	8.2	10.6	−1.3	2.00	−1.07
8 Selling Price Growth Rate	6.4	8.6	−1.2	1.00	−0.30
9 Industry (SIC) Growth, Long-Run	9.3	19.2	0.4	1.00	0.05
STRENGTH OF COMPETITIVE POSITION			−0.5		
10 Market Share	23.3	22.9		5.00	1.16
Relative Market Share	60.6	38.9			
DIFFERENTIATION FROM COMPETITORS			0.7		
11 Price Relative to Com- petition	1.030	1.037	−0.0	0.01	−0.01
12 Relative Product Qual- ity	23.5	41.7	0.8	5.00	0.30
13 Price Diff. from Com- petitors	0.040	0.037	−0.0	0.01	0.13
CAPITAL AND PRODUCTION STRUCTURE			4.8		
14 Investment/Sales	58.3	43.8	2.5	5.00	−1.91
15 Vertical Integration	59.8	57.2	−0.7	2.00	0.50
16 Value-Added per Em- ployee ($000)	29.3	44.3	1.5	5.00	0.50
17 Capacity Utilization	80.6	87.3	0.4	5.00	0.28
18 Replacement Value/GBV of P&E	185.4	180.0	−0.1	10.00	0.11
19 Employees Unionized (%)	51.3	0.0	1.2	5.00	−0.11

Source: Strategic Planning Institute (1980).

Indal Division is using a lot of cash to fund significant share gains in a fast growth market. Expenditures on building a stronger market position (what is called the decision use of cash) are the major contributor to the PAR cash flow/investment rate of − 5.7 percent. The interpretations of the individual cash flow factor coefficients are somewhat more defensible than in the PAR ROI model, for there is less collinearity in this model. Otherwise, the same caveats apply.

The red flag raised by the cash flow PAR analysis of Indal is the large disparity between the PAR and actual cash flow rates. Two questions are suggested immediately: The first is whether the levels of investment need be sustained at the present high levels if market shares stabilize, and the second is how soon a payoff will be realized from the cost advantages that should accrue from a larger experience base relative to the competitors.

Analysis of Past Performance: the Report on Look-Alikes.

The data base is now large enough to permit another approach to the question, What profit performance can reasonably be expected from this type of business, given average management effectiveness and average luck? The Analysis of Look-Alikes does not have an associated model; it goes straight into the data base and directly selects businesses that are similar to the one being studied on important structural features. The basis for similarity is defined by management. For example, Indal management said they wanted to find those businesses that came the closest to satisfying the following matching criteria (where the larger the weight, the more important the variable).

MATCHING CRITERIA	INDAL PERFORMANCE LEVEL TO BE MATCHED	RELATIVE IMPORTANCE WEIGHT
Market share	23%	7
Share of top three competitors	38/12/9	19
Fixed capital intensity	34	1
Working capital/revenue	26	3
Value-added	57	4
Real market growth	11	9
Relative product quality	42	8
Gross book value/employee	26	1
Real sales growth	32	9
Market share change	4	13

What management is evidently saying here is, "We want to know how other businesses who have also experienced our rapid rate of sales growth have fared." Growth variables represent a combined weight of thirty-one out of a total importance weight of seventy-four.

A total of twenty-four look-alike businesses were found to reasonably satisfy these criteria. This set was then divided into "winners" and "losers," with winners being those with an actual ROI greater than 23 percent (whereas losers were those with ROIs less than 18 percent). Some indications of the differences can be seen in Table 5.7. Insights into why these differences were so great were obtained by comparing Indal with the winners on more than three hundred characteristics available in the data base. In general the winners differed by the following:

- Growing their unit volume at a slower rate (suggesting that price increases of winners were better able to reflect material price increases and maintain margins)
- Having lower sales force and other marketing expenses as a percent of sales (7 percent for winners versus 12.5 percent for Indal)
- Lower inventory/sales ratio
- Lower perceived relative product quality (thirty-six for winners versus forty-five for Indal).

These differences do not necessarily suggest that Indal's strategy is inappropriate for its particular environment. They do raise some interesting questions about pricing increases and marketing expenses, which merit further thinking.

Table 5.7 Report on Look-alikes Performance (1978–1980)

	THIS BUSINESS	ALL LOOK-ALIKES ($n = 24$)	LOSERS LOW ROI ($n = 10$)	WINNERS HIGH ROI ($n = 10$)
PAR ROI	28	24	17	31
Actual ROI	17	24	4	41
Cash Flow/Investment	−14	−4	−12	3
Market Share Gain	4	3	3	3
ROS (Pretax)	8	10	2	17
Investment/Sales	44	45	60	43
Working Capital	26	20	22	19
Capacity Utilization	87	74	74	84

Competitive Analysis: The LIM Report

The Limited Information Model (LIM) is an abbreviated form of the PAR model, which can be used to assess the strengths and weaknesses of competitors. Only eighteen profit-influencing factors are used rather than the full thirty-two of the PAR model;[15] consequently, the

Table 5.8 Competitor A Limited Information Model Estimate of Normal ROI

FACTORS	PIMS MEAN	THIS BUSINESS	IMPACT OF FACTOR ON ESTIMATE OF ROI (%)	
1. Market Share (%)	23.6	36.0		
2. Relative Market Share (%)	61.7	76.0	4.1	
3. Relative Product Quality	25.9	−20.0	−4.7	
4. Relative Price	103.5	101.0	0.0	
5. Percent Employees Unionized	48.3	0.0	3.5	
6. Percentage of New Product Sales/Sales	11.9	3.0	1.2	
7. R&D Expense/Sales (%)	2.4	3.5	−0.8	
8. Marketing Expense/Sales (%)	10.8	9.0	0.7	
Competitive Position & Action Impact				4.0
9. Investment/Sales (%)	56.1	35.0		
10. Investment/Value-Added (%)	96.7	65.0	8.2	
11. Fixed Capital Intensity (%)	52.3	30.0	0.9	
12. Vertical Integration (%)	58.8	55.0	−0.2	
13. Value-Added/Employee ($1,000)	30.0	50.0	4.5	
14. Capacity Utilization (%)	79.6	93.0	1.8	
Capital & Production Structure Impact				15.2
15. Real Market Growth Rate	8.2	10.0	0.4	
16. Share of Four Largest Firms (%)	56.5	83.0	1.0	
17. Percentage of Customers = 50% Sales	12.2	12.0	−0.0	
18. Purchase Amount—Immed. Cust.	5.2	7.0	−2.8	
Market Environment Impact				−1.4
Total Impact			17.9	
Average ROI, PIMS Businesses			22.1	
Estimated ROI, This Business			40.0	

Source: Strategic Planning Institute (1980).

---

15. Gale and Swire (1980).

LIM model accounts for less than 60 percent of the variation in profitability. However, the factors that have been dropped are the most difficult to obtain for each major competitor.

Once the LIM data have been assembled for the three leading competitors, LIM reports of the form shown in Tables 5.8, 5.9, and 5.10 can be obtained. These tables provide useful insights into the particular strengths and weaknesses of Indal's competitors in the

Table 5.9 Competitor B Limited Information Model Estimate of Normal ROI

FACTORS	PIMS MEAN	THIS BUSINESS	IMPACT OF FACTOR ON ESTIMATE OF ROI (%)
1. Market Share (%)	23.6	10.0	
2. Relative Market Share (%)	61.7	14.0	−6.2
3. Relative Product Quality	25.9	−30.0	−5.2
4. Relative Price	103.5	99.0	0.2
5. Percent Employees Unionized	48.3	0.0	1.8
6. Percentage of New Product Sales/Sales	11.9	3.0	1.2
7. R&D Expense/Sales (%)	2.4	3.0	−0.5
8. Marketing Expense/Sales (%)	10.8	8.0	1.3
Competitive Position & Action Impact			−7.4
9. Investment/Sales (%)	56.1	41.0	
10. Investment/Value-Added (%)	96.7	73.0	4.1
11. Fixed Capital Intensity (%)	52.3	30.0	1.0
12. Vertical Integration (%)	58.8	55.0	−0.2
13. Value-Added/Employee ($1,000)	30.0	48.0	4.1
14. Capacity Utilization (%)	79.6	85.0	0.9
Capital & Production Structure Impact			9.8
15. Real Market Growth Rate	8.2	10.0	0.4
16. Share of Four Largest Firms (%)	56.5	83.0	1.0
17. Percentage of Customers = 50% Sales	12.2	12.0	−0.0
18. Purchase Amount—Immed. Cust.	5.2	7.0	−2.8
Market Environment Impact			−1.4
Total Impact			1.0
Average ROI, PIMS Businesses			22.1
Estimated ROI, This Business			23.1

Source: Strategic Planning Institute (1980).

passive components market. By comparing a PAR report on Indal with these LIM reports, it is possible to isolate the factors on which Indal has a competitive advantage or disadvantage. It appears that Indal has a significant quality edge over all other competitors, which is to be expected given its success in penetrating the emerging market for high-precision components. There do not appear to be any features of Indal's capital and production structure that place it at a

Table 5.10 Competitor C Limited Information Model Estimate of Normal ROI

FACTORS	PIMS MEAN	THIS BUSINESS	IMPACT OF FACTOR ON ESTIMATE OF ROI (%)	
1. Market Share (%)	23.6	10.0		
2. Relative Market Share (%)	61.7	14.0	−4.9	
3. Relative Product Quality	25.9	0.0	−2.8	
4. Relative Price	103.5	98.0	−0.2	
5. Percent Employees Unionized	48.3	0.0	1.8	
6. Percentage of New Product Sales/Sales	11.9	4.0	1.1	
7. R&D Expense/Sales (%)	2.4	4.0	−1.2	
8. Marketing Expense/Sales (%)	10.8	12.0	−1.0	
Competitive Position & Action Impact				−7.2
9. Investment/Sales (%)	56.1	60.0		
10. Investment/Value-Added (%)	96.7	110.0	−4.2	
11. Fixed Capital Intensity (%)	52.3	40.0	0.7	
12. Vertical Integration (%)	58.8	55.0	−0.2	
13. Value-Added/Employee ($1,000)	30.0	48.0	4.1	
14. Capacity Utilization (%)	79.6	70.0	−1.3	
Capital & Production Structure Impact				−0.9
15. Real Market Growth Rate	8.2	10.0	0.4	
16. Share of Four Largest Firms (%)	56.5	83.0	1.0	
17. Percentage of Customers = 50% Sales	12.2	12.0	−0.0	
18. Purchase Amount—Immed. Cust.	5.2	7.0	−2.8	
Market Environment Impact				−1.4
Total Impact			−9.5	
Average ROI, PIMS Businesses			22.1	
Estimated ROI, This Business			12.6	

Source: Strategic Planning Institute (1980).

disadvantage. Both Competitor A and Indal have similar PAR estimates of ROI (40 percent and 35.6 percent respectively). However, it is likely that Competitor A is operating much closer to PAR, as it has not been growing nearly as rapidly due to the continuing loss of share. The big question, then, is whether this competitor will reassert itself to either hold or rebuild share. Certainly it has the cash flow to do so, and will have to make some kind of a move fairly soon to alleviate an impending capacity constraint.

Applying the LIM Model to Acquisition Assessments

The ease with which a LIM model can be used also makes it an effective tool for screening and evaluating *acquisitions*. Not only does the PAR ROI help to define the profit potential, but also a significant difference between that PAR and the actual ROI is an indicator that the candidate has been "dressed up" for sale. By combining the data for the candidate and the acquiring business, it is possible to estimate the combined performance should the acquisition be implemented.[16]

Applications of PIMS to the Planning Process: Evaluation of Strategy Options

PIMS can be used during the strategy generation and evaluation phase of the planning process to help answer "what if" questions. These questions are usually framed in terms of the probable consequences of major changes in strategy, such building or harvesting market share, or increasing investment intensity by vertically integrating or automating. Questions that are more narrowly focused, such as the consequences of a drop in the marketing expense to sales ratio, or an improvement in quality, are too difficult to handle in the PIMS framework because of multicollinearity and data problems.

A second legitimate use of PIMS at this stage is to provide a cross-check on the validity of plans already made. Considering the experience of similar businesses starting from the same position, does this business have a reasonable chance of reaching the objectives in the plan?

---

16. Strategic Planning Institue (1980).

The Strategy Analysis Report (SAR)

The Strategy Analysis Report is based on a simulation of the profit, cash flow, and investment consequences of major strategic moves. The relationships in the simulator are defined by the following:

- The current position of the business
- Management assumptions about the environment, planning horizon, capacity availability, and the rate at which the actual ROI will approach the PAR ROI (this PAR ROI will also change during the planning period)
- The consequences of similar moves by other businesses with similar starting positions in similar business environments

This analysis is mostly used to screen out infeasible options so that management can focus on a few feasible possibilities that deserve careful scrutiny. The Optimum Strategy Report nominates the combination of strategy moves that promises to give optimal profit, cash, or value results for the business, also based on the experiences of other businesses under similar circumstances.

The Indal management team used the SAR form of analysis to assess the consequences for

- Short-term performance as measured by discounted ten-year cash flow and five-year average ROI.
- Long-term profit performance (as measured by discounted ten-year income) and economic value creation. The measure of value was the discounted sum of cash flows over the ten years plus the estimated fair market value of the business in ten years' time.

The key management assumptions were that unit growth would continue at 11 percent per year, the selling price per unit would match the increase in materials cost, and the deviation from PAR would shrink from −18 percent in 1980 to −12 percent in 1982, −5 percent in 1985, and to a 0 percent difference in 1990. A 15 percent time discount rate was used throughout the entire ten-year period, although inflation was assumed to drop to 6 percent by 1984.

The results of four simulations of future performance are shown in Table 5.11. All four possible strategies yield large negative cash flows and ROI levels that are well below the corporate target of 35 percent. These results are a consequence of fast market growth, aggressive share gain activities, and the high cost of additional units of investment to satisfy the rising sales level.

Table 5.11 Strategy Analysis Report—Indal Division Base Case

	A₁ (NO CHANGE)	A₂ (SHARE GAIN)	A₃ (MAX. ROI)	A₄ (MAX. ECONOMIC VALUE CREATION)
Strategic Position (1985)				
Market Share (%)	27	40	24	24
Value-Added/Sales (%)	55	55	54	54
Mechanization (%)	48	48	34	34
Key Characteristics (1985)				
Pretax ROS (%)	9	11	9	9
Pretax ROI (%)	17	20	24	24
Sales ($000)	64,646	96,142	56,183	56,183
Investment ($000)	32,517	52,521	20,268	20,268
Total Investment/Sales (%)	50	54	36	36
Working Capital/Sales (%)	26	27	26	26
Relative Product Quality	37	69	31	31
Financial Performance ($000)				
Ten-Year Profits (Discount net Income)	13,154	19,459	11,537	11,537
Ten-Year Cash Flow	(15,521)	(29,599)	(5,963)	(5,963)
Ten-Year Discounted Cash Flow + Residual Value*	4,531	1,018	8,335	8,335
Five-Year Avg. Pretax ROI (%)	16	10	23	23

*Current book value: 10,824

The most encouraging finding is that all four strategies do result in an enhancement of economic value because of the significant residual value of the business at the end of the planning period.[17] However, the two options that permit a slight erosion in market share are much better at creating long-run economic value.

A pivotal assumption underlying this analysis is the speed of the recovery of actual ROI toward the PAR value. A "normal" pattern of recovery spread over a period of ten years was the basis for the results in Table 5.11. This period of time seems awfully long for such a recovery, as most of the gap between PAR and actual ROI is traceable to the recent rapid gains in share, which are only continued in Option A₂ in Table 5.11. If a more rapid recovery to a gap of 3

17. Rappaport (1981).

percent by 1982 and 0 percent by 1985 is assumed, then the financial results of a "no change" strategy look much more attractive: Five-year average pretax ROI goes from 16 percent to 23 percent, and the ten-year discounted cash flow plus residual increases from $4,531,000 to $8,042,000.

Another way to reduce the sensitivity of the results to the recently incurred costs of large share gains is simply to go back to 1979 as the base year rather than 1980. Even though the 1979 share was not so large as in the base case, and only a normal pattern of recovery of actual ROI toward the PAR value in ten years is assumed, the financial results look good: Five-year average pretax ROI is 32 percent, and the ten-year discounted cash flow plus residual is $9,924,000. Now the question is whether the 1980 results are merely a blip in the trend line or an indication of future performance. Clearly, the SAR analysis cannot answer this question, but nonetheless it has served its function in ensuring that important questions are being asked.

Validity Testing.   Although the PIMS program has been extending its capability, consistent emphasis has been placed on limiting the use of these tools to directional indicators that aid management in assessing the trade-offs involved in choosing among strategic alternatives. It is precisely this feature that makes it useful to corporate staffs who have to test the validity of the assumptions and recommendations contained in the strategic plans of many business units. While they clearly lack the detailed information needed to critique the plan from a bottom-up feasibility perspective, they can use PIMS to help them determine whether the business has a reasonable chance of achieving the strategic objectives, given the starting point and the proposed strategy.

Two cautions must be observed by anyone testing the validity of plan assumptions with PIMS. First, if business-level managers get the idea that PIMS is being used to second-guess their plans, they will not cooperate with the data collection process. To avoid this kind of breakdown, PIMS should be positioned as a planning aid; it does not predict the business will not reach the share and profit objectives but merely observes that other businesses in similar circumstances could not achieve this performance. Then the strategic dialogue is properly focused on clarifying the unique features of the situation that might justify the proposed plan.

A less obvious problem with PIMS tests of alternative strategies is the need to maintain the same business definition. Otherwise, the outcomes of the new plan cannot be compared with the results of a continuation of the present strategy, and many of the factors would have to be redefined. This means that strategic moves that change the scope of the business—such as a broadening of the geographic scope or forward vertical integration into component assembly—cannot be easily explored.

Special Applications of the PIMS Data Base

The evolution of the PIMS program has seen continuing efforts to provide new services that utilize the existing data base. These new services are usually extensions of the PAR concept to such questions as, What level of marketing or productivity is normal for a given business? If a corporation has most of its business units in the data base, there is a capability for portfolio analysis, which we describe in the following chapter.

A second direction for development has been the creation of new data bases for special industry situations that do not fit the normal pattern of PIMS industries. Financial services, retailing, and start-up businesses each fall in this category.

Productivity Analysis

In productivity analysis, the data base is used to address two related questions: What is a "normal" or PAR level of productivity for a business of this type? Is this business a suitable candidate for mechanization to enhance productivity?

Productivity is defined as value-added per employee, to yield a measure of labor output that is comparable across businesses.[18] Great variations in this measure have been observed, from a low of $10,000 to more than $60,000 per employee. The major determinants of productivity are fixed investment, relative market share, rate of new product introduction, unionization, real market growth, and capacity utilization. A PAR model, based on these factors, is used to determine whether the business is appropriately productive, given its level of fixed investment. The deviation of actual from PAR is considered a measure of operating effectiveness relative to other businesses.

Productivity improvement actions will depend on whether the PAR for the business is low or the business itself is below PAR. Businesses that are below PAR are best treated with shop-level productivity programming such as those to improve either managerial effectiveness or worker motivation. When the business has a low PAR

---

18. Gale (1980).

value, the solution is less obvious. One response is to invest heavily in mechanization and automation to allow each worker to add greater amounts of value. Unfortunately, as the evidence in the Appendix to this chapter shows, increased investment intensity usually reduces profitability. Only in certain conditions—large market share, plus low rate of new product introduction, high capacity utilization, and rapid real growth—is a business likely to be a good candidate for increased mechanization.

Marketing Assessment Program

The marketing assessment program is an adaptation of the PAR concept to the question of what level of marketing costs (sales force and advertising and sales promotion) is normal for a given business, and the impact on ROI and market share of being above or below the norm. Separate models have been developed for both consumer and industrial goods, and in both cases account for high proportions of the variance in marketing cost ratios.[19]

This class of PAR models is somewhat more difficult to use, because some of the presumed determinants of normal marketing expenditure levels clearly work in both directions. For example, market share is both a cause and consequence of advertising expenditures. Other variables with a two-way influence are trading margin and relative price. However, many variables such as frequency and amount of purchase, importance of purchase, and percentage of sales from new products are not likely to be results of marketing cost ratios. As a result, using these PAR models to fine-tune advertising and sales force budgets is decidedly inappropriate. They do, however, provide information on how these budgets might be changed if environmental factors or cost structures are substantially changed.

Special Data Bases

Each of the following projects was undertaken in response to limitations in the structure and format of the main data base.

Start-up Businesses.   The start-up businesses project deals with the special problems encountered during the first four years of a new entry to a market.[20] The vast majority of PIMS businesses are well established, so their experience provides little guidance to such ques-

---

19. Buzzell and Farris (1976), (1977).
20. Biggadike (1977) and Robinson (1984).

tions as: Should we launch a proposed new venture? Should we continue this existing start-up? Should we acquire a newly launched business? What can be done to improve the performance of this start-up situation?

By 1984 this data base contained 196 start-up businesses with between four and eight years of results. Among the major findings were the following:

- Establishing a strong market position by Year 4 is much easier if the market is growing rapidly (33 percent real annual growth or more) and there is no competition or at most one competitor at time of entry.

- Both superior quality and a broad product line help build share, but substantially increase start-up losses.

- Start-up businesses with aggressive marketing programs (more than 3 percent of sales expended on marketing) had shares of 37 percent on average in Year 4, whereas those with marketing expenditures of less than .6 percent of sales had shares of 5 percent.

A useful feature of this data base is the inclusion of the plans and initial performance goals for each start-up. Consistently, the plans were found to underbudget marketing expenditures and overestimate market penetration.

Service Businesses.   Limited progress has been made in enticing retailers to employ PIMS. However, in 1980 there were twelve retailers participating in a study with the inclusion of a few special variables to reflect the importance of type of location and age of stores.[21] The payoff from including these variables was demonstrated by the finding that businesses operating in shopping center malls had ROIs of 27 percent, and significantly outperformed freestanding or downtown locations with ROIs of 10 percent and 8 percent respectively.

A similar approach has been used with financial services businesses, where the standard variables were augmented with unique profit variables such as the number of branches, employee turnover rate, average employee experience, and the branch intensity of staff. Initial experience with eighty-five businesses found that the dominant profit factors were very similar to those operating in consumer and industrial markets. If anything, their profit impacts were more pro-

---

21. Buzzell and Dew (1980).

nounced in the financial services sector. Market position, quality, and investment intensity were especially significant influences. For example, financial services businesses with market shares of less than 3 percent lost money, whereas shares of 14 percent or more were associated with ROIs that averaged 46 percent.

Putting PIMS into Perspective

The continuing developments in the PIMS planning models are taking place against a backdrop of increasingly critical evaluations by analysts outside the program, and anecdotal evidence of uneven and uninformed usage within client companies. Serious questions have been raised about the potential for measurement errors, deficiencies in the models, and the proper interpretations of the findings. Most of the interpretation problems stem from the highly questionable practice of deriving prescriptions about strategy that rely on unsupported causal inferences. Fewer concerns have been directed at the basic logic of the analysis of pooled business experience, for even the critics recognize that the resulting data base is far superior to any of the present or prospective alternatives. The issue then becomes one of fully understanding the limitations and properly adjusting for them when interpreting results of a PIMS analysis.

Specification Problems

Here the issue is whether the regression models include all the relevant variables and have been properly structured. So far, the preferred solution has been to build an all-encompassing model that applies to every industry setting.[22] The alternative is to specify separate regression models for homogenous sets of data.[23] Mounting evidence suggests that differences between industries are sufficiently large and persistent to warrant the added complexity of separate equations for each industry. This study also found there was homogeneity within the industry groups.[24] That is, relationships among strategic variables did not change if the business was a leader or a follower, a market pioneer or a late entrant, and so on.

---

22. Schoeffler (1977).
23. Bass, Cattin, and Wittink (1977).
24. Phillips, Chang, and Buzzell (1983).

Simultaneous Relationships.   Implicit in the use of a single regression equation is the assumption that the direction of influence is from the strategy factors to ROI, and that the level of ROI does not have a simultaneous influence on at least some of the strategy factors. This problem is worrisome, for there is evidence of such reciprocal relationships operating on marketing expenditures, and one study did find that ROI seemed to influence the level of market share attained.[25] If reciprocity exists, then even greater caution must be exercised when interpreting the coefficients.

Choice of Variables.   Many commentators complain about the excessive reliance on ROI as the criterion of profitability. It appears that this reliance is mainly attributable to user behavior, for PIMS analysis need not be restricted to this criterion. As we saw in the discussion of the Strategy Analysis Report, it is possible to incorporate contemporary concepts of economic value creation into the models.

On the independent variable side of the equation, there are problems with (1) omitted variables, including the goals the business was trying to achieve when performance was measured and the structure of the organization; (2) inadequate utilization of information in the data base, especially those variables relating to environmental turbulence, which has been found by organization theorists to have significant *indirect* effects; and (3) the possibility that some variables have an impact on profitability which is primarily due to the way they are constructed.[26] Investment intensity, which is the ratio of working capital and fixed capital (at net book value) to sales or value-added, is most often cited as an example of this problem. In effect, there is an investment term on both sides of the estimating equation, which makes an inverse relation of ROI and I/S inevitable. However, Schoeffler reports that a similar relationship exists when ROI is replaced with residual income as the criterion, although the strength depends on the size of the financial charge on the investment used in the business.[27]

Alternative Models.   Some member companies have elected to deal with these problems by specifying models that are tailored to the dominant strategic issues in their markets. For example, one chemical manufacturer has developed a three-variable ROI model that does

---

25. Schendel and Patton (1976).
26. Anderson and Paine (1978).
27. Schoeffler (1978).

not use investment intensity at all. The three variables are (1) a competitive advantage index, (2) turnover, and (3) capacity utilization. Although these three variables account only for 30 percent of the variance in ROI in the semifinished materials sector, the coefficients are stable and much more meaningful to management.

Measurement Error

The reliance on line management as the source of the periodic and annual data is both a strength and a weakness of PIMS. The resulting depth and breadth of data are unparalleled, but there is a cost in terms of the following:

- Susceptibility of inputs to differences in accounting treatment.
- Differing and hence incompatible interpretations of important variables between businesses. This is especially a problem with judgmental variables such as relative quality.
- Lack of management time and resources to ensure accurate data, especially with difficult variables such as share of served market.
- Overtime variability in data inputs by a business—leading to spurious evidence of change—because of the inevitable changes in the management team that is preparing the inputs.

Despite the best efforts of PIMS staff to ensure the data are free of error, by eliminating outliers, conducting consistency checks, standardizing inputs, and training managers, errors still remain. Finally, there is the possibility that line management will consciously (or unconsciously) perceive it to be in their best interest to subtly shade their inputs toward ensuring a high PAR value. Again, internal consistency checks can help isolate these problems, especially because there are usually several questions addressing a single variable.

The best response to these potential hazards is informed awareness. According to one recent study, excessive sensitivity that leads to paralysis is not appropriate: "The high reliabilities observed for the measures of product quality and other relative competitive strategy variables across [industry] samples suggest that stable traits underlie the measures and that variation due to time related and random error factors is small. Moreover . . . the concepts are measured with equal fidelity across diverse types of businesses. On balance this suggests a very high quality data collection process."[28]

Interpreting and Applying PIMS Findings

Cross-sectional data have one profound limitation that the PIMS analyses have not been able to escape: There is no basis for assessing causality. Until models are built that explicitly incorporate lagged effects, most of the findings from PIMS analysis can be interpreted only as evidence of association. Strictly speaking, it is not possible to go beyond this and predict the consequences for profitability of changes in the independent variables. Yet, the temptation to do so is almost overwhelming. A further complication is the high degree of multicollinearity, which means that one cannot put a specific interpretation on the influence of individual factors.

Beyond methodology there are other, more profound reasons for treating with extreme caution the strategy prescriptions drawn from PIMS results.[29] The first problem is the difficulty of assessing the extent to which evidence of higher profits is compensation for taking higher risks. By only observing outcomes, we do not know whether risks are reflected in the profitability of the survivors or the costs incurred by the failures. Furthermore, the outcomes cannot necessarily be interpreted as representing the objectives of the competitors. Those who ended up with low shares probably did not intend to do so. In the absence of data on goals and objectives, this cannot be assessed, and prescriptions based on observed outcomes become correspondingly difficult.

A final barrier to the derivation of strategic prescriptions stems from the need to use general factors to describe business units, which raises all sorts of problems if one believes that competitive advantage resides more in the specific details of the situation. Hammermesh, Anderson, and Harris have questioned whether PIMS and other planning models do a disservice by "focusing their attention on abstractions . . . [instead of] the essential details."[30] They were specifically referring to the issues of choice of market segments and the application of R and D resources to create a competitive advantage. Certainly these industry-specific factors will dictate strategic choices. But who is going to decide which factors deserve attention? The

---

28. Phillips, Chang, and Buzzell (1983).

29. Wensley (1982).

30. Hamermesh, Anderson, and Harris (1978).

experience of others in similar situations should be one source of guidance.

Conclusion

Most PIMS presentations seem to conclude with a pithy comment to the effect that sophisticated use of models means you do not *ignore* what the model says, but neither should you *believe* what the model says. While PIMS is a unique vehicle for describing and explaining phenomena, and separating the important from the unimportant, it is not a substitute for careful analysis and informed judgment when the task turns to generating and evaluating strategic alternatives. There is absolutely no substitute for an intimate knowledge of the business, but PIMS can support the process of converting knowledge into actionable insights.

Alphabetized Glossary of PAR ROI Factors

ROI = Net Income/Investment

Pretax net income, *including* special nonrecurring costs, minus corporate overhead costs, as a percentage of average investment including fixed and working capital at book value, but excluding corporate investment not particular to this business.

Definitions of Factors Influencing ROI

■ CAPACITY UTILIZATION: The average percentage of standard capacity utilized during the year. Standard capacity is the *sales value* of the maximum output this business can sustain with (1) facilities normally in operation, and (2) current constraints (e.g., technology, work rules, labor practices, and so on). For most manufacturing businesses, this will consist of two shifts, five days per week. For process businesses, a three-shift, six-day period is typical.

■ EMPLOYEES UNIONIZED (%): The percentage of total employees of this business who are unionized.

■ FIFO VALUATION? Is the accounting method used for inventory valuation FIFO or another method (e.g., LIFO)?

■ FIXED CAPITAL INTENSITY: Gross book value of plant and equipment expressed as a percentage of sales. Gross book value includes original value of buildings, real estate, manufacturing equipment, and transportation equipment.

■ IMMEDIATE CUSTOMER FRAGMENTATION: The proportion of the total number of immediate customers accounting for 50 percent of total sales, expressed as a percentage. For example, if five of a business's one hundred immediate customers represent 50 percent of the business's sales, immediate customer fragmentation is five percent.

■ INDUSTRY CONCENTRATION RATIO: The amount of industry shipments accounted for by the four largest firms in your industry, expressed as a percentage.

■ INDUSTRY (SIC) GROWTH, LONG-RUN: The annual long-term (ten-year) growth rate of the SIC industry in which this business is located, expressed as a percentage.

■ INVENTORY/SALES: The sum of raw materials, work-in-process inventory, and finished goods inventory (each net of reserve for losses) as a percentage of sales.

■ INVESTMENT INTENSITY INDEX: A factor combining
   1. INVESTMENT/SALES: Investment expressed as a percentage of sales. Investment may be measured in any of the following ways.
      ■ Net book value of plant and equipment plus working capital
      ■ Equity plus long-term debt
      ■ Total assets employed minus current liabilities attributed to the business.
   2. INVESTMENT/VALUE ADDED: Investment expressed as a percentage of value-added. Value-added is adjusted for profits so that only average profit (PIMS mean ROI times investment) is included.

$$\frac{\text{Investment}}{\text{Value-added} - .5 \, (\text{Net Income} - \text{PIMS mean ROI} \times \text{Investment})}$$

Value-added is net sales, including lease revenues, minus total purchases (which include the cost of raw materials, energy, components, assemblies, supplies and/or services purchased or consumed).

- INVESTMENT PER EMPLOYEE ($000): Average investment, expressed in thousands of dollars, per employee.

- MARKET POSITION: A factor combining
  1. MARKET SHARE: The share of the served market for this business, expressed as a percentage.
  2. RELATIVE MARKET SHARE: The market share of this business relative to the combined market share of its three leading competitors, expressed as a percentage. For example, if this business has 30 percent of the market and its three largest competitors have 20 percent, 10 percent, and 10 percent: $30 \div (20 + 10 + 10) = 75\%$.

- MARKET SHARE GROWTH RATE: The annual growth rate of market share, expressed as a percentage.

- MARKET SHARE INSTABILITY: The instability of the market share of this business, measured as the average percentage difference from the exponential market share trend.

- MARKETING EXPENSE/SALES: The sum of sales force, advertising and sales promotion, and other marketing expenses, expressed as a percentage of sales. Does not include physical distribution. Sales are the net sales billed, including lease revenues, of this business.

- NEW PRODUCT SALES/TOTAL SALES: Percentage of sales accounted for by new products. New products are those products introduced during the three preceding years.

- NEWNESS OF P AND E (NBV/GBV): Newness of plant and equipment, measured as the ratio of net book value to gross book value.

- PRICE RELATIVE TO COMPETITION: The average level of selling prices of your products and services, relative to the average level of leading competitors. The average price of your competitors is 100 percent; if your average prices are 5 percent higher, your price relative to competition is 105 percent.

- PURCHASE AMOUNT OF IMMEDIATE CUSTOMERS: The typical amount of your products or services bought by an immediate customer in a single transaction. A contract covering a period of time is regarded as a single transaction.

- REAL MARKET GROWTH, SHORT-RUN: The annual growth rate of the size of served market, deflated by the selling price index, expressed as a percentage.

- RELATIVE COMPENSATION: The average of hourly wage rates relative to leading competitors and salary levels relative to competitors. Competitors' wage rates and salary levels are 100 percent; if your wage rates and salary levels are 5 percent higher, your relative hourly wage rates are 105 percent, relative salaries are 105 percent, and your average relative compensation is 105 percent.

- RELATIVE PRODUCT QUALITY: The percentage of sales from products and services that, from the perspective of the customer, are judged superior to those available from leading competitors *minus* the percentage of sales from those judged inferior. For example, if 60 percent of the sales of this business are from products considered superior, and 20 percent are from those considered inferior, relative product quality is

$$60\% \ - \ 20\% \ = \ 40\%$$

Note that the mean of relative product quality is about 22 percent, indicating that the typical PIMS business has product quality judged higher than that of its competitors.

- RELATIVE INTEGRATION BACKWARD: The degree of *backward* vertical integration (i.e., toward suppliers) of this business *relative* to its leading competitors (less than, the same as, more than).

- RELATIVE INTEGRATION FORWARD: The degree of *forward* vertical integration (i.e., toward customers) of this business *relative* to its leading competitors (less than, the same as, more than).

- R AND D EXPENSE/SALES: The sum of product or service R and D expenses plus process R and D expenses, expressed as a percentage of sales. Product or service R and D expenses include all expenses incurred to secure innovations or advances (or both) in the products or services of this business, including improvements in packaging as well as in product design, features, and functions. Process R and D expenses include all expenses for process improvements for the purpose of reducing the cost of manufacturing, processing or physical handling of goods (or a combination of these) by this business.

- SELLING PRICE GROWTH RATE: The annual growth rate of selling prices charged by this business, expressed as a percentage.

■ STANDARD PRODUCTS/SERVICES? Are the products or services of this business more or less standardized for all customers, or are they designed or produced to order for individual customers?

■ VALUE-ADDED PER EMPLOYEE ($000): Value-added, expressed in thousands of dollars, per employee. Value-added is adjusted for profits.

$$.001 \times \frac{\text{Value-Added} - .5\,(\text{Net Income} - \text{PIMS mean ROI} \times \text{Investment})}{\text{Total Number of Employees}}$$

■ VERTICAL INTEGRATION: Value-added as a percentage of sales. Both value-added and sales are adjusted for profits so that only *average* profit (PIMS mean ROI times investment) is included.

$$\frac{\text{Value-Added} - .5\,(\text{Net Income} - \text{PIMS mean ROI} \times \text{Investment})}{\text{Net Sales} - .5\,(\text{Net Income} - \text{PIMS mean ROI} \times \text{Investment})}$$

Selected PIMS Findings[31]   *Appendix*

The PIMS model has been tested in many countries, economic environments, and industry settings. In each of these settings, the important determinants of profitability are the same, although their precise relationship may vary. This Appendix reviews some of the general findings on the operation of these variables. In particular, we look at the following:

- Market position
- Product quality
- Investment intensity
- Productivity
- Growth of the served market

The importance of these variables has been established by their performance as highly significant predictors of profitability in a complex, thirty-two variable regression equation. However, it is difficult to illustrate the nature of the relationships when they are embedded in this equation. Moreover, the precise details of the estimating equation have not been made public. For both these reasons, our review of the findings is based on analyses of cross-tabulations of selected variables. Unfortunately, the advantage of easier interpretation is gained at a considerable cost in a multicollinear data set such as this. The reader is cautioned that the following figures also reflect the simultaneous impact of numerous excluded variables on profitability. While the results are intriguing, they are certainly not actionable in this form.

---

31. The tables in this appendix are reproduced with the kind permission of the Strategic Planning Institute. The tables represent relationships found in the data base as of 1984.

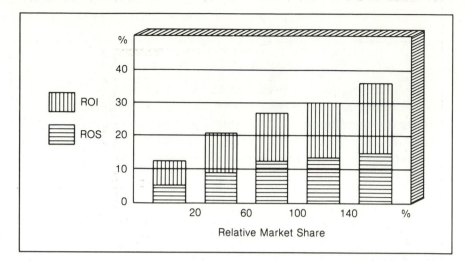

Figure A.1 Market position boosts rates of return

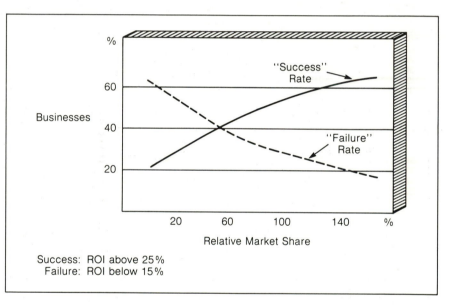

Figure A.2 Market position: neither death warrant nor free pass

Success: ROI above 25%
Failure: ROI below 15%

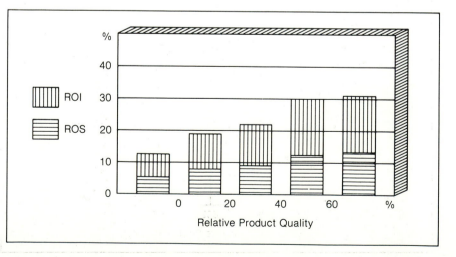

Figure A.3 Relative product quality boosts rates of return

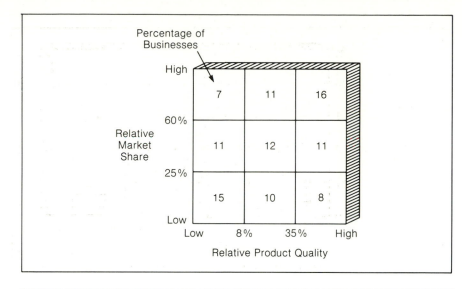

Figure A.4 Relative market share and relative product quality are correlated

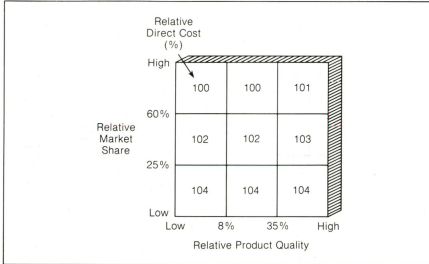

Figure A.5 Share affects cost; quality has little effect on cost

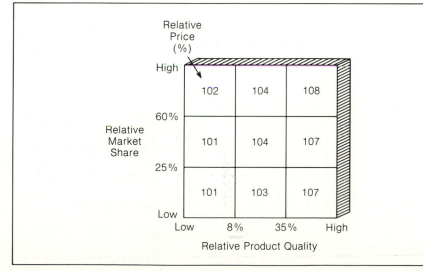

Figure A.6 Quality affects price; separate from quality, share has little effect on price

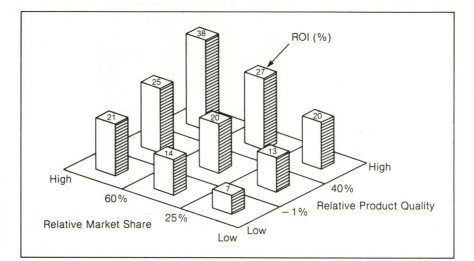

Figure A.7 Quality and share both drive profitability

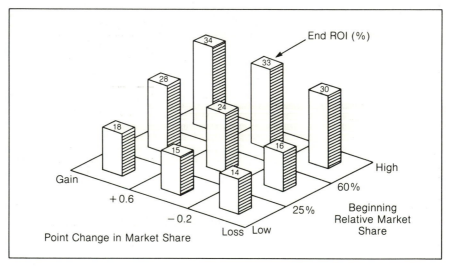

Figure A.8 Current market position helps future ROI

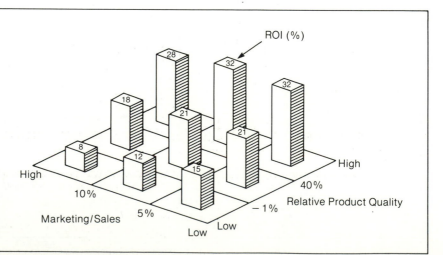

Figure A.9 Heavy marketing is no substitute for low product quality

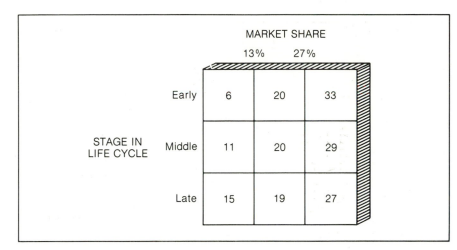

Figure A.10 Low market share, early in the life cycle, is unprofitable

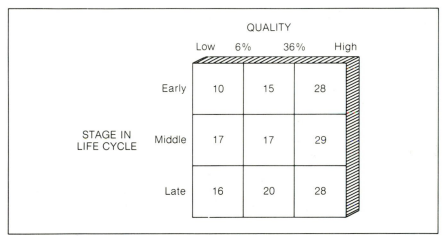

Figure A.11 Low quality, early in the life cycle, is unprofitable

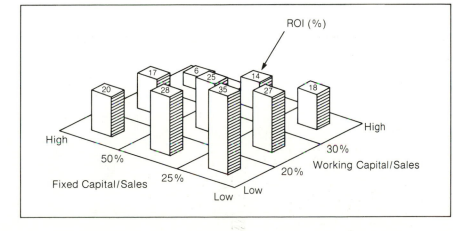

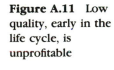

Figure A.12 Any kind of investment intensity hurts profitability

164

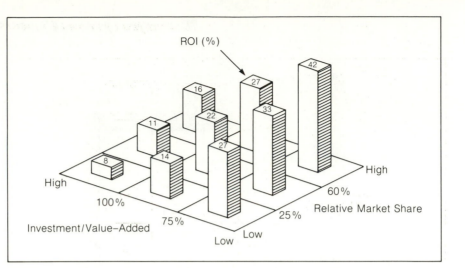

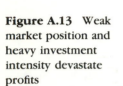

Figure A.13 Weak market position and heavy investment intensity devastate profits

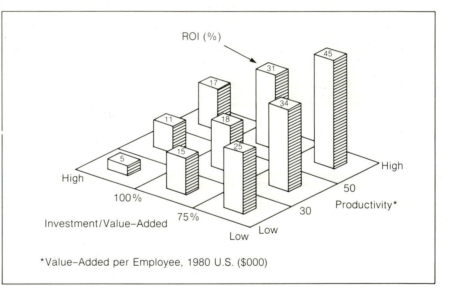

Figure A.14 Investment intensity is a major drag on profitability, but high productivity can offset some of the damage

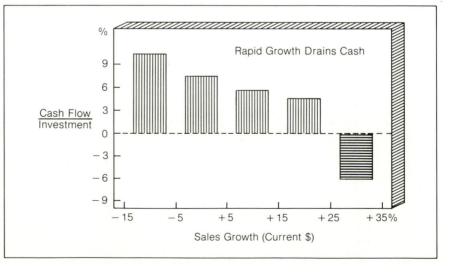

Figure A.15 Rapid growth drains cash

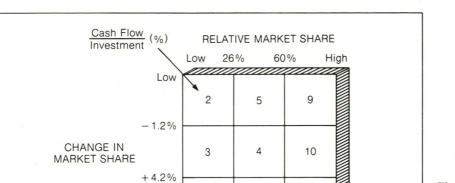

Figure A.16
Having share generates cash, but gaining share uses cash

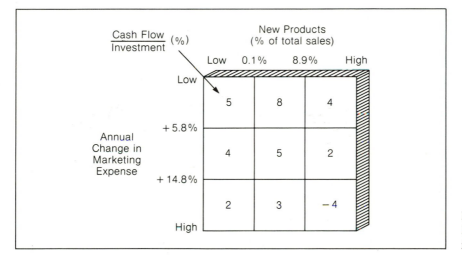

Figure A.17
Investing for the future absorbs cash

The Growth-Share Matrix and Market Share Strategies

Chapter **6**

Portfolio models have been virtually synonymous with strategic market planning since the early seventies. During this period, many different models have been vigorously promoted to managers wrestling with the problems of diversified firms with tens or hundreds of products in markets of widely varying prospects. Their appeal came from the underlying logic that objectives, strategies, and resource allocations should recognize that all products and markets are not equally attractive to the firm. The choices and trade-offs required by this logic were made much easier by the ability of portfolio models to graphically communicate the strategic position of businesses and products.

All portfolio analyses begin with a classification and display of the present and prospective positions of businesses and products according to the attractiveness of the market and the ability of the business to compete within that market. The first of the portfolios to be widely used was the growth-share matrix—sometimes called the cash quadrants model. Market growth serves as the indicator of market attractiveness, and relative market share corresponds to competitive position. While the resulting display is often insightful, the real appeal of this matrix comes from the powerful implications for strategy of different combinations of growth and share dominance. By applying the companion concepts of the life-cycle and experience curve, we can judge which products are investment opportunities, which should be sources of investment funds, and which should be divested or harvested. These guidelines are logically consistent and invariably provocative.

Clouds on the Horizon. It was inevitable that widespread knowledge and usage of the growth-share matrix would lead to disenchantment with the inherent simplifications. Too often the complexities of competitive markets blew holes in the thin fabric of assumptions and empirical support that held the model together. Serious questions have been raised as to whether the growth-share matrix should be used as (1) a *diagnostic aid* that can be used to synthesize prior strategic judgments about the current or prospective position of a business unit, or product line within a business, (2) a *conceptual framework* that guides the generation of strategic options and facilitates the negotiation of objectives for business units, or (3) a *prescriptive guide* to the choice of appropriate strategic options and resource allocations within the firm.

Despite numerous problems, the growth-share matrix remains a useful framework for analysing market share building, holding, or harvesting strategies. For these insights to be useful, however, one must be sensitive to the underlying premises and must avoid the many pitfalls. The purpose of this chapter is to describe how and when the growth-share matrix can be productively used. In the next chapter, we introduce multifactor portfolio matrices that have proven more adaptable to current approaches to portfolio management.

The Growth-Share Matrix

For the growth-share portfolio matrix, each business or product is classified jointly by the rate of present or forecast *market growth* and a measure of *market share dominance*. These dimensions were chosen by the Boston Consulting Group, because market growth served as a handy proxy for the need for cash, while relative market share was a proxy for profitability and cash-generating ability.[1]

Relative market share—for the purpose of this portfolio—is the ratio of the market share of the business to the share of the largest competitor in the same market. High relative market shares were assumed by BCG analysts to be more profitable, for if the experience curve applies, the largest competitor should have the lowest costs at the prevailing price level. The choice of this measure was given further credibility by findings from the PIMS study of a significant relationship of market share and return on investment.[2] If all other factors are equal, the greater the relative share, the greater the cash flow.

---

1. Henderson (1970), (1972), (1973).
2. Buzzell, Gale, and Sultan (1975).

Market growth rate was chosen first because it is a rough proxy for the product life cycle, which has well-known and predictable consequences for cash requirements. In high-growth markets, the need for substantial infusions of fixed and working capital often outstrips the ability of the business to generate cash. But market growth also has indirect effects on the cost of gaining or holding share. It should be easier to gain share in high-growth markets by capturing a disproportionate share of incremental sales from new users and new uses. By contrast, the keynote during maturity is stability and inertia in distribution and purchasing arrangements. A substantial growth in share by one competitor comes at the expense of another competitor's capacity utilization and will be resisted vigorously. As a result, such gains are both time-consuming and costly.

Each business or product is represented in the portfolio by a "bubble" centered at the relative share and current market growth rate. The area of each bubble is proportional to the sales revenue, the largest business having the largest bubble and the others correspondingly smaller. Finally, the grid is divided into four quadrants defined by the two cross hairs. The horizontal line is usually set at the level of nominal GNP growth (inflation rate plus real GNP growth), which has recently been in the range of 10 to 12 percent. Similarly, a vertical cross hair is placed at a relative share of 1, which is the dividing line for a market leadership position. Another line is often placed at a relative share of 1.5 on the grounds that dominance is not established unless the business is at least 50 percent larger than the closest competitor. These lines are strictly for orientation purposes; nothing profound happens just because a business falls slightly to one side or the other of a line. Both axes are continuous variables, so what matters is the distance from the dividing line.

Growth-share matrices can and should be constructed for several levels in the organization, so long as the position in the matrix has meaningful cash flow implications. The top portion of Figure 6.1 shows the portfolio of businesses managed by Black and Decker in 1976. Simply looking at aggregate businesses obscures areas of relative strength or weakness within distinct segments of a business, such as the McCulloch Division, which has its own portfolio.

Typical Cash Flow Patterns in the Growth-Share Matrix. If market share and growth behave as expected, then this portfolio matrix tells a compelling cash flow story. Each quadrant in the matrix has distinct cash flow characteristics that have been given evocative labels, which are now deeply embedded in business jargon.

1. *Cash cows* have dominant shares in slow- or no-growth markets. They are profitable and should throw off considerable cash

Figure 6.1 Growth-share matrix for the Black
and Decker Manufacturing Company—1976

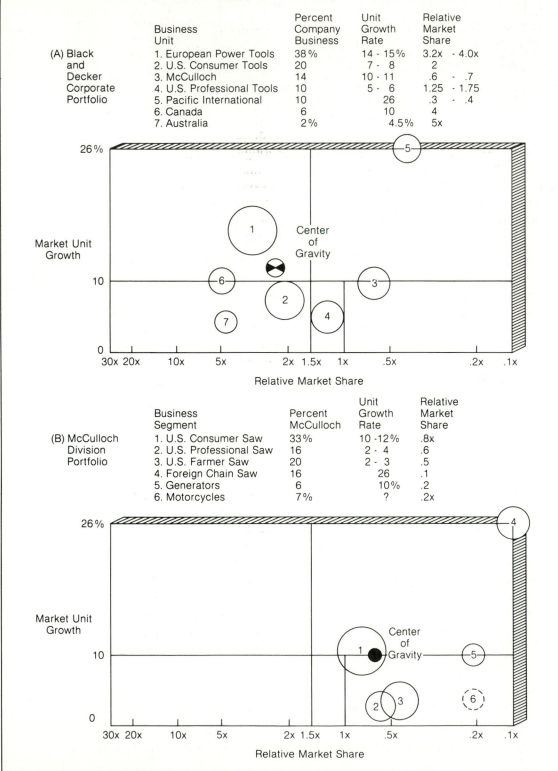

	Business Unit	Percent Company Business	Unit Growth Rate	Relative Market Share
(A) Black and Decker Corporate Portfolio	1. European Power Tools	38%	14 - 15%	3.2x - 4.0x
	2. U.S. Consumer Tools	20	7 - 8	2
	3. McCulloch	14	10 - 11	.6 - .7
	4. U.S. Professional Tools	10	5 - 6	1.25 - 1.75
	5. Pacific International	10	26	.3 - .4
	6. Canada	6	10	4
	7. Australia	2%	4.5%	5x

	Business Segment	Percent McCulloch	Unit Growth Rate	Relative Market Share
(B) McCulloch Division Portfolio	1. U.S. Consumer Saw	33%	10 -12%	.8x
	2. U.S. Professional Saw	16	2 - 4	.6
	3. U.S. Farmer Saw	20	2 - 3	.5
	4. Foreign Chain Saw	16	26	.1
	5. Generators	6	10%	.2
	6. Motorcycles	7%	?	.2x

because their need for new assets is likely to be smaller than depreciation.

2. *Stars* are also profitable because of their strong share position. They may or may not be self-sufficient in cash, depending on whether cash flow from operations can fund the additions to capacity, working capital, and new products needed to keep up with rapid growth.

3. *Problem children* have small relative shares—and correspondingly weak cash flows from operations—with large appetites for cash to fund rapid growth. The problems are compounded if further investments are made to build share to tenable long-run levels.

4. Small-share businesses in slow-growth markets have been tagged with the pejorative label of *dogs*. We would expect them to have modest cash flow from operations, which is usually absorbed in maintaining their market position as well as in funding necessary equipment replacements and upgrades and additions to working capital. As they are unlikely to ever become a significant source of cash to be deployed elsewhere in the company, they are more appropriately called *cash traps*. As there can usually be only one leader and most markets are mature, the greatest number of products and businesses falls into this quadrant. Yet, this quadrant is also least susceptible to generalizations about cash flow, because of the tendency we observed earlier for profitability differentials in mature markets to narrow significantly.

Other Perspectives on the Growth-Share Matrix.   One question the growth-share matrix does not answer directly is whether the growth of the business or product is keeping pace with market growth. All things being equal, if the business is growing faster than the market, it is building share and using even more cash than would be forecast by its position in the matrix. Conversely, slower than market growth suggests that market share is being harvested to generate cash.

Two useful matrices have been developed to help diagnose relative growth patterns. One is the growth-gain matrix, shown in Figure 6.2 for Northwest Industries.[3] This company was investing heavily in 1980 to grow its beverage and tubular steel business. Meanwhile, the company was de-emphasizing chemicals and connecting devices, which were businesses with low relative shares and few growth opportunities. Another diagnostic aid is the sector graph shown in

---

3. This matrix is sometimes called the "share-momentum graph" (Lewis 1977).

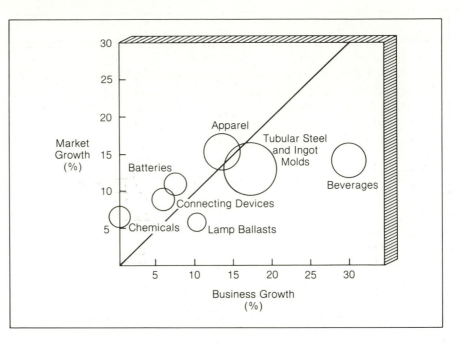

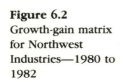

Figure 6.2
Growth-gain matrix
for Northwest
Industries—1980 to
1982

Figure 6.3 for the home health-care market in 1980. This matrix shows which competitors are gaining or losing within an industry or market, and helps to clarify the direction the business is moving in the growth-gain matrix.[4] Overall, the home health-care market is growing at annual rate of 30 percent including inflation. The three broad categories of competitors are traditional home health-care suppliers, independent and chain drugstores, and department store/catalog sales companies. No competitor has a dominant position, and the significant category of "others" represents at least two hundred separate organizations. However, most of the fast-growing leaders are subsidiaries of larger companies such as American Hospital Supply (AHS) or National Medical Enterprises (NME). These companies have the financial resources to fund high growth plus inflation.

Guidelines for Strategies

Strategy guidelines—which sharply narrow the range of feasible strategies for a business unit or product—are jointly shaped by the following:

1. What is *feasible,* given the position of the business in the growth-share matrix. Inasmuch as the market growth rate is

---

4. Callow (1982).

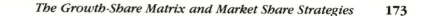

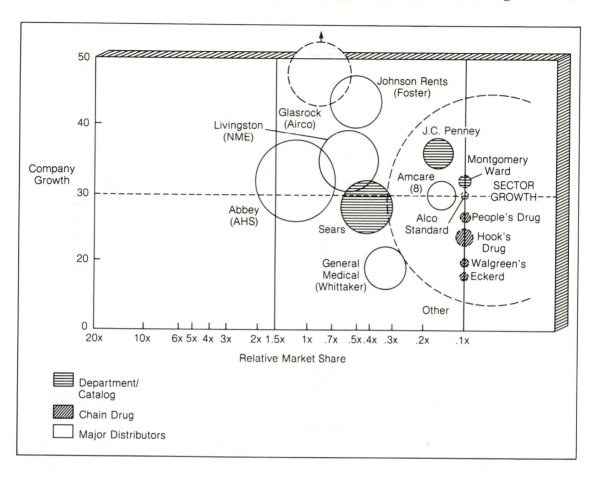

Figure 6.3 Home health centers sector graph 1978–1980

usually noncontrollable, market share becomes the key strategic variable.

2. The *objective* of portfolio management, which is to make the whole (business or corporation) greater than the sum of the parts.[5] This synergy is achieved when there are some products or businesses that *generate* cash—and provide acceptable reported profits in the short run—and others that *use* cash to support long-run growth. Figure 6.4 shows the pattern of cash flows implied by this objective.

A portfolio is *balanced* when the needs for cash can be satisfied by the sources of cash, without jeopardizing their market position. Among the indicators of balance are the size and vulnerability of the cash cows—and the prospects for stars, if any—and the number of

---

5. Henderson and Zakon (1980).

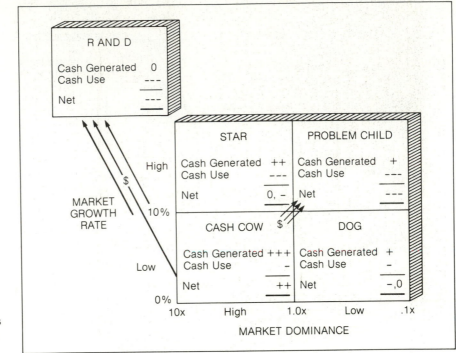

Figure 6.4
Managing cash flows
in the growth-share
matrix

problem children and dogs. Close attention must be paid to those businesses or products with large cash appetites. Unless the company has abundant cash flow—or external fund sources—it cannot afford to sponsor many such products at one time.

The Strategic Success Sequence.   Strategic success is the sequence of share building and holding moves needed to achieve a balanced portfolio. Cash generated by the cash cow is invested in building the market share of problem children by providing advantages that can effectively be sustained. If the investment is successful, they will become stars, and when market growth inevitably slows, they will be the cash cows of the future. To be avoided is the disaster sequence of Figure 6.5, where the problem children limp along in a weak competitive position because they are undernourished with capital, and eventually become dogs when the market matures.

In this scheme, one of the worst scenarios is to have the star lose position and become a question mark as market growth slows. But is this outcome always disastrous? For some companies—3M and Hewlett-Packard being visible and vocal practitioners—this sequence is attractive. They prefer to keep their margins on star products high as long as possible and risk erosion of market share. The purpose is

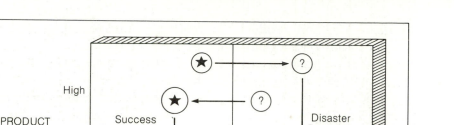

Figure 6.5 The strategic success sequence

to generate funds for R and D on a stream of new products designed to obsolete the dying star just as market share begins to slip rapidly. They are willing to trade the prospect of long-run market share dominance for the greater certainty of short-run profits in the belief their R and D will continue to deliver new generations of products.

Strategies for Leaders in Low-Growth Markets

The overriding consideration is the preservation of market position, for this is the source of future cash flow streams. This priority must be pursued in the face of the natural tendency for cost advantages to shrink, which we saw in the analysis of cross-sectional experience curves in Chapter 2. Contrary to the superficial connotations of the cash cow label, these products and businesses are not to be harvested or milked. Only when their position is secure can free cash flow be diverted to support research and growth areas elsewhere in the company.

Continued dominance is best ensured—although hardly guaranteed—through maintenance of quality, cost, and performance leadership, while keeping abreast of product and process technology. Companies are increasingly adopting this back-to-basics approach. Ralston Purina management is refocusing their investments toward their mature core businesses because "we want to spend our time doing what we do best." This means increasing the depth of geographic coverage in the animal feed market and launching a variety of new pet food products to maintain dominance.[6] Meanwhile, money-losing distractions such as a Colorado resort, mushroom growing, tuna canning, and a hockey team are being spun off.

A leader in a mature market has several options that the other competitors in the market may have problems following. One is to take advantage of a greater scale of operations and increase vertical integration. This is normally profitable only for the leaders.[7] Sometimes it is possible to raise the stakes in the industry by increasing the minimum efficient scale (as measured by the minimum feasible capacity addition). Capital-intensive computer systems to improve distribution service are an effective example of this approach.

Meanwhile, pressure to overinvest through product proliferation and market expansion should be resisted unless prospects for primary demand growth are unusually attractive, or a key competitor has exposed an unexpected area of vulnerability.

Strategies for Leaders in High-Growth Markets

The strategic success sequence identifies two distinct strategic thrusts for high-growth businesses. The conventional option is to reinvest heavily to hold share or even build share. Specific actions to support this thrust include the following:

- Maintaining a large share of the new users or new application segments that are the source of growth in the market.

- Protecting the existing market segments from competitive inroads by reinvesting earnings in aggressive price reductions, product enhancements, improved market coverage, and production process improvements.

- Investing ahead of market growth to maintain the share of production capacity. This also has the effect of deterring aggressive competitive entries.

These strategy prescriptions for stars borrow heavily from the lessons of the experience curve. There is, however, a revisionist alternative to the standard success sequence, which is to maximize current cash flow and invest in innovation. Here, the indicated actions are umbrella pricing (until the share loss becomes untenable) and cautious capacity additions. The new capacity should preferably be designed to

---

6. Business Week (31 January 1983).

7. Buzzell (1983).

accommodate the next generation of products being rolled out of the laboratories and field-testing sites.

Strategies for Followers in Low-Growth Markets

The prototypical dog is at a cost disadvantage, with few opportunities for growth at a reasonable cost. The market is stagnant, so there is little new business to compete for, and efforts to gain market share will be resisted strenuously by the dominant competitor. Clearly, the slower the present and prospective growth, and the smaller the relative market share, the more pressing the need for action. A wide range of possibilities exists, which can be arrayed from most to least attractive.

(A_1) Adapt the strategy to minimize weaknesses. This invariably means reducing the scope of the business. Ideally, the focus should be toward specialized segments of the market that can be dominated and protected from competitive inroads. This strategy is explored in detail in the companion volume in this series. A variation on this theme is to find segments where a small scale of operations hurts least. These could be regional markets in which high importance is attached to local service or to customers who demand extensive customization. The ultimate reduction in scope is to withdraw from competitive markets and simply produce for captive consumption.

(A_2) Harvest the business, aggressively or gradually, depending on the seriousness of the situation. To harvest is to consciously throttle back all discretionary and support costs to some minimum level that will maximize the cash flow over the foreseeable life of the business.

(A_3) Divest the business, wholly or in part. Even here, there are many options to consider. There may be a low-overhead buyer who could extract acceptable margins by eliminating corporate overhead charges. These buyers may include members of the current business management team using a leveraged buy-out. They are particularly well placed because of intimate knowledge of organizational slack, cost inefficiencies, and opportunities being missed by the business as currently operated. The business might fit the requirements of another competitor by giving them a production or market coverage capability that would otherwise be costly and time-consuming to develop. Finally, there is the "kennel of dogs" solution, in which a new corporate entity is created from the dogs of several companies. Here it is hoped the whole will be at least as great as the sum of the parts.

Strategies for Followers in High-Growth Markets

The basic strategy options are fairly clear-cut: either invest heavily to get a disproportionate share of new users or applications, or buy existing market share by acquiring a competitor—and thus move the product toward star status—or drop out by selling the business or by licensing the technology.

An increasingly attractive option is a joint venture where one partner provides the technology and manufacturing capability, while the other has market access and service capability. Consideration also should be given to focusing strategies, but only if a defensible niche can be found and resources are available to gain dominance. At the extreme, a whole new segment may be created, as was done by Bic with disposable pens and Savin and Canon with low-cost office copiers suitable for decentralized copying.

Balancing the Portfolio

The growth-share matrix in Figure 6.6 shows how one company—actually a composite of a number of situations[8]—upgraded its product portfolio to better balance the sources and uses of cash.

The *present* position of each product is defined by the relative share and market growth rate during a representative time period. Since business results normally fluctuate, it is important to use a time period that is not distorted by rare events. The *future* position may be either (1) a momentum forecast of the results of continuing the present strategy or (2) a forecast of the consequences of a change in strategy. It is desirable to do both and compare the results. The specific display of Figure 6.6 is a summary of the following strategic decisions.

- Aggressively support the newly introduced product A to ensure dominance (but anticipate share declines due to new competitive entries).
- Continue present strategies of Products B and C to ensure maintenance of market share.
- Gain share of market for Product D by investing in acquisitions.
- Narrow and modify the range of models of Product E to focus on one segment.
- Divest Products F and G.

---

8. Adapted from Day (1977).

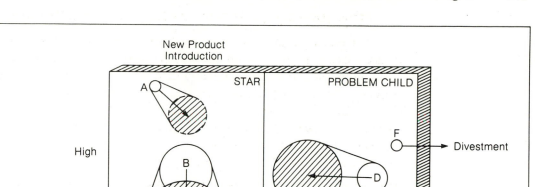

Figure 6.6
Balancing the
product portfolio

These are decisions. Whether they are correct and will achieve the intended results depends on the pressures felt by operating managers to subvert the decisions and the vulnerability of the measures to distortion.

Implementing Portfolio Strategies

Managers are effective at tailoring their behavior to the evaluation system as they perceive it. Whenever market share is used to evaluate performance, managers will be tempted to manipulate the product-market boundaries to show a static or increasing share. The greater the degree of ambiguity or compromise in the definition of the boundaries, the more tempting these adjustments become. The risk is that the resulting narrow view of the market may mean overlooking threats from substitutes or the opportunities within emerging market segments.

These problems are compounded when share dominance is also perceived to be an important determinant of the allocation of resources and top management interest. Managers who do not like the implications of being associated with a dog may try to redefine the market so they can point to a larger market share or a higher than average growth rate. Regardless of their success with the attempted redefinition, their awareness of how the business is regarded in the overall portfolio will ultimately affect their morale.

The forecast of market growth rate may also be manipulated, especially when advancement and additional resources are perceived to depend on association with a product that is classified as a star. This may lead to wishful thinking about the future growth prospects of the product. Unfortunately, the quality of the review procedures in most planning processes is not robust enough to challenge such distortions. Further dysfunctional consequences will result if ambitious managers of cash cows actually attempt to expand their products through unnecessary product proliferation.

Some of these problems have been blamed on the use of a "vulgar and destructive" vocabulary for classifying products and businesses.[9] Despite the unfavorable connotations of *dogs* and *manage for cash,* and the extreme resistance they encounter in organizations that value growth, these terms remain widely used. A greater risk is that a premature closure on the objectives and strategy options appropriate to a classification may signal line management that it is no longer necessary to consider a broad array of options[10]—even though some may be better suited to environmental changes. In this way, the labels may unwittingly become self-fulfilling prophecies. This is a problem when technological or market changes present opportunities for investment to build competitive advantage in otherwise unattractive markets.

Pitfalls in the Measures.   The Achilles' heel of a growth-share matrix is the measurements; for if the share and growth estimates are dubious, so are the interpretations. The possibilities for distortion can be seen in the following insert.[11]

---

9. Andrews (1981).

10. Hamermesh (1980) and Palesy (1980).

11. Goold (1981).

Dangers in the Measures

The two growth-share matrices below present sharply contrasting pictures of corporate health and diversity. Company A is in comparatively few businesses, most of which have weak positions in slow-growth markets. Company B is much more diverse and has a stronger and more rapidly growing portfolio.

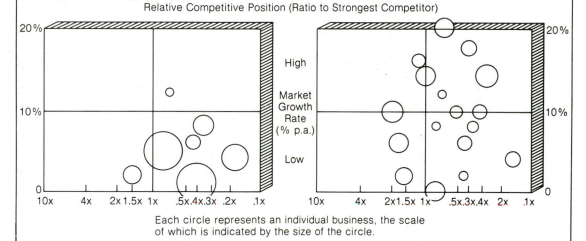

Each circle represents an individual business, the scale of which is indicated by the size of the circle.

The strategic priorities for the two companies are dramatically different—even though A and B are simply different portfolios for the same British manufacturing company. The version labeled Company A is based on aggregated divisional definitions, while Company B uses specific product-market segments. Because the company does not participate fully in every industry but prefers to focus on attractive, protected segments, the B portfolio does not aggregate to the A portfolio.

For purposes of portfolio analysis, a business segment or product-market is correctly defined if it is possible to establish and defend a competitive advantage in the segment alone, without needing to participate in other related segments. As we have seen in each of the preceding chapters, this is easier said than done. Among the questions to be resolved are the following:

■ Should the definition of the product-market be broad to encompass related products and activities that may influence the experience base and ability to achieve scale economies, or should it use narrower customer-oriented definitions to gain insight into how a differentiated competitive position is converted into either premium prices or lower marketing costs?

■ Should the focus be on the total product-market or on the portion served by the business?

The answers to these questions can profoundly influence both the position of the business and the strategic guidelines to follow. As we have emphasized throughout this book, the appropriate measures must be grounded in a detailed understanding of the cost and market position of the business.

Challenging the Premises of the Growth-Share Matrix

Whether one considers the growth-share matrix a well-defined and valid model or simply a metaphor, it does have a singular capacity to reduce the complexities of diversified firms or heterogeneous business units and provide order to the thinking process. Yet, skeptics protest that the inherent simplifications come at too high a price, because critical details are omitted from the analysis. This criticism will be true when the fundamental premises about important variables and relationships that are used to simplify the portfolio situation are violated. Five premises deserve especially careful handling because of their potential to yield misleading signals:

■ Share has a direct effect on profitability.

■ High-growth markets are more attractive, because gaining share in high-growth situations is easier.

■ Cash flow is systematically related to the *position* and *direction* of the product or business in the growth-share matrix.

■ Interdependencies among businesses are limited to the generation and use of cash.

■ The objective of portfolio management is to achieve cash balance.

While these premises are not entirely independent, each provides a different perspective on the issues to be resolved in managing a portfolio of businesses or products. The rest of this section discusses each of these critical premises in turn, with the exception of the second premise, which is discussed earlier in Chapter 4.

The Relationship of Share and Profitability

The first premise has been stated explicitly by Bruce Henderson, the progenitor of the growth-share matrix: "In a competitive business, it [market share] determines relative profitability. When it does not seem to do so, it is nearly always because the relevant market sector is misdefined or the leader is mismanaged."[12] This is a straightforward inference from the experience curve concept. Unfortunately, it is also susceptible to all the problems of cloudy signals from the experience curve, which we encountered in Chapter 2. Indeed, these difficulties are merely a preview of all the difficulties that have been encountered with this premise during its short and stormy history.

The first problem is that the experience curve speaks only to *relative* profitability. Too often, this key point has been overlooked in interpretations of portfolio positions that implicitly assume that two products with the same relative share position (and growth rate) are equally profitable. But some industries are inherently more profitable for all participants than others; the average drug and cosmetic competitor is much more profitable than the average plumbing fixture or hydraulic cylinder manufacturer.

Recognition of further flaws in this premise was delayed by early findings from the PIMS data base, which concluded that "a difference of ten percentage points in market share is accompanied by a difference of about five points in pretax ROI."[13] This reinforced the pivotal role of market share as a strategic variable with an intrinsic value worth pursuing. Indeed, some analysts have used this interpretation of the value of market share to account for the behavior of Japanese firms. Typical is the author who argues that "Japanese business executives are not motivated by profits. They are committed to expanding market share which they consider the only secure item a company can own."[14]

Despite the apparent support for the notion that share is a determinant of profitability, there is growing evidence that it is unimportant in many settings, and where it appears to be important, there are competing explanations for the role it plays.

Conditions Under Which Market Share is Important. There is virtually no end to the variables that can inhibit or accentuate the relationship of share and profitability:

- Size of business. In some industries, it is possible to prosper either as a small, low-overhead, geographically focused

12. Henderson (1979).

13. Buzzell, Gale, and Sultan (1975).

14. Ballon, Tomita and Usami (1976).

competitor or as a large national or international company.

- Type of industry. Profitability differences attributable to market share are most pronounced within high-technology industries. In the service sector, large banks, hospitals, and hotel chains often suffer from diseconomies of scale, which combine with managerial complexity to adversely impact their profitability.

- Stage of life cycle. Recent results from a PIMS study show that profitability differentials narrow as the product matures. On average, a company with twice the share of its leading competitors would have a direct cost advantage of 3.5 percent in "less mature" markets and only 1.2 percent in mature markets.[15]

- Unionization appears to dissipate the advantage of large market shares because of the adverse effect of restrictive work rules on productivity or union bargaining (or both), resulting in a larger fraction of value-added ending up as wages.

Market Share Versus Strategic Fundamentals.   Plans or strategies with the sole objective of building, holding, or harvesting share presume a direct causal linkage from market share to profitability. This interpretation is consistent with the presence of scale economies and experience effects and the exercise of market power. High-share firms not only have lower costs but also have more leverage with suppliers and distributors because of their size. However, there are compelling reasons why this causal explanation may be partially or completely wrong.

It could be that the direction of causality is from profits to share; businesses that are lucky or uniquely endowed select initially defensible and profitable strategies that give them more profits to reinvest so they can grow faster than their less fortunate rivals. Another possibility is that what we are seeing is just the simultaneous consequence of a third variable, such as quality of management, that jointly impacts market share and profitability. Good managers make the right strategic moves in pursuing cost and market advantages that achieve both high shares and high profits.

The most persuasive explanation is that each of these mechanisms is operating over time to yield the share-profit relationship we get whenever a snapshot is taken of a market. A movie would show

---

15. Buzzell (1981).

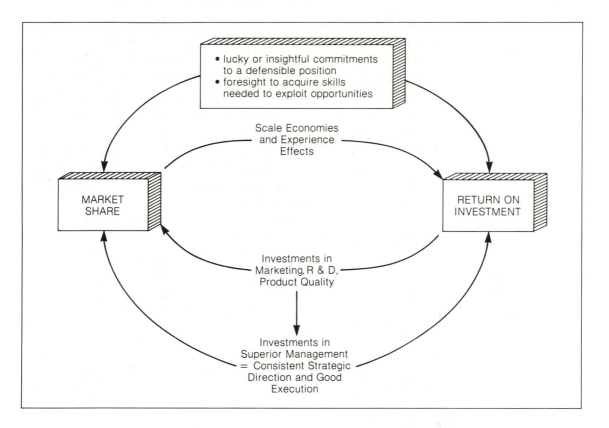

something closer to Figure 6.7. The relative contribution of each mechanism will vary depending on when we take the picture. Early in the evolution of the market, first-mover or fast-follower advantages will dominate. As the market matures, the question is whether management can capitalize on the advantage of an initially high share and redeploy their resources to cope with changes in technology, market requirements, and so forth. Several studies that look at changes in the PIMS data base over a period of years provide support for this multiple mechanism view of the share-profit relationship. They suggest that the direct causal impact of share is much less than commonly assumed and may account for as little as 10 to 20 percent of the relationship.[16]

What does this mean for the formulation or evaluation of market share strategies? First, be careful to separate the question of how a firm first got its share position from how it will keep or build share in the future. Getting share depends on making commitments in the

Figure 6.7 Multiple influences on the relationship of market share and profitability

16. Rumelt and Wensley (1980) and Jacobson and Aaker (1984).

face of uncertainty that later turn into defensible positions.[17] This is best done when the rules of the game in an industry are unwritten (as with embryonic technologies) or are being changed by outside shocks such as airline deregulation, the advent of microcomputers, or a sudden glut or scarcity of critical raw materials. The second message is that market share is better viewed as an outcome of strategic moves or as a measure of success rather than as an intrinsically valuable asset to be bought or sold. In short, focus on the fundamentals. The value of this perspective can be seen by studying successful low-share businesses.

The Profitability of Low-Share Positions.   At most, market share accounts for 15 percent of the observed variation in profitability among businesses in the PIMS data base. This means that while share is relevant, there are many other ways to achieve superior profitability and overcome a weak share position. All such strategies are distinguished by selectivity; high-performing low-share businesses are acutely sensitive to market segment differences, pick their spots carefully, and avoid trying to do everything.[18] They do not copy the strategies of market leaders. Instead, they choose particular bases of competition, such as product quality. They then control expenditures in other areas of competition such as product R and D, product-line breadth, or marketing so that they can achieve high margins despite limited sales volume.

Cash Flow Patterns in the Growth-Share Matrix

There are two facets to the third premise, relating to the position and direction of the business in the matrix. The first is that rapid market growth creates a drain on cash. The ability of the business to generate cash depends on the share position. Second, the need for cash will be accentuated if the business is also building share, but gaining share in high-growth markets is still easier (and presumably cheaper).

The good news is that the PIMS data confirm a systematic relationship between cash flow and position in the growth-share matrix.[19] In Figure 6.8, cash cows have the highest cash flow as a percentage of investment, while question marks have the lowest cash flow rate. The bad news is that less than 10 percent of the variance in cash flow rates is explained by relative share and market growth. Another 55

---

17. Rumelt (1981).

18. Woo and Cooper (1982).

19. Gale and Branch (1981).

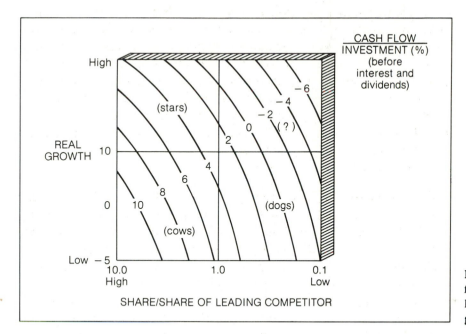

Figure 6.8 Cash flow rate contour lines for the growth-share matrix

percent of the variance is explained by changes in selling price, market share, investment intensity, rate of new product introduction, and marketing expense.

The findings on the cash costs of share building in growth versus mature markets are also troublesome for this premise. Essentially, the relationship is so modest as to be managerially uninteresting.[20] This should not be surprising in light of the problems with the notion that it is easier to gain share in growth markets, which were identified in Chapter 4.

An important corollary to the premise about cash flow patterns is that every business segment or product line in the matrix has the same investment intensity. However, if a problem child requires relatively few assets per dollar of sales, it may not be a drain on cash flow. This is one area to examine thoroughly if a business or product has a significantly different cash flow pattern than would be expected. The analysis of any such apparent inconsistencies between theory and reality can often lead to useful strategic insights.

Interdependencies Among Businesses

There is an implicit and potentially dangerous premise of the growth-share matrix that interdependencies among businesses are limited to their generation and use of a common resource: cash. That

---

20. Burnett (1983).

is, there should be minimal cost or demand cross-elasticities between products and businesses in the portfolio.

This premise may be invalid for two reasons. The first is the ubiquity of shared experience. We saw in Chapter 2 that this could have a major impact on the cost positions of competitors and could potentially override the relationship of market share and relative cost.

Strategic Field Theory.   A more fundamental challenge to this premise comes from the growing recognition that interdependencies should be exploited and not neglected. According to this view, it is the creation and management of linkages—by sharing techniques, skills, and knowledge across business and product boundaries—that give a corporation long-run competitive advantage. The test is whether most of the businesses participate in and fortify the core "fields" of activities and expertise that give coherence to the corporation.[21]

A strategic field map is used to portray potential and actual synergies, and test for overall coherence. This is a plot of linkages along two dimensions: product-market segments and value-added steps. Linkages are highlighted by placing together the products with the most similar cost structures. When we do this for Procter and Gamble, as in Figure 6.9, the map reveals that the field strengths of P and G depend on management's ability to share know-how in such areas as packaging, directed advertising, and couponing, and to achieve cost sharing across businesses. Such linkages are achieved with structures and systems that communicate essential insights and pool ideas between functional areas in different businesses.

The numerous value-added linkages across products and markets help reveal both P and G's competitive strengths and the rationale for extensions into Charmin, Folgers and over-the-counter drugs. The recent acquisition of Norwich Eaton gave it ready access to an over-the-counter market with complacent competitors, products that utilize their advertising clout, synergistic channels, and the potential for achieving low manufacturing costs.[22]

Cash Balance as an Objective

The strategic guidelines emerging from the growth-share matrix emphasize the balance of cash flows, by ensuring there are some businesses and products that use cash to sustain growth and others that supply cash. A corollary to this premise is that most corporations

---

21. Lewis (1984).
22. Silverman (1984).

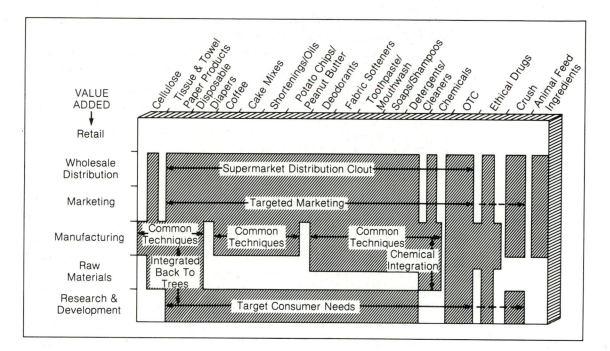

suffer from continual constraints in the amount of outside capital they can raise—even if they can offer a portfolio of attractive projects to the market. There have been sharp attacks on both the premise and the corollary, on the grounds that

- there are other objectives than cash balance.

- diversified firms can raise capital for attractive projects, by raising equity capital, reducing the dividend payout rate, or increasing the debt/equity ratio. As a result, capital rationing is seldom required.

- choices among strategic investment options should be based on the ability of an investment to enhance the economic value of the corporation.[23]

What is an Appropriate Portfolio Objective?   Business objectives have many dimensions beyond balancing cash flows. This point was recognized by Seymour Tilles in one of the earliest discussions of the portfolio approach.[24] Tilles's point was that an investor pursues a balanced combination of risk, income, and growth when acquiring

Figure 6.9 Procter and Gamble strategic field products/markets

---

23. A discussion of value-based capital allocation is beyond the scope of this chapter. See Alberts and McTaggart (1984) for arguments as to why this is a more fundamental approach to strategy evaluation.

24. Tilles (1966).

a portfolio of securities. He further argued that "the same basic concepts apply equally well to product planning." The problem with concentrating on cash flow to maximize income and growth is that strategies to balance risks are not explicitly considered.

What must be avoided is excessive exposure to a specific threat from one of the following areas of vulnerability.

- The economy (e.g., business downturns)
- Social, political, and environmental pressures
- Supply continuity
- Technological change
- Unions and related human factors

It also follows that a firm should direct its new product search activities into several different opportunity areas, to avoid intensifying the degree of vulnerability.

The desire to reduce vulnerability is a possible reason for keeping, or even acquiring, a dog. Thus, firms may integrate backward to assure supply of highly leveraged materials. If a dog has a high percentage of captive business, it may not even belong as a separate entity in a portfolio analysis.

A similar argument could be used for products that have been acquired for intelligent reasons. For example, a large Italian knitwear manufacturer owns a high-fashion dress company selling only to boutiques to help follow and interpret fashion trends. Similarly, because of the complex nature of the distribution of lumber products, some suppliers have acquired lumber retailers to help learn about patterns of demand and changing end-user requirements. In both these cases, the products and businesses were acquired for reasons outside the logic of the portfolio, and should properly be excluded from the analysis.

Dogs may serve other functions that deserve inclusion in the portfolio. Consider the guard dog at work in the low-growth home laundry bleach market.[25] Clorox, the industry leader with 52 percent of the liquid bleach and 60 percent of powdered bleaches, is introducing a new brand called Wave. The purpose is evidently to blunt the expected introduction of a new Procter and Gamble bleach. Although Clorox claims their move is not a feint, it is unlikely they expect Wave to achieve a significant share. They may even lose money on the launch. But the losses will not be nearly as much as they would be if Procter and Gamble were unimpeded.

---

25. Seeger (1984).

Summary

The growth-share matrix was born in the heady days of strategic planning when the strategic prescriptions spoke directly to the needs of decision makers to separate cash flow winners from cash flow losers. The ideas remain compelling, but after fifteen years of experience with the simplifications, pitfalls, and potential for distortion, the users are far more cautious. They have learned that the ability of the growth-share matrix to yield useful diagnostic insights hinges on the validity of five underlying premises:

- Share has a direct effect on profitability.
- High-growth markets are more attractive.
- Cash flow can be predicted by the position and direction of the product or business.
- Interdependencies are limited to cash.
- The objective is cash balance.

In reality, each of these premises may be dominated by the details of the situation. So long as this is recognized and reflected in the interpretation, the growth-share matrix will remain a useful conceptual tool for helping managers ask insightful questions about complex environments.

Portfolio Management with the Market Attractiveness– Competitive Position Matrix

For most companies, the portfolio classification of their products and businesses is simply a means to two more important ends:

■ The negotiation of explicit strategic missions (or investment strategies), between business unit managers and corporate management, that reflect different portfolio prospects.

■ The adjustment of administrative systems to ensure that resources are allocated according to the negotiated mission. Specific adjustments are required in the handling of capital budgeting, the degree of autonomy of management teams, and the type of incentive compensation.

This means using portfolio models as the basis for a system of management, rather than simply as an analytical tool. A 1979 survey of Fortune 1000 companies estimated that 36 percent of the companies had adopted a portfolio approach,[1] and close to half the adopters were using it as the basis for a management system. These numbers were growing at 15 to 20 percent per year. The growth in acceptance was confirmed four years later by a similar survey of diversified Canadian companies that found 51 percent were using a portfolio ap-

---

1. Haspeslagh (1982).

proach, and a further 19 percent were considering its use.[2] Few of the users viewed portfolio models strictly as analytical tools.

The portfolio matrix has undergone considerable reshaping so that it can support the planning process. Most of the changes have been aimed at overcoming the most objectionable simplifications of the growth-share matrix so that the resulting display will be a more realistic assessment of the position of the business. This is largely achieved by using a comprehensive array of strategic factors to describe the dimensions of the matrix. The result is a multifactor portfolio model that can be adapted to a wide variety of industries. This flexibility makes these models especially useful as diagnostic aids as well as common frameworks for negotiating objectives and strategies within a planning system.

Multifactor Portfolio Models

The most popular multifactor portfolio model is the market attractiveness–competitive position matrix developed jointly by McKinsey and General Electric in the early seventies.[3] Within this family of models there are a number of variants such as the Shell Directional Policy Matrix and the Arthur D. Little (Industry Maturity-Competitive Position) matrix. Many of these models were developed by major consulting firms to differentiate their services—and attract the attention of prospective clients. A representative sample of these models is described in the Appendix to this chapter. For the rest of this section, however, we limit our attention to the construction and application of the market attractiveness–competitive position matrix.

Underlying this matrix is the notion that market or industry attractiveness should reflect differences in the average level of long-run profit potential for all participants in the market, while differences along the competitive position dimension should be related to the profitability of the business relative to the competition. This is a static picture that will deteriorate over time unless new sources of advantage are found. Hence, it is desirable to classify a business or product market on both dimensions, both in the present and in the future.

The same basic steps are followed in the development of all multifactor matrices.[4] However, it is important to distinguish the steps leading to an assessment of the present position, from the more

2. Canada Consulting Group (1984).
3. Farquhar and Shapiro (1983).
4. Abell and Hammond (1979), Wind and Mahajan (1981), and Hax and Majluf (1983).

creative application of the portfolio matrix to the analysis of the future situation:

SITUATION ASSESSMENT

> STEP 1: Establish the level and units of analysis (business units, segments, or product-markets).
>
> STEP 2: Identify the factors underlying the market attractiveness and competitive position dimensions.
>
> STEP 3: Assign weights to factors to reflect their relative importance.
>
> STEP 4: Assess the *current* position of each business or product on each factor, and aggregate the factor judgments into an overall score reflecting the position on the two classification dimensions.

STRATEGY DEVELOPMENT

> STEP 5: Project the future position of each unit, based on forecasts of environmental trends and a continuation of the present strategy.
>
> STEP 6: Explore possible changes in the position of each of the units, and the implications of these changes for strategies and resource requirements.

In early 1984, a potential application of the business screen emerged as a team of managers met to cope with the mounting problems of their division. The situation they faced is briefly described in the following boxed insert. For more than a year, the diversity of operations and fast-changing environments had been diffusing their limited management energy and financial resources. Most of the time of management was absorbed in day-to-day "fire fighting" and containing losses in several troubled segments. A major corporate review was impending, and the early signals from headquarters were not encouraging. Somehow, the management team had to come to a consensus on where they would focus their limited resources.

Managing Diversity: The Case of ATG Corporation

In late 1984, the Calumet-Fremont Division operated in the following business segments.

1. Heavy-duty clutches for off-road equipment
2. Pressure relief valves for piping systems

3. Flexible diaphragms made of composite materials
4. Aerospace fittings and connectors
5. Heavy-duty hydraulic pumps
6. Industrial fuel injection systems
7. Expansion joints for bridges and piping systems

When asked to explain the diversity of products and markets, the general manager of the division commented, "This is a tough business to manage or even comprehend . . . . It was put together as a collection of misfits and castoffs from other divisions in the belief there would be some overlaps in markets or production processes we could exploit. We even compounded the problem with several acquisitions where promised synergies just didn't materialize because we didn't understand the new businesses we were entering. For example, we bought a small manufacturer of pressure relief valves to complement our line of fuel injection pumps. Unfortunately, this valve line just doesn't fit; the customers are different and it is sold as a commodity while our fuel injection pumps are sold as specialty items with a lot of consultative selling.

"The result of this patchwork evolution is that we are barely profitable. Last year our operating profit before taxes was 2.1 percent on sales of $52 million. This year will certainly be better, because capital goods sales have been strong, but we will suffer again if there is a downturn.

"As I see it, the key issues for this division are

- properly utilizing our corporate engineering capabilities to develop new products.
- managing a pooled sales force that is spread thin trying to cover a wide variety of unrelated markets.
- the absorption of management time by problem segments.
- the absence of a dominant position in any of the markets we serve.
- a large number of market opportunities to pursue—but a shortage of resources to deal properly with more than a few of them.

What I need is some way to get my management team to agree that these are the issues, and reach a consensus on how resources will be allocated. We just can't keep up the pace of crisis management and knee-jerk reaction to new opportunities. . . . Too often we view new products as the solution to our weak competitive position—but we're always underestimating the development time and the speed of response of more focused competitors."

NOTE: This is a partially disguised description of an actual situation. The essential features of the strategic situation are accurately portrayed.

Step 1: Establishing the Units of Analysis. These matrices can be constructed at several levels in the organization to display business units within a corporation, business segments within an SBU, or even product lines within a business segment. The level should be strategically meaningful, which means that strategic plans are drawn up for each planning unit, and strategic choices for these units can be made relatively independently of decisions for other units.

In practice, the analysis is usually undertaken at several levels to address different questions. Senior management of the ATG Corporation had already constructed an overall matrix that displayed the fifteen divisions within the company, as well as the position of these divisions in key international markets. The management of the Calumet-Fremont Division limited their attention to the seven business segments they managed.

Most of the problems are encountered in the definition of the specific planning units, for all the reasons we have encountered throughout this book. The Calumet-Hecla division was no exception, especially as plans continued to be developed separately for operating units as they were acquired, without reference to overlaps and shared resources. During the planning process, considerable time was spent in identifying meaningful planning units. The five original operating units were divided and recombined into seven new planning units within distinct product-markets.

Step 2: Identifying the Relevant Factors. In some industries or market environments, such as pharmaceuticals, virtually all competitors achieve adequate profits. In other industries, such as tires or pulp and paper, only the strongest competitors will report acceptable profits over the long run. For purposes of diagnosis, however, it is not desirable to use such extreme cases to define what is a highly attractive versus an unattractive market. Instead, these judgments should be made in the light of the markets the company is presently serving, would like to serve, or could serve with its capabilities. Thus, the factors will vary considerably among a financial services company such as Shearson/American Express, a semiconductor manufacturer such as Texas Instruments, and a company primarily in industrial and consumer products based on chemicals and plastic, such as DuPont. Although each of these companies is diversified, there is sufficient relationship among the SBUs that the factors underlying market attractiveness and competitive position are meaningful for each SBU. Conglomerates find the portfolio concept unattractive, for the lack of relationship among the businesses makes comparisons on standard factors difficult if not impossible.

Two complementary approaches to identifying factors can be used to evaluate all the businesses or product-markets in the portfolio. One approach is to select from a standard checklist, such as Table 7.1, those factors that have historically been determinants of industry profitability or relative profitability. Another approach is to select several pairs of businesses, in which one member of each pair is a priori agreed to be an unattractive business, and the other is attractive to the company. Factors can then be derived by identifying the important differences between the two businesses. Whichever approach is emphasized, it is essential that the management team be immersed in the choice and justification of the factors. After all, it is their "theory of the firm" that is being revealed here—in the sense of representing their collective judgments as to which market and business factors will most influence profitability.

Each factor may increase or decrease market attractiveness or competitive position. The relationship is frequently complex. For example, is a competitive structure with a few large competitors of the same size superior to a situation in which there are many smaller competitors? What constitutes a rapid growth rate? In the chemical industry, expansion of capacity is often constrained by uncertainty of feedstock supply. If this is the case, or if there are competing uses for the feedstock, the market is regarded as attractive. Conversely, if there is a surplus of feedstock, suppliers of the feedstock may reduce prices or invest in more capacity to increase consumption. This situation is unattractive.[5] As these examples suggest, a great deal of

Table 7.1 Factors Contributing to Market Attractiveness and Business Strength

ATTRACTIVENESS OF YOUR BUSINESS	STRENGTH OF YOUR COMPETITIVE POSITION
A. Market Factors	A. Market Position
■ size (dollars, units) ■ size of product market ■ market growth rate ■ stage in life cycle ■ diversity of market (potential for differentiation)	■ relative share of market ■ rate of change of share ■ variability of share across segments ■ perceived differentiation of quality/price/service

5. Robinson, Hichens, and Wade (1978).

Table 7.1—*Continued*

ATTRACTIVENESS OF YOUR BUSINESS	STRENGTH OF YOUR COMPETITIVE POSITION

ATTRACTIVENESS OF YOUR BUSINESS

- price elasticity
- bargaining power of customers
- cyclicality/seasonality of demand

B. Economic and Technological Factors

- investment intensity
- nature of investment (facilities, working capital, leases)
- ability to pass through effects of inflation
- industry capacity
- level and maturity of technology utilization
- barriers to entry/exit
- access to raw materials

C. Competitive Factors

- types of competitors
- structure of competition
- substitution threats
- perceived differentiation among competitors

D. Environmental Factors

- regulatory climate
- degree of social acceptance
- human factors such as unionization

STRENGTH OF YOUR COMPETITIVE POSITION

- breadth of product
- company image

B. Economic and Technological Position

- relative cost position
- capacity utilization
- technological position
- patented technology, product, or process

C. Capabilities

- management strength and depth
- marketing strength
- distribution system
- labor relations
- relationships with regulators

Source: Adapted from Abell and Hammond (1979).

judgment and analysis may be necessary before accurate judgments of the relationship of factors with dimensions can be made.

Step 3: Weighing the Factors.   The management team identified six factors as primary indicators of a strong versus a weak competitive position:

1. Relative market share (company share of market as a proportion of the share of the top three competitors)
2. Variability of market shares across end-use segments (as a measure of positioning within market niches)
3. Degree of differentiation (number of product attributes on which there was a real or perceived difference that customers valued)
4. Technological position (both product and process)
5. Relative cost position (using the dominant competitor as the reference point)
6. Service capability (again relative to the dominant competitor)

Quickly the question arose as to whether each of these factors should be of equal importance. The answer—while obviously no—does not necessarily lead to the conclusion that weights should be assigned to each factor (and normalized to sum to 100 percent) to reflect the differences in importance. The problems are: first, that many of the factors, such as market share and relative cost position, are interrelated. Second, a factor such as technological position may be of minor significance in one market, while a dominant determinant of survival in another market being swept by a new generation of technology. The most compelling reason for not using standard weights is that they introduce an unwarranted element of scientific objectivity into a highly judgmental assessment process. The success of this assessment lies in the extent to which critical assumptions about the business are surfaced and tested so that the management team can reach a consensus. Such shared judgments are less likely if the process becomes too mechanistic. Hence, we recommend skipping this step and going directly to the ratings of each business segment on each factor.

Step 4: Classifying the Current Position of the Business Segment in the Portfolio.   The basis of this classification is a rating of each business segment on each of the factors underlying the business strength and market attractiveness dimensions. The magnitude of this task can be seen from the worksheet in Figure 7.1 summarizing the judgments on the attractiveness of the market for heavy-duty clutches for off-road equipment. Profile charts provide a useful display of the overall assessment. For example, each market attractiveness factor was rated on a five-point scale.

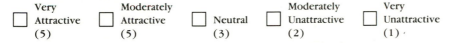

| Very Attractive (5) | Moderately Attractive (5) | Neutral (3) | Moderately Unattractive (2) | Very Unattractive (1) |

With the profile chart overview, it was not difficult to arrive at an overall assessment that the off-road market for heavy-duty clutches was modestly attractive; there was virtually an equal balance of favorable and unfavorable factors. In short, there was a consensus by the management team that this market was not very profitable for the average competitor, largely because of the bargaining power of

Figure 7.1 Profile of assessment of attractiveness of market for heavy-duty clutches for off-road equipment

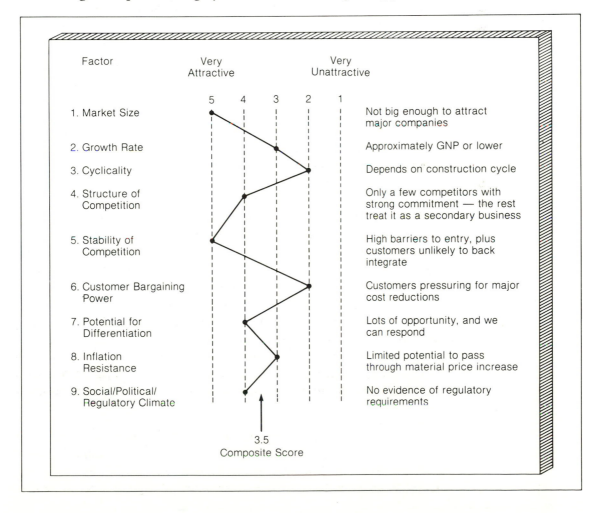

the few large customers. But in this market, the division was not an average competitor; it had a commanding 65 percent of the market achieved with high product quality, superior technology and a long record of product innovation, and low costs as a result of vertical integration and a nonunion manufacturing operation with highly flexible numerically controlled machine tools. Not surprisingly, the division was highly profitable and could sustain profitability even in the depths of the capital goods cycle when order volume could drop by as much as 40 or 50 percent. Overall, the division had a strong competitive position.

Having arrived at composite judgments for each business segment on the two dimensions, it was simple to locate their current positions in one of the nine cells of the portfolio classification matrix (as shown for the division in Figure 7.2). In this display, the area of the circle is proportional to the sales of the business segment, and the shaded wedge is proportional to the current market share.

Figure 7.2 Market attractiveness–competitive position portfolio classification

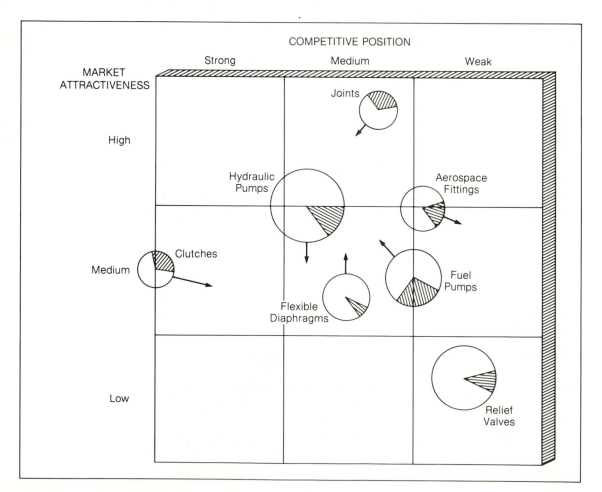

Step 5: Projecting the Future Position of Each Business Segment.
Step 5 proved much more difficult than the assessment of the current position. First, it required a forecast of changes in the factors influencing market attractiveness that would be in effect in three and five years' time. The starting point for this analysis is the product life cycle, to capture the basic shifts in customer behavior, market segmentation, replacement demand, and substitute products that can be foreseen. But future market attractiveness will be dictated by other considerations:

- How will competitors' strategies and commitments change? (Will there be new competitors, and if so, how will they enter?)

- How will product and process technology change?

- What is the longer-term domestic and international economic climate? (This question is especially important to an inflation-sensitive capital goods manufacturer suffering somewhat because of a strong U.S. currency.)

- What environmental changes will take place? (Are there social or regulatory changes that will enhance or inhibit product demand?)

- Will the bargaining power of large customers change, and will this lead to possible changes in product sourcing?

Many of these judgments were highly qualitative and arguable. In some cases, it was necessary to describe the future market environment in terms of several different scenarios.

Equal problems were encountered in forecasting the future competitive position of the business if *no major changes in strategy* were undertaken during the forecast period. These judgments were again made for each of the underlying factors on the assumption that the business would adapt effectively to environmental changes but not undertake any new initiatives that would require a change in the business definition or the thrust of the strategy.

The future position of the business segments, reflected by the length and direction of the vectors in Figure 7.2, gave little solace to the management team. Unless significant changes in strategy were made, the portfolio would look even weaker in the future. This conclusion was important in itself. The real value came from forcing the thinking of the functional managers into the future to arrive at this unpleasant conclusion. In the process, major uncertainties were surfaced and conflicts in assumptions brought into the open. Many of the strategic issues for the division were defined during the dialogue about the future. Here is where strategic thinking really began.

Step 6: Evaluate Changes in Strategy.   At this point, the compelling question is how to reshape the portfolio to a more satisfactory configuration. Unfortunately, this question is largely beyond the capacity of the market attractiveness—competitive position matrix. At most, this portfolio model can offer some strategy guidelines in the form of generic or natural strategies, such as those illustrated in Figure 7.3.[6] The thrust of these generic strategies is to concentrate resources in businesses that are securely positioned in attractive markets, disengage resources in the opposite circumstance, and decide whether businesses in intermediate positions should get more or fewer resources.

Figure 7.3 Generic strategy options

While generic strategies are suggestive, they are no substitute for careful analysis of the feasible strategic options for each business or

MARKET ATTRACTIVENESS	COMPETITIVE POSITION		
	strong	medium	weak
high	PROTECT POSITION •invest to grow at maximum digestible rate •concentrate effort on maintaining strength	INVEST TO BUILD •challenge for leadership •build selectively on strengths •reinforce vulnerable areas	BUILD SELECTIVELY •specialize around limited strengths •seek ways to overcome weaknesses •withdraw if indications of sustainable growth are lacking
medium	BUILD SELECTIVELY •invest heavily in most attractive segments •build up ability to counter competition •emphasize profitability by raising productivity	SELECTIVITY/MANAGE FOR EARNINGS •protect existing program •concentrate investments in segments where profitability is good and risk is relatively low	LIMITED EXPANSION OR HARVEST •look for ways to expand without high risk; otherwise, minimize investment and rationalize operations
low	PROTECT AND REFOCUS •manage for current earnings •concentrate on attractive segments •defend strengths	MANAGE FOR EARNINGS •protect position in most profitable segments •upgrade product line •minimize investment	DIVEST •sell at time that will maximize cash value •cut fixed costs and avoid investment meanwhile

---

6. This figure is a composite of matrices from several sources, including Abell and Hammond (1979), Ohmae (1982), and Robinson, Hichens, and Wade (1978).

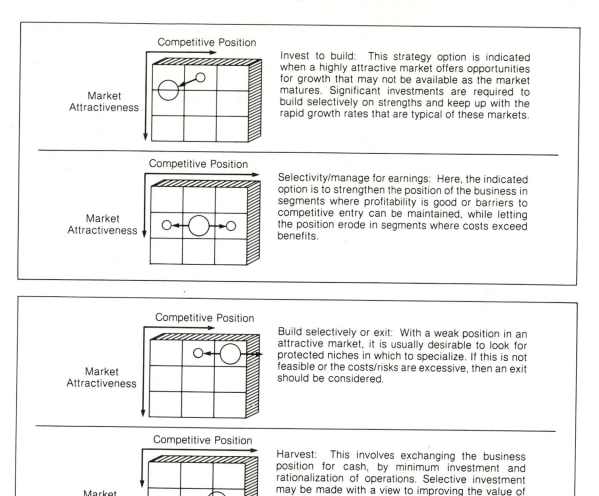

Invest to build: This strategy option is indicated when a highly attractive market offers opportunities for growth that may not be available as the market matures. Significant investments are required to build selectively on strengths and keep up with the rapid growth rates that are typical of these markets.

Selectivity/manage for earnings: Here, the indicated option is to strengthen the position of the business in segments where profitability is good or barriers to competitive entry can be maintained, while letting the position erode in segments where costs exceed benefits.

Build selectively or exit: With a weak position in an attractive market, it is usually desirable to look for protected niches in which to specialize. If this is not feasible or the costs/risks are excessive, then an exit should be considered.

Harvest: This involves exchanging the business position for cash, by minimum investment and rationalization of operations. Selective investment may be made with a view to improving the value of the business if it is to be eventually sold.

Figure 7.3—cont'd

business segment. Some of these options can usefully be portrayed as changes in the portfolio position that reflect the anticipated consequences of alternative investment thrusts. These alternatives may also shift the relative significance from one dimension of the portfolio matrix to the other, as shown in the following examples.

The choice of strategy must of necessity be grounded in the realities of the situation facing each business. Still, it is useful to test the compatibility of the chosen strategy with the generic strategy. Significant discrepancies become an issue only if there is no compelling reason to account for them. Even here, however, specific considerations should always dominate the generic pre-scriptions.

Generic strategies have a number of drawbacks that reduce their usefulness. They presume the business or business segment is autonomous—whereas interdependencies are more likely the case. Furthermore, they do not account for the degree of imbalance of the portfolio. Thus, the ability of the Calumet-Fremont Division to undertake major initiatives with specific product lines is significantly constrained by the general weakness of the portfolio. Finally, the feasibility of a generic strategy, and the corresponding risks and resource requirements, depend largely on the situation.

Limitations of Multifactor Portfolio Models

The widespread and growing acceptance of multifactor portfolio classification is seen by many as a sensible response to the misleading simplifications of the growth-share matrix. Ironically, it is this greater complexity that exposes this portfolio model to both conceptual and methodological criticisms.

Conceptual Limitations.   There is a distinct possibility that the outcome of a multifactor portfolio analysis could simply be a tautological recommendation to invest preferentially in those areas of greatest market attractiveness and strongest competitive position.[7] It is hardly surprising that some companies have found a correlation between the position of a business in a portfolio matrix and the discounted rates of return for specific investment projects proposed by these businesses.[8] If this is the case, why not simply evaluate strategies and projects on standard financial criteria and eliminate the time-consuming development of a portfolio classification? In this view, a positive net present value of risk-adjusted cash flows is de facto evidence of competitive advantage. The weakness in this argument is the extreme susceptibility of the NPV calculations to bias and wishful thinking, and the absence of any disciplined requirement to evaluate the competitive market assumptions from which the financial forecasts are derived. On the other hand, a properly executed portfolio classification should be based on exactly these considerations. Thus, it is more productive to think of the two methods for assessing investment proposals as complementary—for each method has its own merits that tend to protect one from the shortcomings of the other.

---

7. Wensley (1981).
8. Hussey (1978).

Measurement Problems. The conceptual problems are compounded by a frequently noted tendency of management teams to classify a business or product line in an intermediate or medium position on most factors. Either they do not appreciate the issues, or the group members cannot agree among themselves and resolve their conflict with a compromise. The result often is an unwarranted concentration of businesses in the center block—and the matrix loses its discriminating power. This problem may lead managers to be more concerned about unimportant differences in the placement of the business or product line in the matrix, rather than with critical problems with the underlying assumptions.

There are several further problems that are endemic to any composite rating based on multiple factors. First, two businesses or product lines can be assigned identical positions in the portfolio matrix despite dramatic differences in the profile of ratings on the underlying factors. It is possible for one to be high where the other is low, and yet the summed score is the same.[9] In short, a host of information is lost in the process of compressing the complex individual judgments into a single score. While the overall rating of the business on the two dimensions is helpful in communicating a generalized statement about the business, it should not deflect attention from the specific factors. A further reason for caution in dealing with overall ratings is the problem of weighting of factors. Although experience suggests that specifically assigned weights are more trouble than they are worth, having equal weights for each factor is also not a panacea. Here, the problem is that the choice of individual factors may be biased toward an area of market attractiveness or business strength. Thus, one has to be careful to not have three factors relating to market share and one factor for technological position if both are judged to be equally important.

Implementing Portfolio Analysis

Portfolio models—and strategic planning that incorporates a portfolio logic—offer benefits to both business unit and corporate management. However, there are barriers and pitfalls to overcome on the road to realizing these benefits.

Some barriers are inherent in the distortions and simplifications that occur during the construction and interpretation of portfolio

---

9. Wind and Mahajan (1981).

classifications. In particular, portfolio models are poor at reflecting the strategic advantages from interdependencies such as shared sales forces, shared R and D, and so forth. While the potential for misleading insights from these problems is considerable, there is no excuse for their occurrence if the underlying premises of the models are properly understood.

More daunting barriers are confronted when a portfolio is used as more than a diagnostic aid. When the portfolio serves as the bargaining table around which corporate and business management negotiate investment strategies, then there is likely to be major reallocation of resources. This implies a redistribution of power that is likely to be resisted unless the introduction of a portfolio perspective is adroitly handled.

The Benefits of Portfolio Analysis.   A review of the various roles that the portfolio analysis played during the planning process of the Calumet-Fremont Division reveals a number of distinct benefits that accrued primarily to the operating managers. The portfolio provided a structure for analysis that

- helped the management team separate the important issues from the unimportant,
- facilitated the communication and sharing of judgments and assumptions about strategic issues,
- helped isolate information gaps and set priorities for data collection and analysis, and
- forced the management team to project their thinking into the future and consider significant shifts in strategic direction to achieve a more desirable portfolio configuration.

Further benefits resulted when the management team used their portfolio analysis to help justify the investment strategies they were recommending for each business segment. For the first time, corporate management had a clear understanding of the plight of the division, as well as the opportunities. Second, division management gained a much better understanding of corporate expectations, because there was a verbal and graphic framework for communicating in strategic, not just financial, terms.

Evidently, many other companies have had similar experiences. Two surveys—one in 1979 in the United States and a second in Canada in 1983—found that 70 percent of the managers interviewed credited portfolio planning with a sizable to dramatic improvement in the quality of business unit plans. An even higher proportion (84 percent) said there was a sizable to dramatic improvement in corporate management's understanding of individual businesses.[10]

There was also a strong consensus that portfolio planning had lead to significant improvements in corporate management's ability to allocate resources across businesses. A good deal of this benefit came from better control of marginal businesses; there was less wastage of resources on continual subsidization of these businesses. As companies became more experienced with portfolio planning, the businesses with growth opportunities felt liberated from short-run performance pressures and were more likely to propose major growth programs. This further benefited the resource allocation process by ensuring these opportunities were not underfunded.

A Program of Implementation.   Successful users of portfolio analysis and planning have learned some hard lessons about implementation pitfalls.[11] Their experience suggests that prospective adopters should do the following:

- Avoid getting bogged down in trying to introduce the approach throughout the company; instead, move quickly to establish early success by, for example, picking a winner in one division.

- Ensure that line managers understand the basic thinking behind the portfolio approach and participate actively in the analysis. Effective portfolio planning requires strategic thinking at all levels in the organization.

- Treat each business as a portfolio to be managed. Then portfolio analysis and planning become a multilevel activity, combining the detailed view of issues at the segment level and an aggregate perspective on all the businesses for decisions on resource commitments.

- Avoid pejorative labels that deflect management attention from the task of developing feasible strategies grounded in the details of the business situation. For the same reason, generic or natural strategies should be used only as guidelines that are suggestive of the possibilities for the business.

- Invest corporate management time in the review process. Portfolios are facilitating frameworks that encourage

---

10. Haspeslagh (1982) and Canada Consulting Group (1984).

11. These data are drawn in part from Haspeslagh (1982) and Hamermesh and White (1984).

substantive discussion between corporate and business level. But senior management must show their commitment to this approach by the degree of care and attention they give to the review of the resulting strategic plans.

■ Tie resource allocation to the strategic market plan that is negotiated during the review process. A portfolio approach has no teeth unless there are formal links to the capital budgeting process. In particular, the generation and evaluation of capital investment proposals must be made within the context of the investment strategy for each business. No capital should be allocated to businesses or business segments unless it fits explicitly with the strategic thrust.

■ Establish the degree of autonomy, the structure of reporting relationships, and the type of incentive compensation for each business in light of its position and strategic thrust within the portfolio.[12]

Finally, successful implementation must recognize that portfolio analysis and planning approaches deal with only a subset of the strategic challenges facing a business. They are not designed to deal with the development of new business opportunities and may even inhibit creative thinking about these questions, because the focus is solely on the situation of the established businesses and the correction of resource allocation imbalances. Also, by treating each business as autonomous, they inhibit the exploitation of potential strategic advantages derived from the interdependencies between businesses. Despite these limitations, portfolio perspectives on the formulation of business strategies are clearly here to stay, for they deliver significant benefits to both operating and corporate management.

12. Hamermesh and White (1984).

## Other Portfolio Classification and Analysis Models	# *Appendix*

By now it will be evident that a portfolio of businesses, or product lines, can be examined from a number of perspectives. Indeed, it sometimes seems that the possibilities are limited solely by the imagination of the analyst who is trying to structure complex strategic analyses into meaningful patterns. Virtually any combination of performance or descriptive variables can be used for this purpose, although most suffer from extreme ad hocracy and a consequent lack of a sound theoretical or conceptual grounding. The following are indicative of the variety of methods that have been utilized.

ADL Industry Maturity–Competitive Position Matrix

This portfolio model was developed by the consulting firm of Arthur D. Little and Company.[13] It is probably the third most widely used model, in part because it is an interesting hybrid of the BCG growth-share matrix and a multifactor matrix. The two dimensions used to evaluate each business or segment are as follows:

- *Industry maturity.* A business is judged to be in an embryonic, growing, mature, or aging industry on the basis or parameters such as growth rate, growth potential, the distribution and stability of market shares, number of competitors, customer stability, ease of entry, and technological stability.

- *Competitive position.* To classify a business into one of five categories of competitive position (dominant, strong, favorable, tenable, weak), the following determinants of a strong position are considered: capacity utilization close to optimum, satisfactory current profitability, distinctive product advantages protected by patents, and high forward or backward integation relative to competition.

The emphasis on a life-cycle framework is both a strength and a weakness, as we saw in Chapters 3 and 4. If this framework is viable, it is a useful tool for assessment, especially in conjunction with other portfolio models. ADL has used their experience with this matrix to propose basic strategy guidelines for each combination of industry maturity and competitive position (as shown in Figure 7.4).

13. Patel and Younger (1978).

		Embryonic	Growing	Mature	Aging
Dominance	{	All-out push for share	Hold position	Hold position	Hold position
	{	Hold position	Hold share	Grow with industry	
Strong	{	Attempt to improve position	Attempt to improve position	Hold position	Hold position or Harvest
	{	All-out push for share	Push for share	Grow with industry	
Favorable	{	Selective or all-out push for share	Attempt to improve position	Custodial or maintenance	Harvest
	{	Selectively attempt to improve position	Selective push for share	Find niche and attempt to protect	Phased withdrawal
Tenable	{	Selectively push for position	Find niche and protect it	Find niche and hang on or Phased withdrawal	Phased withdrawal or Abandon
Weak	{	Up or Out	Turnaround or Abandon	Turnaround or Phased withdrawal	Abandon

Figure 7.4
Strategic guidelines
for ADL matrix

Directional Policy Matrix

The directional policy matrix was developed by Shell Chemicals U.K. It is a close relative of the market attractiveness–business strength matrix. The major differences are greater precision in the assessment of factor ratings, and somewhat more explicit strategy guidelines.

While usage of this model has waned, it still finds acceptance in the chemical and related capital-intensive industry situations. The derivation of the two dimensions can be seen in the adaptation of this matrix by Chloride Electrical.[14]

Score

(A) *Competitive position rating:*

    (1) *Relative Market Share*

        Preeminent market position   4

        One of the market leaders   3

14. Hughes (1981).

Below the market leaders but a viable stake	2
Low market share	1
Negligible share of the market	0

(2) *Production Capability*

Q: Lower than average relative cost structure?	2
Q: Consistently reliable supplier?	1
Q: Strong managerial resources?	1
Total (out of 4)	

(3) *Servicing Capability*

Q: Wider than average product range?	1
Q: Better than average product range?	1
Q: Leader in successful product innovation	1
Q: Strong brand image?	1
Total (out of 4)	

(4) *Other* (to be specified)

(B) *Business sector prospects rating:*

(1) *Market Size*

Sufficiently large to justify any future expansion	4
	3
Variants within this range	2
	1
Already restricting business growth	0

(2) *Market Growth* (in volume %)

Very high (>5% above GDP)	4
Average (GDP ± 1%)	3
Low (no market growth up to GDP less 1%)	2
Declining	1

(3) *Market Quality* (total out of 4)

Q: High, stable profitability?	2
Q: Evidence of low product price elasticity?	2

(4) *Competitive Structure*

Monopoly producer	4
	3
Variants within this range	2
	1
Free competitive market	0

(5) *Role of Technology* (total out of 4)

Q: Is the current technology of production restricted to those who developed/already use it?	2
Q: Is the technology free from the risk of substitution?	2

(6) *Social/Political/Environmental Considerations*
    Relative Status quo

Strong improvement	4
Improvement	3
No change	2
Deterioration	1
Severe deterioration	0

(7) *Other* (to be specified)

The flavor of the strategy guidelines can be gained from Figure 7.5. However, the precision of these guidelines is questionable, and they should be approached with the same degree of caution accorded to any strategy prescriptions.

PIMS Portfolios

As we noted earlier in the chapter on PIMS, it is possible to submit all the businesses in the corporate portfolio to this type of analysis. The positions of the businesses can be portrayed in at least two different ways:

1. The PAR matrix is a representation of each of the businesses contributed by a company to the PIMS data base in terms of

Figure 7.5
Directional policy matrix

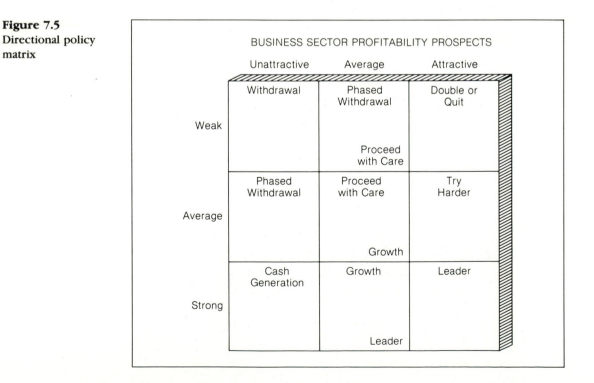

(1) the deviation of the PAR ROI of each business from the mean ROI in the data base and (2) the deviation of actual from PAR ROI for the business. The former is treated as a measure of strength of strategic position, while the latter is a measure of the adequacy of operating performance. The value of this analysis hinges on the extent to which deviation from PAR is really a consequence of operating efficiency rather than of measurement and estimation error.

2. A variant of the PAR matrix compares the actual and desired position of each business in terms of the dimensions of *cash used* versus *cash generated.* This matrix can be useful when applied simply to comparing actual positions, but the inclusion of the desired position (in terms of businesses with similar characteristics) helps to highlight any imbalances in the portfolio.

Classification by Financial Criteria

Numerous financial factors have also been employed for the classification of businesses:

1. The Ronagraph is a plot of return on net assets versus rate of internal deployment of funds, defined as the percentage of funds generated that are reinvested in the business.[15] The observed patterns are then tested for congruency with the industry maturity.

2. A matrix of ROI versus ROS (return on sales) can be insightful when these ratios are emphasized in performance evaluations. The advantage of this matrix is the demonstration that it is possible to achieve high investment returns with low sales returns.

3. The position of a business unit in terms of the reinvestment ratio versus growth in net assets will yield direct insights into the cash surplus or deficit position.

Technology Portfolios

Recent interest in the problems of integrating technology into the strategic planning process has led to portfolio perspectives based on three emerging principles of technology management:

1. The direction and timing of technology evolution can be

---

15. Patel and Younger (1978).

anticipated—it is not as unpredictable and unquantifiable as many believe.

2. Technology should be treated as a strategic resource rather than as an isolated, project-based phenomenon.

3. Investments in technology must be congruent with the business strategy to be effective.

The technology portfolio is a useful tool to facilitate the integration of technology investments. There are two dimensions to this portfolio:

1. Importance of the specific technology to the business strategy, based on criteria such as value-added, rate of technological change, and potential markets and their attractiveness.

2. Relative technological position is basically a measure of the firm's investment in a given technology relative to the competition. Criteria for assessing this position include number of patents, human resource strengths, product history, cost, and current and projected expenditures.

Each of the technologies employed by the business or firm can be assessed and displayed in a matrix defined by these two dimensions. The primary value of the display is to isolate discrepancies between the position of the technology and the strategy implied by the business portfolio and strategic plans.

Strategic Decision Support Systems

Chapter **8**

It is fitting that this concluding chapter deal with the prospects for analytical approaches specifically designed to serve a supportive role in the strategic decision-making process. There is a growing body of opinion that this is the logical next direction in the development of methods of strategy analysis.

Conditions are certainly conducive to the application of decision support systems to strategic issues. First, as we have seen throughout this book, the generic models of strategy analysis are often difficult to adapt to specific circumstances. Skillful usage of portfolio, life-cycle, PIMS, or experience curve analysis depends on knowing when these methods are even appropriate, and how to take idiosyncrasies of the market and competitive situation into account while interpreting their signals. Even when a particular model clearly adds value to the process, it will still illuminate only part of the strategic landscape. This means using several different models at the same time. But even so, many significant questions that are amenable to decision support systems remain unanswered.

The changing nature of strategic decisions also creates an incubator for decision support systems:

> By competitive necessity one makes more decisions more quickly,
> they are often "bigger" decisions, more and more data exist,
> increasingly sophisticated judgment must be applied, multiple
> managers are involved, and the competitive environment is
> constantly shifting. It is a common condition that data exist,
> somewhere in the organization, but are not easily assimilated,
> found, optimally formatted, or readily manipulated.[1]

The capacity of decision support systems to organize and make accessible data banks that yield strategic insights also makes them an

---

1. Lillis and McIvor (1983).

invaluable partner to the other strategy analysis methods. Too often the quality of insights from these methods is compromised by the absence of proper input data.

Finally, trends in the technologies that underlie decision support systems are rapidly enhancing their feasibility. The growing availability of interactive personal computer hardware with abundant memory and user-friendly software is the most obvious driving force. Parallel developments in communication technology, permitting local entry and control of data and access to centralized banks, will have major impacts in the future. In some markets, developments in data collection utilizing automated checkouts, credit card diary panels, and integrated order initiating and processing networks will further encourage adoption.

In summary, the conditions are right and the need is pressing. A big question remains as to whether decision support systems can add value to strategic decisions. To assess this prospect, we first review progress with each of the components: strategic intelligence, models, and optimization.[2] Particular attention is paid to strategic intelligence. This component of a DSS yields the fundamental currency of planning, which is information, and the inputs to the data banks that feed the strategy analysis models. Then the experience of leading-edge users such as Kodak, Xerox, and General Electric is examined for clues as to the pitfalls and payoffs.

What are Decision Support Systems?   A good picture comes from the following characterization.

> The impact is on decisions in which there is sufficient structure for computer and analytic aids to be of value, but where managers' judgment is essential.
>   The pay-off is in extending the range and analysis capability of managers' decision processes to assist them in improving their *effectiveness.*
>   The relevance for managers is in the creation of a decision support tool, which remains under their *control* in that it does not attempt to automate the decision process, impose solutions, or predefine objectives.[3] (Emphasis in original.)

Although the impact of the system should be greater than the sum of the parts, few users have progressed beyond putting the compo-

----

2. Many of the examples in these sections are adapted from Montgomery (1985). Permission to adapt portions of this paper is gratefully acknowledged.

3. Keen and Scott Morton (1978).

nent parts in place. Separate examination of the component parts is warranted, because the issue is decision relevance and not the completeness of the system.

Strategic Intelligence

Decision support systems for strategic marketing need to provide for environmental monitoring, especially the competitive and customer environments. For example, a firm will want to monitor a competitor's capacity (both current and intended), its product announcements, its market share by product-market, speeches by its key executives, its financial performance and capabilities, its personnel activities (especially in technical areas), and even the consultants they are using. The objective is to identify and evaluate the competitor's strategy, assess its capabilities, and understand its goals, objectives, and assumptions about its environment. The end product of all this is hopefully an enhanced ability to predict a competitor's likely actions or reactions in the marketplace. Further, a firm must attend to potential sources of new competition—technical substitutes, new entrants (especially foreign), forward integration by supplier, and backward integration by buyers.

Strategic Intelligence Systems (SIS)

An SIS is the feeder to the analysis and use stages of the intelligence cycle (shown in Figure 8.1), in which data are transformed into decisions with the aid of models.[4] An SIS performs three crucial functions: *directing* the intelligence activities, *collecting* data, and *transforming* data into information that is available at the point of decision. The development of an SIS is an iterative and evolutionary process, driven in part by the increasing sophistication of management needs for relevant information.

Directing Intelligence Activities. Ideally, one would like to know everything possible about all the strong and weak influences on the long-run performance of the business. This would probably be more like a nightmare than an ideal, for there is no end to the data one could conceivably collect. To avoid being overwhelmed, it is im-

---

4. Montgomery and Weinberg (1979).

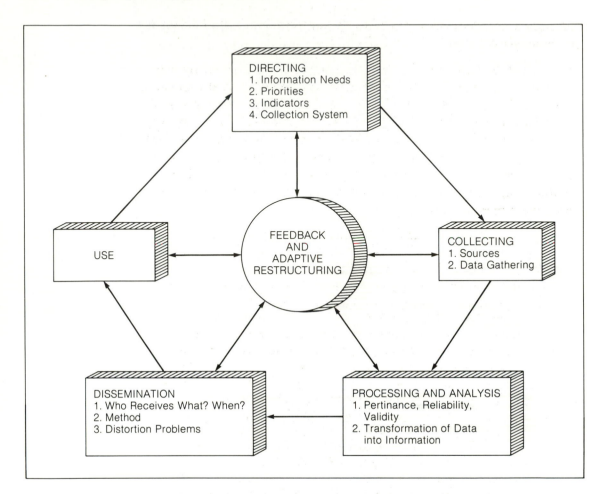

Figure 8.1
Strategic intelligence
systems

Source: Montgomery
and Weinberg (1979).

portant to set priorities on which of all the possible events require attention. These priorities should consider (1) the importance of the event in terms of speed and possible magnitude of impact, (2) the likelihood the event will occur, and (3) the costs of anticipation and reaction. Both importance and costs will also be influenced by the strategy being pursued. The desire to "gain share via a new product innovation" requires extensive primary intelligence about the customer's willingness to accept the change, the nature and likely response of the competitors being displaced, the potential reaction of the wholesalers and retailers, and in some cases the acceptability of the product by the government. Other strategies such as "defense via distribution" may require less first-hand knowledge and more focus on the distribution and competitive tactics. Strategies aimed at harvesting may demand little intelligence except the ability to identify a catastrophe that may force and accelerate the harvest or even an abrupt exit.[5]

Collecting Intelligence.   Useful intelligence is collected by selective scanning of the environment. Scanning entails both surveillance and search. Surveillance is a broad viewing and monitoring activity for the purpose of detecting signals that suggest a strategic response. By contrast, search implies a highly directed investigation, triggered by changes uncovered during surveillance. Montgomery and Weinberg describe how one company utilized the finding from their ongoing competitive surveillance that a major competitor had sold an important manufacturing operation:[6]

> Since the company knew from its own operations that this manufacturing activity was the most profitable portion of its own vertically integrated chain of activities, the question arose as to why the competitor had sold this operation. Two potential reasons seemed apparent: (1) the competitor, a closely held company, was in a serious cash bind and was forced to sell this profitable operation in order to improve its financial position or (2) the competitor had made a breakthrough that would render the old technology either obsolete or at least substantially less valuable. Set against the background of data the company had, both answers seemed plausible. Learning the true answer had important strategic significance. If done for financial reasons, this could signal either competitor vulnerability or a reduction in his vulnerability depending upon the results of a further investigation. On the other hand, if the competitor had made some technological breakthroughs, then the company could no longer assume a stable environment. Clearly early resolution of these uncertainties was required.

The array of sources of data is formidable, but their contribution of useful intelligence is often limited. A good deal of experience is required before deciding which sources should be utilized and believed. Some of the possibilities and limitations are shown in Table 8.1.

Processing and Analysis.   The first analysis question concerns the pertinence, reliability, and validity (accuracy) of the data. Data is pertinent if it is responsive to the needs of decision makers. Reliability

---

5. Rothschild (1979).
6. Montgomery and Weinberg (1979).

Table 8.1 Sources of Intelligence

SOURCE	EXAMPLES	COMMENT
Government	Freedom of Information Act Government Contract Administration	1974 amendments have led to accelerating use. Examination of competitor's bids and documentation may reveal competitor's technology and indicate his costs and bidding philosophy.
	Patent filings	Belgium and Italy publish patent applications shortly after they are filed. Some companies (e.g., pharmaceutical) patent their mistakes in order to confuse their competitors.
Competitors	Annual reports and 10Ks	FTC and SEC line of business reporting requirements will render this source more useful in the future.
	Speeches and public announcements of competitor's officers	Reveal management philosophy, priorities, and self-evaluation systems.
	Products	Systematic analysis of a competitor's products via back engineering may reveal the competitor's technology and enable the company to monitor changes in the competitor's engineering and assembly operations. Forecasts of a competitor's sales may often be made from observing his serial numbers over time.
	Employment ads	May suggest the technical and marketing directions in which a competitor is headed.
	Consultants	For example, if a competitor has retained Boston Consulting, then portfolio management strategies become more likely.
Suppliers	Banks, advertising agencies, public relations firms, and direct mailers and catalogers, as well as hard goods suppliers	Have a tendency to be more talkative than competitors since the information transmitted may enhance supplier's business. Can be effective sources of information on such items as competitor's equipment installations and on what retail competitors are already carrying certain product lines. Suppliers biases can usually be recognized.

Table 8.1—*Continued*

SOURCE	EXAMPLES	COMMENT
Customers	Purchasing Agents	Generally regarded as self-serving. Low reliability as a source.
	Customer engineers and corporate officers	Valued sources of intelligence. One company taught its salespersons to perform elementary service for customers in order to get the salespersons past the purchasing agent and on to the more valued sources of intelligence.
Professional Associations and Meetings	Scientific and technical society meetings, management association meetings	Examine competitor's products, research and development, and management approach as revealed in displays, brochures, scientific papers, and speeches.
Company Personnel	Executives, sales force, engineers and scientists, purchasing agents	Sensitize them to the need for intelligence and train them to recognize and transmit to the proper organizational location relevant intelligence which comes to their attention.
Other Sources	Consultants, management service companies, and the media	Wide variety of special purpose and syndicated reports available.

Source: Montgomery and Weinberg (1979).

asks whether there are systematic biases in the data that are inherent in the source, as in the selectivity or optimism in sales force reports. Validity pertains to the accuracy or truthfulness of the data itself.

The basic steps in processing data to convert it into useful information are as follows:

- Transmission from point of entry to the point of usage.
- Storage of data in a form that permits later retrieval.
- Aggregation of many data points into a smaller set of pertinent information.
- Analysis of the data in order to find patterns and measure relations among variables. This step is facilitated by the models discussed in the next section.

Table 8.2 Basic Steps in Processing Data

NAME	DESCRIPTION	BRIEF EXAMPLES
1. Transmission	1. Moving data from one point to another	1a) Manager in one company who receives information personally or by telephone from line managers and distributes information personally or by weekly newsletters
		1b) Highly mechanized interactive computer system to make data base reachable by numerous managers
2. Accumulation	2. Storing data in one place; implies some notion of retrievability	2a) Corporate libraries or computer systems
		2b) Not frequently observed in practice, managers tend to keep data in their heads or in individualized data bases ("little black book")
3. Aggregation	3. Many data points brought together into a smaller set, which is usually more easily accessed	3a) Use of computer program to reduce thick Nielsen reports to much shorter documents
		3b) Page length limitation on planning documents

■ Mixing. This includes all conscious efforts to bring together the apparently unrelated data spread throughout an organization to identify linkages. Often this is done during participatory planning meetings within business units, and across organizational levels and functions.

A number of examples of each of these steps are described in Table 8.2.

Models for Decision Support Systems

Models can range from something as simple as a way to organize data—in which the underlying structure is quite implicit—to an explicit set of structural relationships such as PIMS. The explicit models also vary by the degree to which they are tailor-made to fit

Table 8.2—*Continued*

NAME	DESCRIPTION	BRIEF EXAMPLES
4. Analysis	4. The analysis, usually formal, of data in order to seek and measure relations	4a) Use of econometric consulting firms to provide forecasts of the economy 4b) Use of Shell's Directional Policy Matrix to locate businesses for a portfolio analysis
5. Mix	5. Passing of data around to a variety of managers looking for possible links. The data is often not well ordered	5a) CEO insists on plans which show multiple inputs at each phase 5b) Open planning meetings in which managers must give and defend plans before colleagues
6. Pattern Recognition	6. A more informal, less analytic process than analysis (4) in which patterns or relations are sought. Can be a result of the other five functions described.	6a) Combining plant closing, financial and product change information to recognize a competitor is short of cash 6b) Special purpose competitor studies & role playing or the use of adversary teams

Source: Montgomery and Weinberg (1979).

a particular decision situation. Most of the models we have looked at in this book have fairly general structures that accommodate many circumstances. This is not so for the models that are usually built into a decision support system. The structure of these models is handcrafted for a particular class of problems (sales force allocation or new product entry strategies) or for a unique industry setting (financial services or pharmaceuticals, for example). For strategic market decisions, the most useful models are those used to generate conditional sales forecasts. In this section, we also look into the potential value of optimization models that seek to identify the best strategy.

Conditional Sales Forecasting Models

A major step in the generation, evaluation, and selection of strategic options is the construction of conditional sales forecasts. Such forecasts project revenues, units, and market shares given different strategic moves by the business and various assumptions about competitive actions and the economic environment. While such conditional forecasts may be constructed directly, the use of models generally facilitates this process. Their contribution may include the following:

- Helping managers focus upon areas of agreement and disagreement in the construction of conditional sales forecasts. The specificity of model-based analysis facilitates this process.

- Facilitating sensitivity analysis to determine which factors (firm actions, competitor actions, or environmental events) have the greatest leverage on the outcomes and which are of secondary importance.

- Identifying the measures to be obtained with marketing research. The construction of a model-based conditional forecast will suggest what factors should be measured in order to make such a forecast. Further, sensitivity analysis of a model may suggest that a few factors are vital in determining outcomes. Measurement attention should then focus on vital factors where there is disagreement about market impact.

- Providing a basis for analyzing and projecting market measurements.

The contribution of models to these conditional sales forecasting tasks can be best seen from several examples where the complexity of the environment swamped conventional approaches. The first is Xerox's introduction of the 9700 Electronic Printing System, a computer-controlled laser-scanning computer printer.[7] When launched in 1978, the 9700 was Xerox's largest development project outside its main business. However, the project was nearly killed when IBM announced its own high-speed laser-scanning system. In what has been described as a controversial decision, Xerox decided to keep the project alive for one more year by allocating just enough funds to keep the key elements of the technical team together. This core team was told to use the year to generate a credible market forecast.

In order to generate a credible market forecast, the study team first developed a model of the process whereby customers would

7. Oren, Rothkopf, and Smallwood (1980).

Figure 8.2 Xerox
forecasting system

Source: Oren, Rothkopf, and Smallwood (1980).

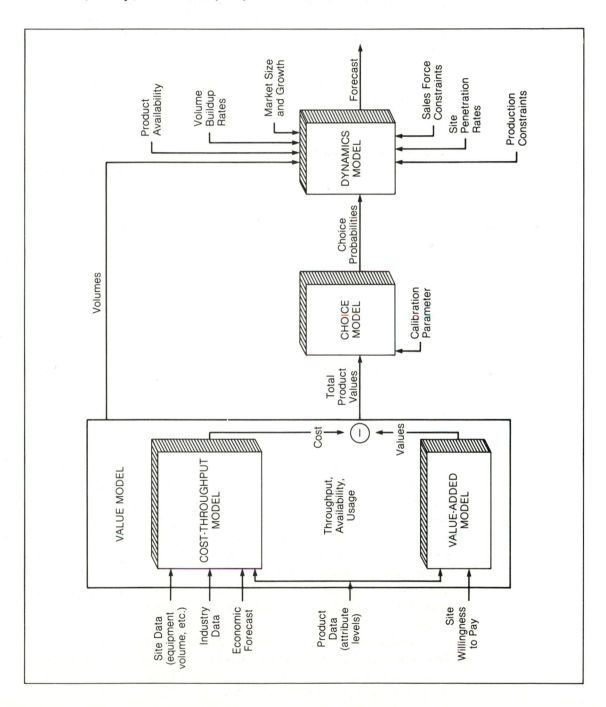

choose among computer printers. For a given computer site, the model predicts the customer's product choices and level of usage of the chosen printer. The forecasting system incorporated three interrelated models: a value model, a choice model, and a market dynamics model. These are shown in Figure 8.2. The value model was built up from two submodels that balance cost and value-added. The cost throughput submodel determines the minimum cost configuration of impact and nonimpact computer printers given the existing hardware on the site, the site's workload, paper costs, and printer availability. The output of this submodel is an optimal printer configuration for the site as well as the direct costs, throughput, availability, and usage of computer printers at the site. The value-added submodel establishes a dollar value for intangible product attributes such as brand name, reliability, and copy quality. Direct costs and value-added then become inputs to the choice model. The output of the choice model is a product choice assuming all alternative products are fully available and each customer is fully aware of all of the alternatives. The market dynamics model then modifies the estimated choice to reflect differences in product availability, awareness, and penetration rates. It also accounts for customer resistance to change. The final output is a detailed forecast of product requirements and usage over time.

The model was constructed prior to any field marketing research. It dictated ahead of time the measures that would be needed to construct the forecast. Telephone and personal interviews were conducted with a stratified sample of about one hundred installations from International Data Corporation's computer site files. These interviews provided the data to estimate both the value and the choice models. When the field data were collected, the analysis proceeded quickly because of the availability of the model to provide a sensible structure.

Forecasts were then created for a wide variety of competitive product scenarios. Each of these scenarios consisted of competitive products and their associated attributes, product introduction dates, product launch strategies (e.g., timing of city openings), sales force sizes, and production constraints. In one set of scenarios, top management wanted to see what would happen to the 9700 unit forecasts if a major competitor were to introduce a low-cost, high-speed computer printer using a new technology. To their surprise, a series of forecasts based upon successively lower prices for this competitor's potential product were found not to noticeably reduce the demand forecast for the Xerox 9700 until the hypothetical printer had greatly reduced the forecast for other nonimpact printers. This meant the competitor would cannibalize a great deal of its own demand if it were to choose such a strategy. After exploring many such scenarios, Xerox management became convinced that the 9700 product should be launched.

In addition to the fundamental "go" decision on the 9700, the model also influenced other elements of the prelaunch strategy. The model assured management that the timing of introduction and the planned geographical constrained product introduction were appropriate. Tests of alternative pricing strategies suggested an unusual pricing plan that would effectively eliminate the usual incremental pricing charge between 1 million and 1.4 million impressions per month. This pricing scheme was adopted and remained in use for five years after the launch of the 9700. Management continued to utilize the forecasting system to help with the evaluation of proposed product enhancements, such as two-sided printing. These evaluations were used to allocate resources and set priorities for enhancements.

The model-driven forecasting system turned Xerox around on the 9700. As of June 1981, the 1,000th 9700 was installed. This translates into a revenue base of approximately $10 million per month. The forecasts have stood up well over time. However, the fundamental impact of the model-structured forecasting system was to focus the debate over the future of the 9700 printer on the assumptions. The decision process changed from a negotiation over plausible forecasts in absence of credible data, to a dialogue over critical assumptions.

RCA's entry strategy into the satellite communications business provides another example of a model-based analysis playing a major role in a strategic decision. The model was a probabilistic simulation of the interactions and relationships among a collection of important variables.[8] The variables included the size and mix of potential markets, competitive actions from both terrestrial and other satellite carriers, and combinations of satellite characteristics with launch vehicles. After evaluating approximately three hundred strategy alternatives using the model, the model development team recommended an immediate and independent RCA market entry using a particular satellite. The investment requirement was on the order of $125 million over the first five years. Although this recommendation was at variance with management's initial expectations and plans, it was adopted in only slightly modified form within six months of the original recommendation. The model enables the managers and the model developers to compare many more strategy combinations than could ever have been done without the structure and the rapid

---

8. Nigam (1975).

manipulation power provided by the model. RCA has subsequently used this approach in assessing other new business opportunities.

Conditional forecasting models such as those at Xerox and RCA have also been useful for developing brand strategies for frequently purchased consumer products. A good example is the BRANDAID Model for evaluating marketing mix options.[9] This model uses a combination of historical data analysis and field experimentation—overridden as necessary by management judgment—to first develop a momentum forecast. This is a baseline forecast that incorporates what is known about market trends, competitive actions, and the impact of the current marketing program. Then the model takes account of management judgments as to the responsiveness of market demand to price, promotion, and advertising. These "response coefficients" are used to judge the sales and profit impact of changes in the company's marketing program from the levels established for the momentum forecast. If the management team does not believe the market is very advertising-sensitive, then changes in advertising expenditures will have little impact on sales or share—but may have a lot of influence on profits. Both short-run and long-run effects would have to be considered. The model may also be used to determine what would happen if the competitors change their strategy and the company elects to either ignore these moves or aggressively retaliate.

Optimization Models

Optimization models search for the market strategy that will best achieve management's objectives while accounting for possible resource constraints. The potential contribution of such models will be assessed by looking at two recent examples. The first deals with the question of defining the market scope in the context of a firm selecting target end-user markets. The second develops an explicit cash flow and profit model suitable for conducting a portfolio analysis.

Market Selection Model (MSM).   The MSM is used to choose the set of target markets—from among many possible end-user markets—that will best achieve the company objectives.[10] An end-use market is any customer or customer group that can be characterized by a single attribute profile. Each end-use market is described by a set of attributes such as growth, revenue, net income, ROI, cash flow, and

9. Little (1975), (1979).
10. Zoltners and Dodson (1983).

cyclicality. Timing of production demand may also be an attribute of interest to a firm seeking to balance production to avoid capacity constraints. A key aspect of the MSM is the specification of functions that aggregate the attributes in the profile across the end-use markets. This yields an estimate, for example, of total company revenue after aggregating the revenues of the individual end-use markets.

Given a set of end-use markets each described in terms of the attribute profile, MSM will enable management to address any of the following problems.

1. Choose the end-use markets that best match a specified profile on the aggregate market attributes.

2. Identify a set of end-use markets so that certain minimum and maximum constraints on the aggregate attributes are satisfied.

3. Find a set of end-use markets that maximize (or minimize) some aggregate attribute while holding other aggregate attributes within some specified ranges.

MSM was implemented within a division of a large commercial bank, with the following results.

- The division's profits rose 5 percent as a result of the alteration in market emphasis suggested by the model.

- The profit increase was achieved by reducing the division's staff size.

- The analysis indicated that for the twelve end-use markets, one should be dropped, one cut back, and several others should receive more emphasis.

- The division's prospect conversion rates were found to be too low to support the current level of effort.

STRATPORT (for STRATegic PORTfolio planning) is an on-line model designed to both evaluate portfolio strategies and suggest an optimal allocation of marketing resources across strategic business units.[11] The key relationships in the model for each business unit are as shown in Figure 8.3. Using a combination of data and management judgment, the relationships in Figure 8.3 are calibrated for each current and potential business unit. The objective of the STRATPORT optimization model is to find the allocation of marketing resources across the SBUs (current and potential) that will maximize the dis-

---

11. Larréché and Srinivasan (1981), (1982).

Figure 8.3
Relationships in the
STRATPORT model

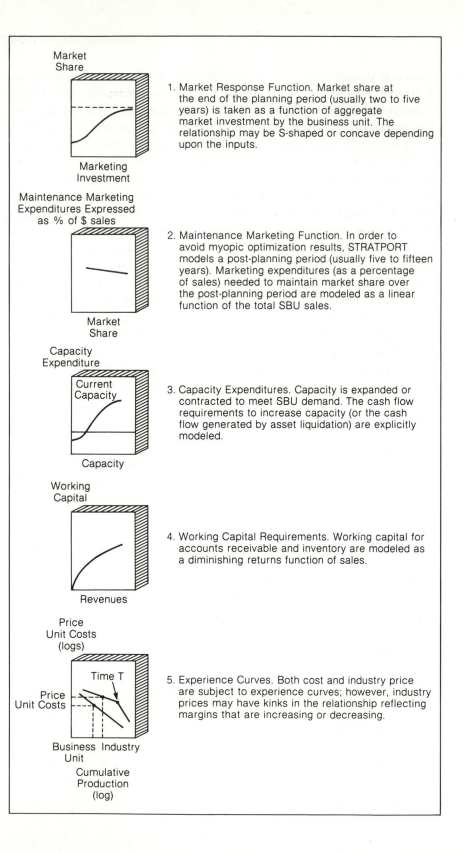

Market
Share

Marketing
Investment

1. Market Response Function. Market share at the end of the planning period (usually two to five years) is taken as a function of aggregate market investment by the business unit. The relationship may be S-shaped or concave depending upon the inputs.

Maintenance Marketing
Expenditures Expressed
as % of $ sales

Market
Share

2. Maintenance Marketing Function. In order to avoid myopic optimization results, STRATPORT models a post-planning period (usually five to fifteen years). Marketing expenditures (as a percentage of sales) needed to maintain market share over the post-planning period are modeled as a linear function of the total SBU sales.

Capacity
Expenditure

Current
Capacity

Capacity

3. Capacity Expenditures. Capacity is expanded or contracted to meet SBU demand. The cash flow requirements to increase capacity (or the cash flow generated by asset liquidation) are explicitly modeled.

Working
Capital

Revenues

4. Working Capital Requirements. Working capital for accounts receivable and inventory are modeled as a diminishing returns function of sales.

Price
Unit Costs
(logs)

Time T

Price
Unit Costs

Business   Industry
Unit

Cumulative
Production
(log)

5. Experience Curves. Both cost and industry price are subject to experience curves; however, industry prices may have kinks in the relationship reflecting margins that are increasing or decreasing.

counted present value of the profit stream over the planning and post-planning periods subject to a cash flow constraint. STRATPORT explicitly allows for different discount rates to be used for each business unit, thereby linking the strategic perspective of portfolio analysis to the risk considerations of financial portfolio theory.

Each of the five basic relationships is difficult to obtain, and some may be beyond the capacity of managers. The greatest difficulties are likely to be found with the aggregate response function of market share to marketing investment. For this relationship to be meaningful, the manager providing the inputs must creatively consider segmentation and positioning options and possible competitive responses while also estimating the sales consequences of interactions among the different elements of the marketing mix. A further difficulty is that the model specifies a continuous function, while experience suggests that strategic alternatives and the corresponding investments tend to be lumpy and few in number. For example, acquisitions and joint ventures will likely create discontinuous market response functions, since they do not happen in degrees. In view of these limitations, the model is best used to help identify a few attractive resource allocation strategies that can then be analyzed in depth.

Building the Capability to Support Strategic Decisions

Effective decision support systems seldom spring to life in their ultimate, full-blown form. Instead, they evolve from simple structures and data bases to incorporate more complex and ambitious models, as managers learn from using the system and want to extend their analyses. The patterns of evolution vary considerably, depending on the sophistication of the organization, the decision requirements, and the availability of data banks. The influence of these three factors can be seen from the following examples.

Experience With a Retailing DSS

The retailing DSS was designed to help a large mass retailer improve its planning activities.[12] The foundation was a straightforward annual marketing planning and resource allocation model with the following structure.

12. Lodish (1981).

Inputs—reference conditions,

—marketing plan alternatives,

—assumed market growth and economic scenarios,

—managerial estimates of the sensitivity of sales to changes in marketing variables.

Outputs—sales and profits anticipated for the marketing plan based on the system inputs,

—an evaluation of the marginal profitability of changes in the marketing mix.

These analyses could be done for a separate department or group of departments, or for different subgroups of stores.

As management gained experience with the system, they realized the estimates of the response elasticities were not as good as they would have liked. Therefore, management added three other components to the system as methods for evaluating these elasticities:

1. A national campaign and event evaluation system was designed to estimate the sales effectiveness of large national campaigns or events seen periodically by the retailer. This system takes internal sales data from a sample of stores and examines the promoted items before, during, and after the national event.

2. A market experiment system was designed to be used when the national campaign and event system did not provide high-quality estimates of sensitiveness. Typically, the sample of stores used here is specific to the design of the particular experiment being conducted.

3. An interactive data base and analysis system was developed to provide managers with a continuous picture of how well the marketing activities were doing. The data base is a nationally representative sample of stores, used to track the effectiveness of past decisions, provide rapid response to ad hoc managerial questions, and act as a general working system for identifying problems early.

System acceptance was assured for the best of all reasons; usage led to demonstrable profit improvements that could not have been achieved otherwise. For example, one experiment provided an estimate of incremental sales per $1,000 of television expenditures as $11,700, whereas magazines, which had been the most heavily used media, yielded incremental sales of only $4,200. After the shift to television, the item being advertised became one of the most successful in the history of the group of stores. Acceptance of the system was enhanced by the effectiveness of an interface person who related the manager's needs to the DSS and translated the output into the manager's terminology. Having a real-time, interactive system also helped by allowing rapid response to critical questions. As a result, many more alternatives could be considered than was possible before the model. All these factors contributed to the decision by top management to develop a longer-range version of the system so that strategic planning scenarios could be evaluated over a five-year planning horizon.

An Incremental System Development Process

The General Electric experience in applying marketing decision support systems is both instructive and cautionary.[13] The diversity of this company means that at least one of almost every conceivable "type" of MDSS exists somewhere. Yet, few of these applications satisfy the requirements for a complete system in which data banks, models, optimization, and interrogation capabilities are integrated. Seldom are the complete systems fully used even when they do exist. The main inhibitors to further acceptance are traceable to uncertainty about product-market definitions and the marketing mix response functions. To properly understand these problems, we need to first understand the variety of existing capabilities (classified in two dimensions in Figure 8.4) and the level of usage.

The sophistication dimension ranges from simple data bases of sales transactions, which are sometimes manipulated manually, to statistical analyses of these data for demand forecasting, to alternative scenario analyses and interactive modeling of strategy alternatives. Most of the automated MDSSs are recent creations. Historically, the responsibility for information systems has been given to the finance function. The problem is that the level of detail required by the finance function is different from the level required to guide market decisions. As a result, information on orders, sales, and margins as well as competitive actions and the external environment has not been tied to meaningful market segments.

The strategic relevance dimension locates each MDSS according to its ability to support strategic versus tactical decisions. Systems that are limited to data base storage and retrieval are predominantly used to support tactical decisions. For example, System D in Figure

---

13. Lillis and McIvor (1983).

Figure 8.4 Range of MDSS capability in GE

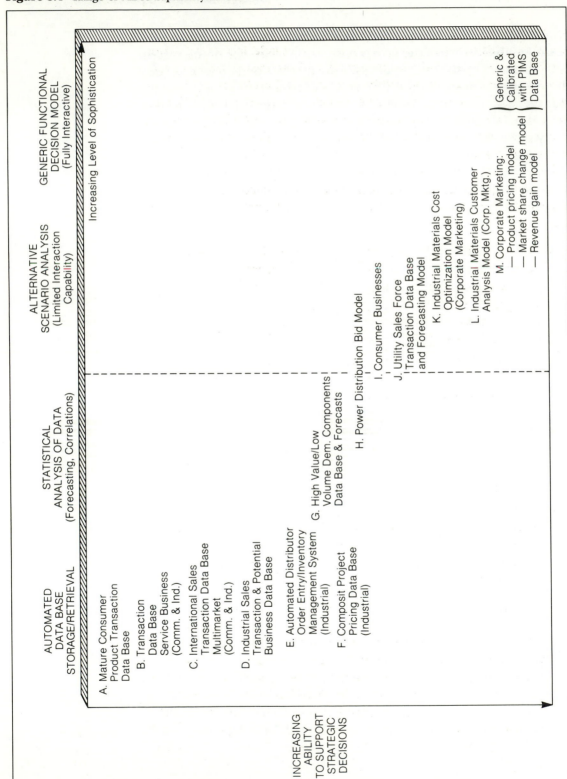

8.4 supports an industrial sales organization. There are three components to this overall system. Two use direct field inputs on major orders pending. These are used to track and forecast pending (available) business based on monthly or quarterly entries by each sales representative. The third component is an actual order-tracking data base, in which the input is part of the order process. The data can be retrieved by customer type, by product category, by sales engineer, or by region.

Systems that are data management and analysis directed are often designed to guide tactical decisions, but may be useful in support of strategic decisions. Two examples give a good flavor of the possibilities:

- A high-value/low-volume OEM component business has built market data bases and analytic programs to forecast parts and service needs of all existing components in use by customers. The data base is worldwide and continually updated with inputs from field sales. A forecasting capability is being incorporated.

- A power distribution bid model takes as input a given customer's bill of material for a specific power project, and combines that with the customer's economic evaluation of the project and the economics of production by GE. The prime output is a bid on these products, but the program also determines production needs, initiates necessary raw material orders, and is linked to a computer-aided design and manufacturing capability.

The most sophisticated systems are those that provide direct strategic decision support by simulating the consequences of alternative environmental scenarios, or testing the revenue, share, or profit outcomes of different strategic moves. Again, specific examples are the best way to understand the possibilities here:

- A utility sales organization has created an extensive data base on worldwide power-generating capacity from field input, along with an interactive model to forecast long-term generating needs by country. It allows managers to change their assumptions about growth rates of population, electricity usage, and GNP to develop various scenarios of future demand for power generation facilities. This type of scenario analysis is particularly suited to the long-range planning horizons dictated by the extended lead times in the industry.

■ Corporate marketing has developed three models of the market share change impacts of changes in six strategic variables. Each model is generic to a broad category of industrial market structure and has been calibrated with the PIMS data base. One application of this model reviewed twenty-one industrial product lines and compared their planned share growth with predicted growth—given their planned efforts in field selling, media and product quality, and their current market position. The purpose was not to second-guess the strategies but to make sure their forecast consequences were not out of line with environmental realities.

The Pattern of Evolution.   Clearly, the majority of the MDSSs are simply data bases of sales transactions. However, they have been most useful when combined with the organizational, economic, and marketing correlates for these transactions. The statistical analyses of the data have been mostly used to forecast demand, and then analyze these forecasts by product line, market segment, and geographic area. Few users in nonconsumer SBUs have progressed beyond this stage of development. The market share change model, which has been shown to be quite effective, gained only one continuing user. A number of possible inhibitors—present in the GE or any other corporate environment—seem to be impeding progress.

■ The gains in performance from bringing data and statistics to bear on problems has been so pronounced that the perceived incremental gain from further model enhancements is low.

■ Many SBUs are structured along product divisions, so that data often do not correspond to relevant market boundaries.

■ Good estimates of market response are hard to obtain in industrial settings, making the empirical foundation unstable and suspect. Part of the problem is that market experimentation is risky in these markets.

■ Until recently, the development of on-line systems has been costly, and subsequent access was often awkward.

For the foreseeable future, it appears that primary emphasis will be given to developing market data and applying statistical models. This pattern will be encouraged by the widespread availability of personal computers for data storage and flexible format reporting.

More sophisticated MDSSs will begin to emerge only when their contribution can be persuasively documented. After all, significant departures from the way decisions have traditionally been made are at stake, and will be embraced cautiously.

Summary: The Challenge of Implementation

The effective introduction of a decision support system—or any strategic planning model—requires an understanding of the costs, benefits, and especially the people involved. What is their capacity to use the new systems? How secure are they in their positions? How traditional are their values? Are they willing to experiment with new ideas and methods? To understand these issues, Barabba has proposed a series of six critical questions that he has employed during the installation of two different decision support systems.[14] In his experience the first one is pivotal, for without an affirmative answer nothing enduring will happen.

1. Have those who manage the organization agreed there is a need that will utilize the change being proposed? And, have they designated a champion—a person or a group of people—to make sure the change comes about?

2. Who has participated in planning for the change? Who has not? The obvious answer is that all stakeholders should participate. This includes those with knowledge who can aid in the solution process and those who need to understand the reason for change to ensure eventual implementation.

3. What, if anything, does the change modify or replace?

   Within Kodak the DSS replaced a system that focused on reacting to current problems. There was no way to foresee or understand a potential problem before it occurred. The DSS, however, forced a disciplined examination of the implicit assumptions about the future.

4. Who within the organization will benefit immediately as a result of the DSS? Who will benefit over the longer term?

---

14. Barabba (1983).

5. Who will suffer immediately? Who will suffer over the longer term?

   Two groups are likely to be affected: those that like stability and those whose organizational influence is based on either a real or a perceived control over information. If the DSS permits these controllers to be bypassed, their role will be diminished.

6. How will the change affect the major relationships within the organization:
   - individual job relationships?
   - organizational relationships?
   - informal relationships?

These questions must yield answers that ensure the DSS or other strategic planning tool enhances management decision making and is not an obstructive step backward. The acquisition of an experience base on how to achieve this objective is a slow and often painful process. Many steps have already been taken on this route and many more will be taken, for the rewards are worth the effort.

Bibliography

Aaker, David A., and George S. Day. "The Perils of High Growth Markets." *Strategic Management Journal* (October-December 1985).

Abell, Derek, F., and John S. Hammond. *Strategic Market Planning: Problems and Analytical Approaches.* Englewood Cliffs, N.J.: Prentice-Hall, 1979.

Abernathy, William J., and James M. Utterback. "Patterns of Industrial Innovation." *Technology Review* 80 (1978): 41–47.

Abernathy, William J., and K. Wayne. "Limits of the Learning Curve." *Harvard Business Review* 52 (1974): 109–19.

Alberts, William W., and James M. McTaggart. "Value Based Strategic Investment Planning." *Interfaces* 14 (January–February 1984): 138–51.

Amit, Raphael, and Chaim Fershtman. "The Experience Curve Revisited: Strategic Implications of the Dynamic Interrelationship Between Scale and Experience Effects." *Strategic Management Journal* (forthcoming 1985).

Anderson, Carl, R., and Frank T. Paine. "PIMS: A Reexamination." *Academy of Management Review* (July 1978): 602–12.

Andrews, Kenneth R. "Replaying the Board's Role in Formulating Strategy." *Harvard Business Review* 59 (May–June 1981): 18–19.

Ayal, Igal. "International Product Life Cycle: A Re-Assessment and Product Policy Implications." *Journal of Marketing* 45 (Fall 1981).

Ballon, Robert J., Iwao Tomita, and Hajime Usami. *Financial Reporting in Japan.* Tokyo: Kodansha International, 1982.

Barabba, Vincent P. "Steel Axes for Stone Age Men." In *Marketing in an Electronic Age,* edited by Robert D. Buzzell. Cambridge, Mass.: Harvard Business School Press, 1985.

Bass, Frank M. "A New Product Growth Model for Consumer Durables." *Management Science* 15 (January 1969): 215-27.

————. "The Relationship Between Diffusion Rates, Experience Curves, and Demand Elasticities for Consumer Durable Technological Innovations." *Journal of Business* 53 (1980): 551–67.

Bass, Frank M., Phillippe Cattin, and Dick R. Wittink. "Firm Effects and Industry Effects in the Analysis of Market Structure and Profitability." *Journal of Marketing Research* 15 (February 1978): 3-10.

Beevan, Alan. "The U.K. Potato Crisp Industry, 1960–1972: A Study of New Entry Competition." *Journal of Industrial Economics* 22 (June 1974): 281–97.

Biggadike, Ralph. *Entering New Markets: Strategies and Performance.* Cambridge, Mass.: Marketing Science Institute, 1977.

————. *Scott-Air Corporation (B).* Colgate Darden School, University of Virginia, 1977.

Bishop, William S., John L. Graham, and Michael H. Jones. "Volatility of Derived Demand in Industrial Markets and Its Management Implications." *Journal of Marketing* 48 (Fall 1984): 95–102.

Booz, Allen, and Hamilton. *New Products: Best Practices—Today and Tomorrow.* Cambridge, Mass.: 1982.

Boston Consulting Group. *Perspectives on Experience.* Boston: Boston Consulting Group, 1972.

————. "The Experience Curve Reviewed: I. The Concept." Boston: Boston Consulting Group (Perspectives, no. 124), 1973.

————. *Strategy Alternatives for the British Motor Industry.* London: Her Majesty's Stationary Office, 1975.

Branch, Ben. "Above-PAR or Below-PAR Profitability." Strategic Planning Institute, Cambridge, Mass.: 1981.

Burck, Gilbert. "The Myths and Realities of Corporate Pricing." *Fortune* (April 1972).

Burnett, Stephen C. "The Ecology of Building, Harvesting, and Holding Market Share." *Research in Marketing* 6 (1983): 1–63.

Business Week. "The New Planning." (19 December 1978).

————. "IVECO: A Brash Attempt to Exploit Its Harvester Connection." (17 May 1982): 132–39.

————. "Matsushita: Seeking Industrial Markets While Staying Strong in Home Products." (17 May 1982): 132–39.

————. "Videodisc Markets Make an Amazing About-Face." (20 September 1982): 119–22.

————. "Who's Excellent Now." (5 November 1984): 76–88.

————. "Black and Decker Saws Off a Loser." (8 November 1982): 45–46.

———. "The Coming Shake-Out in Personal Computers." (22 November 1982): 72–78.

———. "Ralston Purina: Dumping Products That Led it Away from Checkerboard Square." (31 January 1983): 63–64.

———. "Big Times for Tiny TV's." (18 April 1983): 73–74.

———. "Personal Computers: And the Winner Is IBM." (3 October 1983): 76–95.

———. "U.S. Memory Makers Are Regaining Lost Ground." (2 April 1984): 70–72.

———. "The Anatomy of RCA's Videodisc Failure." (23 April 1984).

———. "The New Breed of Strategic Planner." (17 September 1984).

Buzzell, Robert D. "Competitive Behavior and Product Life Cycles." In *New Ideas for Successful Marketing,* edited by John Wright and Jac Goldstrucker. Chicago: American Marketing Association, 1966.

———. "Are There Natural Market Structures?" *Journal of Marketing* 45 (Winter 1981): 42–51.

———. "Is Vertical Integration Profitable?" *Harvard Business Review* 61 (January–February 1983): 92-102.

Buzzell, Robert D., and Marci K. Dew. "Strategic Management Helps Retailers Plan for the Future." *Marketing News* (7 March 1980).

Buzzell, Robert D., and Paul W. Farris. "Marketing Costs in Industrial Businesses." *Marketing Science Institute.* Working paper, 1976.

———. "Marketing Costs in Consumer Goods Industries." In *Strategy + Structure = Performance,* edited by Hans B. Thorelli. Bloomington, Ill: Indiana University Press, 1977.

Buzzell, Robert D., Bradley T. Gale, and Ralph G. M. Sultan. "Market Share—A Key to Profitability." *Harvard Business Review* 53 (January–February 1975).

Buzzell, Robert D., and Frederik D. Wiersema, "Modeling Changes in Market Share: A Cross-Sectional Analysis." *Strategic Management Journal* 2 (January–March 1981): 27–42.

Cady, John F. "Marketing Strategies in the Information Industry." In *Marketing in an Electronic Age,* edited by Robert D. Buzzell. Cambridge, Mass.: Harvard Business School Press, 1985.

Callow, A. Dana. "Planning for Healthcare Distribution: The Application of Strategic Concepts in a Consolidating Marketplace." *Surgical Business* (June 1982).

Canada Consulting Group. *Portfolio Planning in Canada.* Toronto, Ontario: Canada Consulting Group, January 1984.

Cardozo, Richard N. *Product Policy: Cases and Concepts.* Reading, Mass.: Addison-Wesley, 1979.

Carman, James M., and Eric Langeard. "Growth Strategies for Service Firms." *Strategic Management Journal* 1 (January–March 1980): 7–22.

Carroll, Peter. "Business-Specific Strategy." Chicago: Hayes/Hill, Inc., 1980.

Chussil, Mark J. "Responses to PIMS: Fact or Folklore?" *Journal of Business Strategy* 4 (Spring 1984): 93–96.

Collier, Don. "Strategic Planning Systems Design and Operation." *Journal of Business Strategy* 1 (Fall 1980): 76–77.

Conley, Patrick. "Experience Curves as a Planning Tool." *IEEE Spectrum* 7 (1970): 63–68.

Conway, R., and A. Schultz. "The Manufacturing Progress Function." *Journal of Industrial Engineering* 10 (1959): 39–53.

Cox, William Jr. "Product Life Cycles as Marketing Models." *Journal of Business* 40 (October 1967): 375–84.

Cushman, Robert. "Corporate Strategy: Planning for the Future." Paper presented to the North American Society of Corporate Planners, Boston, Massachusetts, October 1978.

Day, George. "Diagnosing the Product Portfolio." *Journal of Marketing* (April 1977): 29–38.

―――― . "The Product Life Cycle: Analysis and Application Issues." *Journal of Marketing* 45 (Fall 1981): 60–67.

―――― . "Strategic Market Analysis and Definition: An Integrated Approach." *Strategic Management Journal* 2 (1981): 281–99.

―――― . "Gaining Insights Through Strategy Analysis." *Journal of Business Strategy* 4 (Summer 1983): 51–58.

―――― . *Strategic Market Planning: The Pursuit of Competitive Advantage.* St. Paul: West Publishing, 1984.

Day, George, and David B. Montgomery. "Diagnosing the Experience Curve." *Journal of Marketing* 47 (Spring 1983): 44–58.

Dean, Joel. "Pricing Policies for New Products." *Harvard Business Review* 54 (November–December 1976): 141–53.

Dhalla, Nariman, and Sonya Yuspeh. "Forget the Product Life Cycle Concept." *Harvard Business Review* 54 (January–February 1976): 102–12.

Dolan, Robert J., and Abel P. Jeuland. "Experience Curves and Dynamic Demand Models: Implications for Optimal Pricing Strategies." *Journal of Marketing* 45 (Winter 1981): 52–73.

Dumaine, Brian. "Chipmaking Machines Come Roaring Back." *Fortune* (3 October 1983): 86–88.

Dutton, John M., and Annie Thomas. "Treating Progress Functions as a Managerial Opportunity." *Academy of Management Review* 9 (1984): 235–47.

Enis, Ben M., Raymond LaGarce, and Arthur E. Prell. "Extending the Product Life Cycle." *Business Horizons* 20 (June 1977): 46–56.

Erickson, Gary, and David B. Montgomery. "Measuring the Time Varying Response to Market Communication Instruments." In *Market Measurement and Analysis,* edited by David B. Montgomery and Dick R. Wittink. Cambridge, Mass.: Marketing Science Institute, 1980.

Farquhar, Carolyn R., and Stanley J. Shapiro. *Strategic Business Planning in Canada.* Ottawa: The Conference Board of Canada, April 1983.

Foster, Richard N. "A Call for Vision in Managing Technology." *The McKinsey Quarterly* (Summer 1982): 26–36.

Fox, Harold W. "A Framework of Functional Coordination." *Atlanta Economic Review* (November 1973).

Fraker, Susan. "High Speed Management for the High-Tech Age." *Fortune* (5 March 1984): 62–68.

Frey, John B. "Pricing Over the Competitive Cycle." Paper presented to the 1982 Marketing Conference, The Conference Board, New York.

Gale, Bradley T. "Planning for Profit." *Planning Review* (1978): 4–7, 30–32.

————. "Can More Capital Buy Higher Productivity?" *Harvard Business Review* 58 (July–August 1980): 78–86.

Gale, Bradley T., and Ben Branch. "Cash Flow Analysis: More Important Than Ever." *Harvard Business Review* 59 (July–August 1981): 131–36.

Gale, Bradley T., and Donald J. Swire. *The Limited Information Report.* Cambridge, Mass.: Strategic Planning Institute, 1980.

Gale, Bradley T., and Richard Klavans. "Formulating a Product Quality Strategy." Cambridge, Mass.: Strategic Planning Institute, 1980.

Ghemawat, Pankaj. "Building Strategy on the Experience Curve." *Harvard Business Review* (March-April 1985): 143-149.

Goold, Michael. "Why Dicey Definitions Are So Dangerous." *Financial Times of London* (16 November 1981).

Griliches, Avi. "Hedonic Price Indices for Automobiles: An Econometric Analysis of Quality Change." *Government Price Statistics.* U.S. Congress Joint Economic Committee, U.S. Government Printing Office (January 1961): 173–96. Reprinted in *Readings in Economics, Statistics and Econometrics,* edited by A. Zellner. Boston, Mass.: Little, Brown, 1968, 103–30.

Gross, Irwin. "Insights From Pricing Research." In *Pricing Practices and Strategies.* Conference Board, 1979.

Hall, William K. "Survival Strategies in a Hostile Environment." *Harvard Business Review* 58 (September-October 1980): 75-85.

Hamermesh, Richard. "Administrative Issues Posed by Contemporary Approaches to Strategic Planning: The Case of the Dexter Corporation." Working paper, Harvard Business School, 1979.

Hamermesh, R.G., M.J. Anderson, Jr., and J.E. Harris. "Strategies for Low Market Share Businesses." *Harvard Business Review* 56 (May–June 1978): 95–102.

Hamermesh, Richard G., and Roderick E. White. "Manage Beyond Portfolio Analysis." *Harvard Business Review* 62 (January–February 1984): 103–09.

Harrell, Stephen C., and Elmer D. Taylor. "Modeling the Product Life Cycle for Consumer Durables." *Journal of Marketing* 45 (Fall 1981): 68–75.

Harrigan, Kathryn Rudie. "Strategies for Declining Industries." *Journal of Business Strategy* 1 (Fall 1980): 20–34.

Harrigan, Kathryn Rudie, and Michael E. Porter. "End-Game Strategies for Declining Industries." *Harvard Business Review* (July–August 1983): 111–20.

Haspeslagh, Philippe. "Portfolio Planning: Uses and Limits." *Harvard Business Review* 60 (January–February 1982): 59–73.

Hax, Arnoldo, and Nicholas Majluf. "The Use of the Industry Attractiveness-Business Strength Matrix in Strategic Planning." *Interfaces* 13 (April 1983): 54–71.

Hayes, Robert H., and William J. Abernathy. "Managing Our Way to Economic Decline." *Harvard Business Review* 59 (July-August 1980): 67–77.

Hearne, Roger W. "Fighting Industrial Senility: A System for Growth in Mature Markets." *Journal of Business Strategy* (Fall 1982).

Hedley, Barry. "A Fundamental Approach to Strategy Development." *Long Range Planning* (December 1976).

———. "Strategy and the Business Portfolio." *Long Range Planning* 10 (February 1977): 9–15.

Heeler, Roger M., and Thomas P. Hustad. "Problems in Predicting New Product Growth for Consumer Durables." *Management Science* 26 (October 1980): 1007–20.

Henderson, Bruce D. "The Product Portfolio." Boston: Boston Consulting Group *(Perspectives),* 1970.

———. "Cash Traps." Boston: Boston Consulting Group *(Perspectives),* 1972.

———. "The Experience Curve Revisited: The Growth-Share Matrix." Boston: Boston Consulting Group *(Perspectives),* 1973.

———. "Cross-Sectional Experience." Boston: Boston Consulting Group *(Perspectives,* no. 208), 1978.

———. *Henderson on Corporate Strategy.* Cambridge, Mass.: Abt Books, 1979.

———. "Caution Based on Experience." In *Shifting Boundaries Between Regulation and Competition,* edited by Betty Bock. New York: Conference Board, 1980.

———. "The Experience Curve Revisited." Boston: Boston Consulting Group *(Perspectives,* no. 220), 1980.

———. "The Application and Misapplication of the Experience Curve." *Journal of Business Strategy* 4 (Winter 1984): 3–9.

Henderson, Bruce D., and Alan J. Zakon. "Corporate Growth Strategy: How to Develop and Implement It." In *Handbook of Business Problem Solving,* edited by Kenneth J. Albert. New York: McGraw-Hill, 1980.

Hirschmann, Winfred B. "Profit from the Learning Curve." *Harvard Business Review* 42 (January–February 1964).

Hopkins, David S. *Business Strategies for Problem Products.* New York: Conference Board, 1977.

Horsky, Dan, and Leonard S. Simon. "Advertising and the Diffusion of New Products." *Marketing Science* 2 (Winter 1983): 11-20.

Hughes, Malcolm. "Portfolio Analysis." *Long Range Planning* (February 1981): 101–3.

Hussey, David E. "Portfolio Analysis: Practical Experience with the Directional Policy Matrix." *Long Range Planning* 11 (August 1978): 2–8.

Jacobson, Robert, and David A. Aaker. "Is Market Share All That It's Cracked Up To Be?" Working paper, University of California, Berkeley, 1984.

Joskow, Paul L., and George A. Rozanski. "The Effect of Learning by Doing on Nuclear Plant Operating Reliability." *Review of Economics and Statistics* 61 (May 1979): 161–68.

Keen, Peter G.W., and M.S. Scott Morton. *Decision Support Systems: An Organizational Perspective.* Reading, Mass.: Addison-Wesley, 1978.

Kiechel, Walter. "The Decline of the Experience Curve." *Fortune* (5 October 1981): 139–46.

Kotler, Philip. *Marketing Management: Analysis, Planning and Control,* 5th ed. Englewood Cliffs, N.J.: Prentice-Hall, 1984.

Larréché, Jean-Claude. "On Limitations of Positive Market Share-Profitability Relationships: The Case of the French Banking Industry." Working paper, Fontainebleau, France: Insead, January 1980.

Larréché, Jean-Claude, and V. Srinivasan. "STRATPORT: A Decision Support System for Strategic Planning." *Journal of Marketing* 45, no. 4 (Fall 1981): 39–52.

———. "STRATPORT: A Model for the Evaluation and Formulation of Business Portfolio Strategies." *Management Science* 28, no. 9 (September 1982): 979–1001.

Levitt, Theodore. "Exploit the Product Life Cycle." *Harvard Business Review* 43 (November–December 1965): 81–94.

Lewis, W. Walker. *Planning by Exception.* Washington, D.C.: Strategic Planning Associates, 1977.

———. "The CEO and Corporate Strategy in the Eighties: Back to Basics." *Interfaces* (January–February 1984): 3–9.

Lillien, Gary L. "The Implications of Diffusion Models for Accelerating the Diffusion of Innovation." *Technological Forecasting and Social Change* 17 (1980): 339–51.

Lillis, Charles M., and Bonnie J. McIvor. "MDSS's at General Electric: Implications for the 90's From Experiences in the '70's and 80's Paper presented to Conference on Marketing and the New Information/Communication Technologies, Harvard University, July 1983.

Little, John D.C. "BRANDAID: A Marketing-Mix Model Part 1: Structure and Part 2: Implementation, Calibration, and Case Study." *Operations Research* 23, no. 4 (July–August 1975): 628–73.

———. "Decision Support Systems for Marketing Managers." *Journal of Marketing* 43, no. 3 (Summer 1979): 9–27.

Lodish, Leonard. "Experience with Decision Calculus Models and Decision Support Systems." In *Marketing Decision Models.* New York: Elsevier Science, 1981.

Loomis, Worth. "Strategic Planning in Uncertain Times." *Chief Executive* (Winter 1980–81.

Machnic, John A. "Multi-Level Versus Single-Level Substitution: The Case of the Beverage Can Market." *Technological Forecasting and Social Change* 18 (1980): 141–49.

Magnet, Myron. "Time Takes the Torture Test." *Fortune* (27 June 1983): 112–20.

Mahajan, Vijan, and Eitan Muller. "Innovation Diffusion and New Product Growth Models in Marketing." *Journal of Marketing* 43 (Fall 1979): 55–68.

McLagan, Donald L. "Market Share: Key to Profitability." *Planning Review* (March 1981): 26–29.

———. "Technology Company Strategy: Growth or Profitability?" *Planning Review* (September 1983): 20–23, 47.

Michael, George D. "Product Petrification: A New Stage in the Life Cycle Theory." *California Management Review* 9 (Fall 1971): 88–91.

Midgley, David F. "Toward a Theory of the Product Life Cycle: Some Testable Propositions." *Journal of Marketing* 45 (Fall 1981).

Minoff, Alan. "Strategy Formulation." Paper presented to the Business Week Strategic Planning Conference, Toronto, Canada, 10–11 November 1980.

Montgomery, David B. "Toward Decision Support Systems for Strategic Marketing." In *Strategic Marketing and Strategic Management,* edited by D. Gardner and H. Thomas. New York: Wiley, 1985.

Montgomery, David B., and George S. Day. "Experience Curves: Evidence, Empirical Issues and Applications." In *Strategic Marketing and Strategic Management,* edited by D. Gardner and H. Thomas. New York: Wiley, 1984.

Montgomery, David B., and Charles B. Weinberg. "Toward Strategic Intelligence Systems." *Journal of Marketing* 43, no. 4 (Fall 1979): 41–52.

Nigam, A.K. "Analysis for a Satellite Communications System." *Interfaces* 5, no. 2 (February 1975): 37–47.

Ohmae, Kenichi. *The Mind of the Strategist: The Art of Japanese Business.* New York: McGraw-Hill, 1982.

Oren, S.S., M.H. Rothkopf, and R.D. Smallwood. "A Causal Market Forecasting System: Theory and Application." *Market Measurement and Analysis,* edited by D.B. Montgomery and D.R. Wittink. Cambridge, Mass.: Marketing Science Institute, 1980.

Palesy, Stephen. "Motivating Line Management Using the Planning Process." *Planning Review* (March 1980).

Pappas, Chris. "Strategic Management of Technology." *Journal of Product Innovation Management* 1 (January 1984): 30–35.

Patel, Peter, and Michael Younger. "A Frame of Reference for Strategy Development." *Long Range Planning* 11 (April 1978): 6–12.

Pessemier, Edgar A. *Product Management: Strategy and Organization.* New York: Wiley, 1977.

Peters, Thomas J. "Strategy Follows Structure: Developing Distinctive Skills." *California Management Review* 26 (Spring 1984).

Peters, Thomas J., and Robert H. Waterman, Jr. *In Search of Excellence: Lessons from America's Best-Run Companies.* New York: Harper & Row, 1982.

Phillips, Lynn W., Dae R. Chang, and Robert D. Buzzell. "Product Quality, Cost Position, and Business Performance." *Journal of Marketing* 47 (Spring 1983): 26–43.

Polli, Rolando, and Victor Cook. "Validity of the Product Life Cycle. " *Journal of Business* (October 1969): 385-400.

Porter, Michael E. "How Competitive Forces Shape Strategy." *Harvard Business Review* 57 (March–April 1979): 137–45.

———. *Competitive Strategy: Techniques for Analyzing Industries and Competitors.* New York: Free Press, 1980.

Rappaport, Alfred. "Selecting Strategies that Create Shareholder Value." *Harvard Business Review* (May–June 1981): 139–49.

Reece, James S., and William R. Cool. "Measuring Investment Center Performance." *Harvard Business Review* (May–June 1978): 28–30.

Rink, David R., and John E. Swan. "Product Life Cycle Research: A Literature Review." *Journal of Business Research* 78 (September 1979): 219–42.

Robinson, Bruce, and Chet Lakhani. "Dynamic Price Models for New Product Planning." *Management Science* 21 (June 1975): 1113–22.

Robinson, S.J.Q., R.E. Hichens, and D.P. Wade. "The Directional Policy Matrix: Tool for Strategic Planning." *Long Range Planning* 11 (1978): 8–15.

Robinson, William T. "Market Pioneering and Sustainable Market Share Advantages in Industrial Goods Manufacturing Industries." Working paper, Purdue University, August 1984.

Rogers, Everett M. *Diffusion of Innovations,* 3d ed. New York: Free Press, 1983.

Rogers, Everett M., with Floyd F. Shoemaker. *Communication of Innovation: A Cross-Cultural Approach.* New York: Free Press, 1971.

Rosenberg, Nathan. "Learning by Using." In *Inside the Black Box: Technology in Economics,* edited by N. Rosenberg. Cambridge, Mass.: Harvard University Press, 1982.

Rothschild, William E. "Comment." *Journal of Marketing* 43, no. 4 (Fall 1979): 53–54.

Rumelt, Richard R. "Towards a Strategic Theory of the Firm." UCLA working paper, 1981.

Rumelt, Richard P., and Robin Wensley. "In Search of the Market Share Effect." UCLA working paper, 1980.

Rutenburg, David. "What Strategic Planning Expects from Management Science." Working paper, 89-75-76, Carnegie-Mellon University, December 1976.

Schendel, Dan, and G. Richard Patton. "Simultaneous Equation Models for Corporate Strategy." Paper no. 582, Krannert School, Purdue, 1976.

Schoeffler, Sidney. "Cross-Sectional Study of Strategy, Structure and Performance: Aspects of the PIMS Programs." In *Strategy + Structure = Performance,* edited by Hans Thorelli. Bloomington, Ill.: Indiana University Press, 1977.

———. "Nine Basic Findings on Business Strategy." *Pimsletter* 1 (1977), Strategic Planning Institute.

———. "Capital-Intensive Technology vs. ROI: A Strategic Assessment." *Management Review* (September 1978): 8–14.

Schoeffler, Sidney, Robert D. Buzzell, and Donald F. Heany. "Impact of Strategic Planning on Profit Performance." *Harvard Business Review* 52 (March–April 1974): 137–45.

Seeger, J.A. "Reversing the Images of BCG's Growth/Share Matrix." *Strategic Management Journal* (January-March 1984): 93-97.

Sherwin, C., and R. Isenson. "Project Hindsight." *Science* 156 (1967): 1571–77.

Silverman, Dean. "Field Analysis: A 3-D Look at Opportunities." *Planning Review* (September 1984): 22–24.

Spence, A. Michael. "The Learning Curve and Competition." *Bell Journal of Economics* 12 (Spring 1981): 49–69.

Stobaugh, Robert B., and Philip L. Townsend. "Price Forecasting and Strategic Planning: The Case of Petro Chemicals." *Journal of Marketing Research* 12 (February 1975): 19–29.

Strategic Planning Institute. *Strategy Seminar for Senior Executives* (20 March 1980).

Sultan, Ralph. *Pricing in the Electrical Oligopoly,* vols. 1 and 2. Cambridge, Mass.: Harvard Graduate School of Business Administration, 1974.

Tellis, Gerard J., and C. Merle Crawford. "An Evolutionary Approach to Product Growth Theory." *Journal of Marketing* 45 (Fall 1981).

Thorelli, Hans B., and Stephen C. Burnett. "The Nature of Product Life Cycles for Industrial Goods Businesses." *Journal of Marketing* 45 (Fall 1981).

Tigert, Douglas, and Behrooz Farivar. "The Bass New Product Growth Model: A Sensitivity Analysis for a High Technology Product." *Journal of Marketing* 45 (Fall 1981).

Tilles, Seymour. "Strategies for Allocating Funds." *Harvard Business Review* 44 (January–February 1966): 72–80.

Tita, Michael, and Robert J. Allio. "3M's Strategy System—Planning In an Innovative Corporation." *Planning Review* 12 (September 1984): 10-15.

Uttal, Bro. "Japan's Latest Assault on Chipmaking." *Fortune* (3 September 1984): 76–81.

———. "Is IBM Playing Too Tough? *Fortune* (10 December 1984): 34–37.

Utterback, James M. "Innovation in Industry and the Diffusion of Technology." *Science* 198 (1974): 620–26.

Wasson, Chester R. *Dynamic Competitive Strategy and Product Life Cycles.* St. Charles, Ill.: Challenge Books, 1978.

Webster, Frederick, Jr. "New Product Adoption in Industrial Markets: A Framework for Analysis." *Journal of Marketing* 33 (July 1969): 35–39.

Wensley, Robin. "Strategic Marketing: Betas, Boxes or Basics." *Journal of Marketing* 45 (Summer 1981): 173–82.

———. "PIMS and BCG: New Horizons or False Dawns in Strategic Marketing." *Strategic Management Journal* 3 (April–June 1982): 147–59.

Wilson, Aubrey. "Industrial Marketing Research in Britain." *Journal of Marketing Research* 6 (February 1969): 15–28.

Wilson, Aubrey, and Bryan Atkin. "Exorcising the Ghosts in Marketing." *Harvard Business Review* 54 (September–October 1976): 117–27.

Wilson, Robert G. "Strategies to Fight Inflation." *Journal of Business Strategy* 2 (Winter 1982): 22–31.

Wind, Yoram. *Product Policy: Concepts, Methods, and Strategy.* Reading, Mass.: Addison-Wesley, 1981.

Wind, Yoram, and Vijay Mahajan. "Designing Product and Business Portfolios." *Harvard Business Review* 59 (January–February 1981): 155–65.

Woo, Carolyn Y., and Arnold C. Cooper. "The Surprising Case for Low Market Share." *Harvard Business Review* 60 (November–December 1982): 106–13.

Yelle, Louis E. "The Learning Curve: Historical Review and Comprehensive Survey." *Decision Sciences* 10 (1979): 302–28.

Yip, George S. "Gateways to Entry." *Harvard Business Review* 60 (September–October 1980): 85–92.

Zaltman, Gerald, and Ronald Stiff. "Theories of Diffusion." In *Consumer Behavior: Theoretical Sources,* edited by Scott Ward and Thomas S. Robertson. Englewood Cliffs, N.J.: Prentice-Hall, 1973.

Zoltners, Andris, and Joe Dodson. "A Market Selection Model for Multiple End-Use Products." *Journal of Marketing* 47, no. 2 (Spring 1983): 76–88.

Index